Memory and the future of Europe

MANCHESTER
1824

Manchester University Press

Memory and the future of Europe

Rupture and integration in the wake of total war

Peter J. Verovšek

Manchester University Press

Published by Manchester University Press
Oxford Road, Manchester M13 9PL
www.manchesteruniversitypress.co.uk

British Library Cataloguing-in-Publication Data
A catalogue record for this book is available from the British Library

ISBN 978 1 5261 4310 5 hardback
ISBN 978 1 5261 6376 9 paperback

First published 2020
Paperback published 2022

Typeset by Newgen Publishing

For my parents

Contents

Acknowledgements

Any project that takes ten years to complete racks up an impressive number of debts along the way. Over the past decade I have lived and conducted research in numerous locations and received the generous assistance of countless friends and colleagues. Unfortunately, due to constraints of space and the deficiencies of my own memory, it is impossible to list them all. My apologies in advance to those who I have unintentionally left out!

I started to conceptualise this project at Yale University in the fall of 2009. At that point I hoped to write a book examining the role of collective memory in political life using the origins and development of the European Union since 1945 as an illustrative case study. Although the subprime mortgage crisis had already started in the United States, it still looked as though Europe had managed to avoid the contagion emanating from the other side of the Atlantic. However, by the time I had started to work on the project in earnest in the spring of 2010, Greece's difficulties financing its sovereign debt had already set off the crisis of the Eurozone, which would ultimately threaten the future of the European Union as a whole.

As a result of these events, the reflective, backward-looking, and optimistic manuscript I had planned to write about the ability of collective memory to help individuals and communities learn the lessons the past, became much more politically relevant, forward-looking, and pessimistic. Thinking and writing in the shadow of a series of existential threats to the EU – from the problems of sovereign debt in Greece in 2010 to Brexit in 2016 and the striking electoral success of far-right populists in the EU parliamentary elections of 2019 – I found that the idea of crisis had come to play a central role in my thinking. A project that was originally supposed to be about the transformational power of the collective memory of what I call the 'rupture of 1945'

Acknowledgements

ultimately became a book that had to seriously contemplate what the loss of this transnationally shared remembrance meant for European politics at a time when the generations of experience were beginning to pass away. I was also forced to reflect on the role that collective remembrance could play in combating the return of nationalism on a continent that had suffered through two world wars brought about by this ideology in the first half of the twentieth century.

Luckily, I was well-prepared to undertake this work, which combined research in collective memory studies with the critical theory of the Frankfurt School. I initially became interested in collective memory when I had the opportunity to help my undergraduate advisor, Richard Ned Lebow, edit a volume on *The Politics of Memory in Postwar Europe* (Duke University Press, 2006) as a Presidential Scholar in the Government Department at Dartmouth College. At that same time I was also receiving my introduction to the Frankfurt School – and to continental philosophy more generally – from Amy Allen in the Philosophy Department.

Although political science and international relations is a relative latecomer to the study of collective memory, I found a lot of support within the discipline during my time at Yale. Seyla Benhabib deserves particular thanks for taking me under her wing. She was instrumental to my development as a scholar and infinitely supportive of my desire to pursue a somewhat unorthodox project combining political theory, international relations, collective memory studies, and history. She deserves much of the credit for whatever merits this book might have.

Bryan Garsten and Adam Tooze also played crucial roles. As a political theorist, Bryan helped me to ensure that this book would appeal to a philosophical audience despite its interdisciplinary nature. He was also a valuable source of support throughout my work, generously giving his time to talk through minor details with me. By contrast, Adam provided me with the perspective of a twentieth-century historian, guiding me through the process of historical and archival research. I am also grateful to other faculty I consulted with at the Department of Political Science during my time at Yale, especially Keith Darden, Stathis Kalyvas, Jolyon Howorth, and Jim Scott. Bruno Cabanes and Jay Winter, both of the History Department, as well as Ron Eyerman of Sociology, were also important sounding boards for my ideas.

It is often said that we learn as much from our peers as from our teachers. That was certainly true in my case. Although there are too many to name, Matthew Longo, Luke Thompson, Lucas Entel, Onur Bakiner, Anna Jurkevics,

Acknowledgements

Erin Pineda, Paul Linden-Retek, Stefan Eich, Kim Lowe Frank, Jennifer Wellington, and Jensen Sass were all generous with their time and attention in helping me to develop my ideas. I am also grateful to the participants at the Yale Political Theory Workshop, where I was able to present this work in its earliest incarnations.

This project builds on a substantial amount of historical and archival research, which required a lot of travel and substantial amounts of funding. I would like to thank the MacMillan Center and the EU Studies Council at Yale for their financial support. I conducted the majority of my archival research during a stay at the Fondation Jean Monnet pour l'Europe in Lausanne, which was generously funded by the Fondation's Bourse Henri Rieben. I owe a debt of gratitude to the director of the Centre, Gilles Grin, as well as Françoise Nicod, the head of the archives at the time, and Philippe Klein, who was always ready to fetch new documents for me to examine.

I am also grateful to Rainer Forst, who hosted me twice in Germany, first at the Excellence Cluster 'The Formation of Normative Orders' at the Goethe-Universität Frankfurt am Main, which was possible due to the support of the German Academic Exchange Service (DAAD). He later invited me back as Junior Fellow at the Institute for Advanced Studies in the Humanities (Forschungskolleg Humanwissenschaften) in Bad Homburg, courtesy of the Alphons and Gertrude Kassel Foundation. I would like to thank all of the participants of Rainer's research group, especially Erin Cooper, as well as the fellows at the Forschungskolleg during my stay there for their thoughtful comments and support.

After leaving Yale I was lucky to get a job teaching at the Committee for Degrees in Social Studies at Harvard University. The staff and my colleagues there – especially Anya Bernstein Bassett, Katie Greene, Jonathan Hansen, Bonnie Talbert, Angela Maione, and Ian Story – provided wonderful support as I worked on this book while also carrying a full teaching load and searching for a tenure-track position. Although we stand on opposite sides of the debate about the EU, Richard Tuck was a wonderful sparring partner and a great supporter of my work. Additionally, I greatly enjoyed discussing my ideas about critical theory and European politics with Peter Gordon. I am also grateful to my colleagues at the Minda de Gunzburg Center for European Studies, especially Art Goldhammer, Vivien Schmidt, and Karl Kaiser, for including me in the intellectual life of the Center.

I did not know what to expect when I arrived to England to take up my position as Lecturer (Assistant Professor) in the Department of Politics at the

Acknowledgements

University of Sheffield in January 2017, especially as my move took place six months after the UK had voted to leave the EU in June of 2016. What I found was a wonderfully ecumenical, pluralistic department that embraced both me and my rather eclectic interests with open arms. For their various contributions to my thinking, research, professional development, and personal well-being, Andrew Hindmoor, Owen Parker, Matt Sleat, Alasdair Cochrane, Ed Hall, Luke Ulaş, Helen Turton, Burak Tansel, and Anastasia Shesterinina all deserve special thanks. I am also grateful to the staff at Manchester University Press, especially my commissioning editor, Caroline Wintersgill, who has been a wonderful supporter of this project since it arrived on her desk. Ana Reberc provided valuable manuscript assistance during her stay in Sheffield as a fellow of the American Slovenian Education Foundation (ASEF). Anja Verovšek also provided welcome assistance in helping me to prepare the index.

Finally, I would not have completed this book without the love and support of my family and friends. Ten years is a long time and there were moments – both in my personal and in my scholarly life – when I believed that this book would never appear in print. Without the steadfast support of those closest to me, it would never have come to fruition. *Hvala vsem!*

Abbreviations

AMTE	Allied Maritime Transport Executive
CAP	Common Agricultural Policy
CFLN	Comité français de la libération nationale
CM	Common Market
ECB	European Central Bank
ECSC	European Coal and Steel Community
EDC	European Defence Community
EEC	European Economic Community
EMU	Economic and Monetary Union
EP	European Parliament
EU	European Union
Euratom	European Atomic Energy Agency
HA	High Authority
MEP	Member of European Parliament
NATO	North Atlantic Treaty Organisation
SPD	Social Democratic Party of Germany

Introduction

We hope vaguely, we dread precisely.
> Paul Valéry, *On European Civilisation and the European Mind* (1922)

Europe in crisis

In the aftermath of the Second World War, 'never again' was more than just a slogan; it was an imperative for political change. During the postwar era (1945–89) collective memories of Europe's 'age of total war' (1914–45) served as the foundation for a broad movement that sought to move the 'savage continent' away from the state-centric nationalism that had led to two world wars towards a new, community-based political order based on 'the image of a peaceful, cooperative Europe, open toward other cultures and capable of dialogue.'[1] Taking shape primarily through the organisation known today as the European Union (EU), the European dream of unification over and above the nation-state has defined politics on the continent since the creation of the European Coal and Steel Community (ECSC) in 1952.

For much of the postwar period the symbolic rupture of 1945 served as the driver of what is undoubtedly 'the most significant political innovation' of the twentieth century. By challenging the assumption that nation-states are the most fundamental and important political actors in international politics, the development of the 'Euro-polity' has significant implications for existing theories of the state, sovereignty, social welfare, democracy, and citizenship, all of which are plagued by an inherent 'methodological nationalism.' Building on collective memories of a nightmarish past to create a better future, the EU has served as 'the theoretical proving-ground of contemporary liberalism.'[2]

Introduction

Despite its many achievements – a list that includes the fact that 'peace in Europe is secure, the economy sound and in spots dynamic, and the EU is a force to reckon with in international economic affairs' – European integration is haunted by both the 'spectre of tedium' and the dangers of bureaucratic 'rule by nobody.'[3] At the beginning of the twenty-first century, these long-standing concerns were reinforced by the problems emanating from the onset of the greatest financial downturn since the Great Depression of 1929. In 2010 Greece's difficulties in financing its sovereign debt metastasised into a full-blown 'crisis of the Eurozone,' affecting not only the states that share its common currency (the euro), but also the EU as a whole.[4] Far from spurring further cooperation, these issues have caused citizens across the continent to turn inward, away from the EU and back towards the seemingly safe harbour of the nation-state.

The problems radiating from the so-called Great Recession arguably reached their zenith on 23 June 2016, when the United Kingdom, driven by English nationalism and neo-imperial dreams of a 'Global Britain,' as well as a backlash against the austerity imposed by the Conservative government, narrowly voted to 'take back control' by leaving the EU.[5] Previously united by a common destiny based on the lessons of 1945, at the start of the third millennium the European continent is increasingly divided. With the rise of nationalistic populist movements across the continent – from Britain in the northwest, Hungary and Poland in the east, as well as Italy in the south – the core liberal values of the postwar settlement embodied by the EU, including rule of law, tolerance, and a respect for human and minority rights, are increasingly threatened by a 'return of fascism.'[6]

The almost universal diagnosis of these problems as a crisis signals their seriousness as a threat to the European project. In ancient Greece the concept of crisis (κρίσις) was 'coined to denote the moment in which the future of the patient was in the balance, and the doctor had to decide which way to go and what treatment to apply.' It thus describes a key moment of action and decision, whose resolution 'will determine whether the "patient" will recover or die.' The problems facing Europe and the EU at the start of the twenty-first century represent such a moment of decision. In the words of Stathis Kalyvas, the situation in the wake of the Great Recession 'has not only challenged our optimistic belief in the bright future of the European integration project, but it has also reminded us why this is, indeed, the most ambitious and far-reaching political experiment of our lifetime.'[7]

Introduction

The premise of this book is that the crisis Europe is facing at the start of the third millennium is potentially existential. Building on the medical metaphor of crisis as a key moment of decision, I seek not only to identify what made the European project successful through much of the twentieth century and diagnose the issues at the root of its problems at the start of the twenty-first, but also to suggest treatments for these pathologies.[8] As a result, I am 'not concerned with pure truth,' but with the more practical task of 'discovering the real causes of the crisis.' Following Max Horkheimer and the writings of the Frankfurt School, I associate critical inquiry with the task of the physician, who searches for concrete solutions to real problems. In the words of Seyla Benhabib, 'The purpose of critical theory is not crisis management, but crisis diagnosis such as to encourage future transformation.'[9]

This starting point dictates the shape of my inquiry. Although it is notoriously difficult to provide a clear definition of the Frankfurt School, 'It has been common to treat critical theory primarily as a distinctive methodology.' One of its unique features is its two-stage approach to social criticism. Starting with an 'explanatory-diagnostic' analysis of the social pathologies of the present, the critic then seeks 'anticipatory-utopian' solutions that – building on the medical roots of the crisis metaphor – seek to provide treatments for the 'diseases of society' (*Krankenheiten der Gesellschaft*) it has identified.[10] Understood in this light, the 'practical interest' of critical theory is not unlike the 'emancipation' of the body from disease.[11]

In line with this approach, I seek to diagnose the pathologies of integration at the beginning of the twenty-first century while also charting possible courses for emancipation from the political, economic, and social storms that have battered the EU since the turn of the millennium. My basic thesis is that the difficulties facing the continent can be traced back to cognitive, motivational, and justificatory deficits resulting from the loss of the shared experience of war and suffering between 1914 and 1945. Through much of the postwar period, this collective memory of total war shared across state borders played a positive, constructive role leading to the foundation of Europe on a community-basis. By focusing on the role of collective memory in the process of continental unification, I show that it was indeed 'the shadow of war, not its crucible, that sparked both the early European integration project and its later deepening.'[12] Unfortunately, with the passing of the generations that experienced and have personal memories of the war, the power of this collective remembrance is starting to fade.

My contribution to the existing scholarship is found primarily in my development of the concept of 'ruptures' (*Brüche*) or breaks that shatter the existing frameworks of collective memory, allowing new ideas and institutions to emerge. I argue that the Second World War, which followed closely on the horrors of the Great War, acted as a caesura that splintered prewar, nationalistic historical narratives. By making these traditional stories untenable, what I call the 'rupture of 1945' inspired new thinking by forcing individuals and communities across the continent to reframe their understandings of the past. By delegitimising national stories of glory, I argue that these violent collective memories of total war functioned as what Jacques Derrida calls a '*coup de force*,' i.e. a form of 'performative and therefore interpretive violence' that allowed Europeans to tell new, transnational narratives to replace the established nationalistic frameworks of history.[13]

Building on this shared remembrance of total war, I argue that in the aftermath of this rupture Europeans were able to imagine and build a common future. While the polity they created was initially established as part of a normative project designed to pacify the bloody nationalism that led to two world wars, my diagnosis is that the gradual forgetting that accompanies the passage of time and generations has undermined the EU's normative and moral dimensions, making economic prosperity its sole *raison d'être*. In this sense, I agree with Michael Loriaux that 'the real spectre haunting the European Union is not so much of failure as of loss of moral horizon.'[14]

Looking forward from this diagnosis to the future of European memory, I argue that in an increasingly globalised, multicultural, and interdependent age, stepping back and decreasing cooperation is not realistic. On the contrary, resolving the issues facing the EU at the start of the twenty-first century will require Europeans to construct a truly supranational understanding of history that does not require personal memories of suffering. However, given that debates about memory are as much about the future as the past, this narrative will need to have a forward-looking as well as a backward-looking dimension.

More specifically, I argue that a successful European identity will have to be based on the capacity of the EU to stand up to international pressures and resolve future problems in ways that the outdated institution of the nation-state cannot at the start of the third millennium. Only such a notion, which links collective memories to future projects, the past to the future through the present, can hope to resolve the European crisis. In this sense – and in line with the tradition of the Frankfurt School – my focus on the role of collective memory in European integration helps to diagnose and explain the problems the EU is facing at the start of the twenty-first century. The basic thesis of this book is that resolving these issues will require Europe to develop a new, more inclusive narrative historical that will allow it to act as a more powerful and more unified entity in the future.

Collective memory and European integration

By treating collective memory as central to the creation of the EU, using it to explain the multiple crises it is undergoing seventy years after the end of the Second World War, and arguing for its role in Europe's future, I both build on and set myself apart from existing studies of European integration. In the first major theoretical assessment of this phenomenon, Ernst Haas defines integration as '*the process whereby political actors in several distinct national settings are persuaded to shift their loyalties, expectations and political activities toward a new centre, whose institutions possess or demand jurisdiction over the preexisting national states.*' Since then, studies of the European project have sought to understand the process of creating 'a new political community, superimposed over the pre-existing ones.'[15]

Building on the subtitle of Haas's *Uniting of Europe* (1958), the existing literature has focused on the role played by 'political, social or economic forces.' Despite its insights and explanatory power, Catherine Guisan notes that 'much of the scholarship on European integration has overlooked, or misinterpreted, the self-understandings of political actors central to the process.' By focusing on functional 'spill over,' economic self-interest, or national power politics, existing approaches have operated at the third-person 'observer' perspective favoured by positivistic social science.[16] Due to its methodological commitments, this literature cannot account for the internal, first-person perspective of the participants in the creation of the European Communities.

In order to take account of the standpoints of the agents involved in this process, a more hermeneutical perspective inspired by the humanities and qualitative social sciences is necessary. In addition to this different methodological approach, taking the perspective of the participant seriously also requires a focus on a new explanatory factor: culture. It is, after all, cultural ideas and practices that shape the basic categories of scholarship, determining what 'Europe' is, who counts as 'European', and how 'Europeanness' is defined.

Introduction

None of these notions are given or obvious. On the contrary, they are 'highly unstable,' requiring constant negotiation by the participants in the process of constructing Europe.[17] Additionally, Kathleen McNamara notes that the continent's 'banal cultural infrastructure' has 'made the EU a natural part of the political landscape, folded into national political identities' in ways that make them difficult for social scientists to discern. While these ideas inevitably remain contested, 'Culture has to be in the equation when explaining a social phenomenon as significant as the integration of former enemy countries.'[18]

From within the broad field of culture, I focus on the role that collective remembrance played in the origins and development of the EU. In response to the European crisis at the start of the twenty-first century, I also reflect on what the loss of this 'moral demand of memory' means for the project of unification as the generations that experienced Europe's age of total war begin to pass away. Throughout this volume I consistently emphasise the importance of this historical horizon in shaping 'how participants in the European founding dealt with their historical memories of war, invasion and mutual exploitation, and how they could trust one another enough to put their war industries under a common authority.'[19]

This perspective is not meant to deny the importance of the factors highlighted in the existing literature. It is merely intended to show that collective memories of the rupture of 1945 acted as an important lens that shaped how the political, social, and economic forces that are usually used to explain this phenomenon were seen and understood by key actors at the time. In so doing, I seek to bring the scholarly conversation about the importance of memory in social and political life together with the public rhetoric about European integration propagated by its leaders.

The idea that the project of integration 'originated in the ruins of the Second World War, aiming at ending nationalist aggression and inter-state war' is hardly new. However, to date it has been largely restricted to the politics of memory propagated by various European institutions.[20] For example, the House of European History, which opened in Brussels in 2017, recounts the EU's official narrative of integration, interpreting it as a learning process that builds on the wars, atrocities, and sufferings of the first half of the twentieth century. Similarly, just as burgeoning nation-states established universities to promulgate national histories, so the member-states of the EU have created the European University Institute in order to research 'the great movements and developments which characterise the history and development of Europe.'[21]

Despite these institutional efforts, scholars of integration are usually sceptical of attempts to root integration in the shared continental experience
of total war. For example, Haas himself admits that memories of the traumatic events of the two world wars 'were undoubtedly primary among the
specific stimuli' that helped to 'launch and then spur the process' of unification. However, he ultimately argues that 'this does not make the past an
active causative agent' for the move towards political community beyond the
nation-state.[22] Haas's scepticism, as well as that of the literature as a whole, is
rooted in two main problems. First, there are those who argue that European
memory is too divided to provide the foundation for a united political community, particularly after the accession of the postcommunist states of East-
Central Europe in 2004.[23] The second issue is methodological, as the influence
of memory on politics is hard to pin down.

As part of the broader 'memory boom' brought about by the desire of
the children of the generation that fought in the Second World War to know
what role their parents had played during that fateful conflict, scholars have
gradually come to recognise that the European push to postnational integration 'springs[s] directly from their unique historical experience.'[24] Analyses
of the major discourses in mass media confirm that references to the Second
World War played and continue to play an important role in public debates
about the EU. Once dismissed out of hand, what Derrida refers to as the
'*universal urgency* of memory' has become increasingly apparent. However, while
almost all of the existing literature mentions the importance of the two world
wars in helping to push the project of integration forward during the postwar
period – at least in passing – few studies have treated collective memory as an
explanatory factor driving the process of European integration.[25]

In focusing on remembrance in this way, this book is part of a new movement
that has 'developed outside the mainstream of political science,' in which
'young scholars have increasingly started to pay attention to memory politics
also on the supranational level.'[26] Two studies deserve particular attention.
In contrast to the larger literature that focuses on the EU as a manager of
conflict, in *A Political Theory of Identity in European Integration: Memory and Politics*
(2012) Guisan argues that the European project should be understood as a
peace-making experiment whose participants shared one main goal: 'to invent
new forms of political life in Europe after the murderous wars of the early
twentieth century.' Through an examination of the speeches and discourses of
key agents of integration, she argues that Europe offers a new model of politics that focuses on 'action in concert rather than domination over the other.'

Focusing on the EU's approach to the politics of memory, she contends that 'the EU offers a viable model for the difficult "politics of recognition"' necessary to achieve peace and reconciliation between former enemies.[27]

As one of the first studies to focus on memory and the EU, Guisan's book opens the intellectual space for my research. I build on her methodological approach, which focuses 'on the self-understanding of important actors in the process' of integration in order to highlight the importance of remembrance as a 'hidden yet vital factor for the success of the enterprise.'[28] However, in contrast to Guisan, I am interested in collective memory as a resource for new political thinking and the creation of new forms of political community in the aftermath of experiences that break the existing narrative frameworks of history. The forward-looking aspect of my project, which seeks to think through possible resolutions to Europe's crisis at the start of the twenty-first century, also differs from her approach.

Although Guisan and I both interpret the experience of integration through the lens of political theory, our philosophical foundations differ considerably. As is clear from my brief reconstruction of her argument, Guisan builds primarily on Hannah Arendt's concept of 'action in concert' and G. W. F. Hegel's understanding of recognition (*Anerkennung*), along with some insights drawn from other thinkers, including Karl Jaspers, Paul Ricœur, and Charles Taylor. By contrast, I draw my inspiration from the Frankfurt School. Using ideas drawn from Max Horkheimer, Theodor Adorno, Herbert Marcuse, Walter Benjamin, and Jürgen Habermas, I focus on how ruptures free the imagination to think things anew. Although I also engage with Arendt, I build more on her reading of Benjamin's ideas on history and memory, her reflections on totalitarianism, and her conception of 'new beginnings' than with the notion of 'action in concert.'[29]

In addition to Guisan, Aline Sierp's scholarship is also an important touchstone for my work. In *History, Memory and Trans-European Identity: Unifying Divisions* (2017), Sierp 'challenges the widespread idea that political experiences in Europe continue to be interpreted in terms of national history.' Instead, she argues that 'the creation of a European memory culture' is visible in 'emerging common European characteristics of national commemoration, which are expressed either through similar approaches to addressing certain topics or through similar institutional acts of remembrance.'[30] Although I am less interested in the operations of the EU as a transnational political space for the politics of remembrance and more in how collective memory serves as a cognitive, motivational, and justificatory resource for integration as such,

Sierp's book is still an invaluable resource. In particular, it helps me to combat the 'presentism' of many existing studies of the politics of memory in Europe, which argue that the remembered past is merely the product of social and political manipulation that serves the needs of actors in the present.[31]

By focusing on ruptures as turning points, I reject presentist readings of the politics of memory by outlining the preconditions that define the crucial moments when memories can be fundamentally reframed through the creation of new historical narratives. In opposing instrumental interpretations of collective memory that conceptualise the past as essentially malleable, I help to identify how and when 'certain windows of opportunity' open, allowing political and cultural leaders to reshape the frameworks of collective memory. In this sense, my work can be seen as part of a move towards recognising the path-dependency of collective memory that sets in as a result of key decisions made at critical turning points. My development of the concept of historical ruptures that break apart existing narratives of the past, allowing new stories to be told, thus helps to explain both the 'constraints that se[t] limits on memory entrepreneurship in the present' and the specific circumstances under which the frameworks of collective remembrance are subject to change.[32]

A critical theory of memory

Social and political theorists have traditionally avoided explicitly addressing issues of methodology. This reluctance is puzzling, since 'the choice is not between having a method and not having one, but rather between deciding to think about method or simply carrying on unreflectively.'[33] This critique does not apply to the critical theory developed by the thinkers who coalesced around the Institute for Social Research (*Institut für Sozialforschung*) and their successors in what has come to be called the Frankfurt School. These figures all agree that methodological reflection is central to a critical theory of society that seeks to address 'great philosophical questions with the most refined methods.' The goal of such research is not merely to reach greater theoretical understanding, but to transcend the division between theory and practice. What makes critical theory distinctive is its belief that 'apolitical reflections on praxis are unconvincing.'[34]

I choose to build on this tradition for three basic reasons. First, critical theory engages with the pathologies of the present in concrete ways that not only seek to understand contemporary problems in real time, but which are also able to 'guide criticism with a practical interest in emancipation.'[35] This focus on developing a 'theory of society at the present time' is particularly well suited for my examination of the European crisis at the start of the twenty-first century, as it is based in the contention that the 'lived experience' of crisis 'afford[s] contemporaries privileged access to the structures of the social world.'[36]

Second, the fact that the Frankfurt School developed its emancipatory approach during the European 'age of total war' between 1914 and 1945 also allows me to combine theoretical insights with historical developments in an immanent manner. As a result of their common historical origins, the thinkers of the Frankfurt Circle were concerned with many of the same issues that faced the founders of the European project. Much like continental integration, the critical theory of the Frankfurt School is the product of two basic impulses: a strong commitment to antitotalitarianism based on the personal experience of war in Europe, as well as the articulation of an emancipatory vision of the good society based on an examination of this 'unmastered' – and perhaps unmasterable – past.[37]

My third motivation is that the Frankfurt School provides a model for an interdisciplinary approach grounded in real-world developments. The practitioners of critical theory are committed to the idea that the elaboration of philosophical concepts must both precede and respond to empirical research.[38] Such data, which has already been informed by philosophical reflection, is supposed to dialectically return to its starting point by enriching the theoretical ideas that the critic had laid out at the start of the project. Adorno notes that the members of the Frankfurt School 'never regarded the theory simply as a set of hypotheses but as in some sense standing on its own feet, and therefore did not intend to prove or disprove the theory through our findings but only to derive from it concrete questions for investigation, which must then be judged on their own merit.'[39]

This critical approach allows theoretical reflection and empirical analysis to mutually reinforce each other. My research therefore combines the 'explanatory-diagnostic' elements of social analysis with the 'anticipatory-utopian' perspective of normative research.[40] Working in these two stages depends on the appearance of a crisis that disrupts existing forms of life, thus serving as evidence for a disjunction between concrete social processes and the background assumptions on which they rest, such as Europe's difficulties at the start of the third millennium.[41]

In the first stage of crisis diagnosis, the theorist seeks to understand the underlying social and political pathologies of the present. Critique in its 'explanatory-diagnostic' moment seeks to penetrate below the surface of the revealed crisis to provide a descriptive account of its deeper 'social-structural causes.'[42] After providing an explanatory diagnosis, critical theory proceeds to a second, explicitly normative stage. In this 'anticipatory-utopian' phase the critic charts possible paths for emancipation from the pathologies of life that gave rise to the need for social critique in the first place. In Marcuse's words, 'Theory ... not only anticipates political practice, runs ahead of it, but also upholds the objectives of liberation in the face of failing practice.'[43]

As a result of its 'practical, emancipatory interest' critical theory is decidedly forward-looking.[44] However, the Frankfurt Circle resists outlining specific prescriptions out of respect for the decision-making ability of the inhabitants of the future: 'In regard to the essential kind of change at which critical theory aims, there can be no ... conception of it until it actually comes about.'[45] While never prescribing concrete utopias, the critic seeks to spur the community to action by imagining and presenting alternative social arrangements. As a result of this approach, critical theory is 'explanatory, practical, and normative, all at the same time.' The social criticism encouraged by the Frankfurt School thus 'challenges the validity of prevailing social institutions and arrangements through reference to some alternative idea of the good society.'[46]

Although it is often not explicitly addressed in this context, memory plays a central role in this process. As Seyla Benhabib points out, true critique cannot be merely 'based upon norms and values derived from the self-understanding of this culture and social structure'; on the contrary, it must draw on resources outside the present, i.e. either on a 'utopian vision' of the future or on the 'retrospective remembrance' of a past that has been betrayed. By bringing these two perspectives together, critique can draw on 'the past that has been eliminated' to chart paths of possible transformation in the present, leading to a more emancipated future. Thus, in the words of Moishe Postone, 'The standpoint of the critic transcends the present and juxtaposes to the existent what ought to be or what could have been had the past not been betrayed.'[47]

This temporal dimension of social and political criticism is reflected in Horkheimer and Adorno's shared conviction that 'all reification is based on forgetting.' Marcuse goes even further, rooting reason itself in the remembered experience of the past. He argues that 'memory ... is the hidden driving power behind the process of thought.'[48] By placing 'retrospective remembrance' at the centre of both empirical analysis and theoretical reflection, critical theory thus provides a model for how to combine philosophy and history through the concept of memory.

Introduction

Roadmap

The argument of this book follows the basic methodological structure of investigation provided by the Frankfurt School. The first step is to clarify and elucidate the basic concepts that guide the rest of my inquiry.[49] Chapter 1 therefore lays out an ontology of collective memory and outlines its critical potential as a resource for social and political change. It builds on the insights of Frankfurt School to develop the concept of a historical rupture as a series of traumatic events that tear existing narratives of the past asunder, allowing collective memory to act as a resource for social and political change.

Despite the broad range of approaches applied to memory since the 1970s, scholars have tended to emphasise the violent, destructive aspects of memory.[50] By contrast, I argue that the tradition of critical theory offers a constructive understanding of memory. Although the past can function as a straitjacket, limiting freedom by forcing events into chains of cause and effect, it can also be a resource for rethinking following historical ruptures. My basic thesis is that the experience of total war between 1914 and 1945 created a caesura in European understandings of the past, which gave Europeans the *cognitive*, *motivational*, and *justificatory* resources to reimagine the future.

In making this argument I highlight the importance of political generations, defined by shared formative experiences, in large-scale political transformations such as the founding of the European project. Radical changes in political organisation, like the partial turn away from the principle of national sovereignty towards community-based solutions that delegate autonomous decision-making powers to insitutions outside the constitutional infrastructure of the nation-state, do not occur overnight.[51] They also cannot be attributed to factors that operate independently of political actors. The broader social environment, such as the need to rebuild destroyed cities, restart the postwar economy, and deal with the military, political, and ideological threat of communism and the Soviet Union, invariably needs to be interpreted and acted upon by individuals. In this sense, 'Politics is a matter of human, and not merely mechanical, interaction between individuals, institutions, or groups.'[52]

After elucidating the basic philosophical concepts that guide the rest of the book, I then proceed with the empirical diagnosis of the origins of the current crisis in the form of a 'critical history of the present.'[53] Part I substantiates my claims about the important role that collective memory played in the construction of the European Communities throughout the postwar period by measuring my ideas against the evidence found in the history of European integration.[54] By drawing on historical and archival sources, I reconstruct the origins and development of Europe to demonstrate the crucial role that memory played in its success as a political project achieved by economic means.

In line with the 'explanatory-diagnostic' perspective that defines the first stage of research within the Frankfurt School, this elucidation of the history of European integration through collective memory studies also helps me to diagnose the crisis of the present. Coming to grips with the problems that Europe faces in the wake of the Great Recession requires an understanding of how the conditions that drove integration throughout the postwar period – i.e. a shared understanding of the moral dimensions of this project as a response to the violence that nationalism unleashed on the continent in the first half of the twentieth century – have started to dry up at the start of the twenty-first century. Only by understanding how the past successes of the EU built on a common memorial foundation is it possible to comprehend how the loss of this grounding has affected the project.

My qualitative, interpretive approach focuses on archival documents and other primary sources. This historical approach is well-suited to the elaboration of theoretical ideas. More specifically, the tradition of critical theory 'is deeply embedded in archival research.' Focusing on primary sources that date back to the time of the events in question respects the Frankfurt School's emphasis on the privileged perspective of the contemporary participant. Insofar as 'lived experience' is crucial to understanding the internal perspective of key agents, archival evidence is key.[55] Given my focus on individuals, engaging with archival sources also enables me to obtain 'a broader, richer, and more robust understanding of the nature of political thinking, and in particular its critical connections with political practice.' As Desmond Dinan points out, 'Contemporary, confidential records … hold the key to figuring out why the main player acted as they did.'[56]

When archives area unavailable or incomplete, I draw on other primary sources to supplement my analysis. As Guisan points out, 'Memoirs, essays and interviews abound and constitute a rich source of information regarding the common past.' Although such resources are often dismissed as propaganda, focusing on the reasons agents use to justify the narratives they tell is crucial in understanding how they sought to legitimise their actions in certain historical moments. As such, even non-archival sources are important as they reveal 'the story behind the story, how individual political actors changed their own minds, how they persuaded others to change their minds in order to pursue their worldly objectives.' I second Guisan's argument that this approach, based on 'a political tradition grounded in the texts of the Republic's actors,' which is 'quite common in the study of American political roots,' is also applicable to European integration.[57]

The chapters grouped together in Part I proceed chronologically. Chapter 2 details the founding of the first European institution, the ECSC, in 1951 and of the European *relance* in 1957, which brought the European Economic Community (EEC) into existence. This initial period is of crucial importance, because 'The four-sided institutional framework that it brought into being – Assembly, Court, Ministerial Council, and High Authority – has continued in the form of the Parliament, Court, Council of Ministers, and Commission.'[58] The chapter documents how crucial postwar leaders, particularly the first President of the European High Authority Jean Monnet, French Foreign Minister Robert Schuman, and German Chancellor Konrad Adenauer, built on their transnational collective memories to found the first European institutions. In so doing, it shows how their shared remembrance of the rupture of 1945 was crucial in helping them to create Europe based on the community model of autonomous decision-making, instead of through more traditional approaches based on international cooperation or confederalism.[59]

Based on my historical and archival research, I show that these three central actors in the first stage of integration all viewed the Second World War as an important historical rupture requiring fundamental changes to the underlying political architecture of the continent.[60] As a result of this process, they came to believe that supranational cooperation was necessary in order to curb the violent tendencies of nationalism. I call this 'the classic narrative of integration.' Although the United Kingdom was invited to participate in the European integration at its earliest stages, its leaders declined, foreshadowing the ambivalent relationship Britain has maintained with the EU since its founding.

My focus on these three leaders is hardly uncontroversial. For example, Alan Milward is critical of the traditional emphasis given to 'the lives and teachings' of these individuals, whom he dismissively labels as the 'European saints.' He argues that focusing on the 'legends of these great men' ignores the true imperatives of integration rooted in the need to reconstruct the economic, social, and political basis of Western Europe after 1945. Milward and his followers therefore argue that the history of European integration cannot be reduced to hagiography. This is certainly true, as far as it goes. However, even he is forced to concede that Monnet, Schuman, and Adenauer 'achieved prominence and success because they were among those who developed an accurate perception of … the need for those limited surrenders of national sovereignty through which the nation-state and western Europe were jointly strengthened, not as separate and opposed entities, but within a process of mutual reinforcement.'[61]

While Milward is right to resist hagiography, his dismissal of the first-person perspective of the participants in the process of integration reveals the methodological blind-spot of much of the existing literature. Milward's positivistic narrative is driven by the assumption that postnational integration was the natural (and perhaps even only) solution to the problems the states of Europe faced after the end of the Second World War. By paying closer attention to the early debates of these individuals, which I lay out in chapter 2, I follow Craig Parsons in arguing that the 'Schuman Declaration and the subsequent creation of the ECSC were not inevitable,' nor were they part of 'a prearranged plan.' By focusing on the role that memory played from the first-person perspective of these participants, I show how the lessons of the past were deployed to overcome the traditional resistance to dismantling the doctrine of sovereignty. Although ruptures can trigger new thinking, 'entrepreneurial leaders must articulate a new vision of unity, formulate specific policy proposals, and shepherd those changes through stormy political seas.'[62]

Chapter 3, which focuses on 'countermemory and generational change' after the passing of the first generation of postwar European leaders, moves the narrative forward by normatively reconstructing the period of European stagnation (1959–84) and the second phase of integration (1985–2003). This leads to the culmination of what I call the 'classic narrative of integration' in the text Habermas and Derrida published in response to the pan-European protests against the American invasion of Iraq on 13 February 2003. The first phase of European integration was followed by a long period of institutional torpor lasting through the 1970s. This 'Eurosclerosis' was due at least in part to outside factors associated with the end of colonialism and the oil crisis. However, it was also the result of a counter-narrative brought to the fore by General Charles de Gaulle, who sought to return the state to the centre of political and economic power in Europe.

The expansion of Europe beyond its Franco-German core forced Europe to confront new understandings of the past. This was strengthened by the accession of the United Kingdom, whose more triumphalist memories of the war meant that the British took a fundamentally different view of the European project from the start. The first expansion of the European Communities to the United Kingdom – after it was vetoed not once but twice by de Gaulle – required the nascent European institutions to confront the alternative memory regime with a different interpretation of the key events of the past. Although some parts of this narrative are based on archival evidence, it mostly builds on other types of primary source documents, including memoirs, speeches, and reporting from the time, due to the fact that most of the archives dealing with this period are still embargoed (the same is true of the even more recent material in chapter 4).

Despite political stagnation and challenges to the vision of the 'founding fathers,' the classic narrative survived de Gaulle's attack. In the mid-1980s a new cohort of European leaders, including Commission President Jacques Delors, French President François Mitterrand, and German Chancellor Helmut Kohl, came to power. While they shared a preexisting disposition towards Europe, their leanings were reinforced by the opportunities offered by the fall of the Berlin Wall in 1989. Mirroring Monnet, Schuman, and Adenauer, the constellation of Delors, Mitterrand, and Kohl reinvigorated the project with a swath of new initiatives, including the completion of the Common Market (CM), the Schengen open-border zone, and the Economic and Monetary Union (EMU) under a shared currency. This second phase of integration also established the memory of the Holocaust as central to the EU's conception of itself, resulting in the culmination of the classic narrative of integration.

Chapter 4 – the last of Part I – traces the difficulties the EU has experienced since the turn of the third millennium through the lens of what I call 'fragmentation and the loss of European memory.' Recent challenges to the classic narrative have taken at least three different forms, including: (1) the desire of the new postcommunist member-states from East-Central Europe, which joined the union in waves after 2004, for recognition of their suffering under communism; (2) the growing economic problems brought about by the Eurozone crisis starting in 2010; and (3) the push towards a return to the nation-state symbolised by Brexit and the anti-European populist movements that have swept across the continent. All of these challenges have confronted the EU and the classic narrative with new interpretations of a past that has increasingly faded from experiential memory.

Chapter 4 analyses these difficulties. The postcommunist states of East-Central Europe questioned the central place of the Holocaust and the image of Auschwitz in the classic narrative of integration.[63] The divisions resulting from this confrontation, which bifurcated Europe along the old lines of the Iron Curtain, were further reinforced by the monetary, banking, and sovereign debt crisis emanating from the Great Recession, which created additional periphery–core cleavages between north and south. This was followed by the Brexit referendum and is further threatened by the rise of populism and the spectre of additional votes to leave the EU. I argue the very different, more triumphalist collective memories Britain carried from the Second World War as a victor whose territory was never occupied by the Nazis have been a disrupting force within integration ever since its entry into the European Communities in 1975. These proximate challenges have been compounded by the rise to power of the first generation of European leaders with no personal memories of Europe's age of total war.

Following the methodology of the Frankfurt School, Part II charts possible paths for the future transformation of Europe by reflecting on the latent, immanent potential of the project to realise its own goals. Chapter 5 therefore examines how the EU can transform personal memories of total war into a more durable social imaginary by drawing on noneconomic social resources, especially in light of the populist challenge to postwar European values. While memories of the continental experience of total war between 1914 and 1945 helped push the founding and development of the Union along through two phases of integration, it is clear that they can no longer play this role. As Neil Fligstein points out, 'Memories of World War II have faded as that generation has passed. Europe now has a new set of challenges to deal with.'[64] This recognition, combined with the differing historical experiences of the leaders and populations of new member-states, poses a number of problems for Europe as 'a community of memory,' especially in light of the ongoing European crisis of monetary union and sovereign debt.[65] Whereas Europeans of the founding generation saw the Schuman Declaration of 1950, and the European movement borne of it, as what Arendt called 'the pardon and the promise' of the postwar world, the foundations of the EU and its guiding narrative have to be rethought for the project to sustain itself into the future.[66]

In chapter 6 I argue that social developments, such as rising rates of inter-European marriage and the advent of the first generation of Europeans that grew up within a continent of open borders, combined with civic education focusing on teaching national history within its European context, can help ground the intra-European solidarity necessary for a true supranational democracy. For the EU to survive, it must find a way to harness the normative resources of the past in the long term. If not, short-term economic calculations will be all that keeps the Union together, to the detriment of the citizens of Europe.

Chapter 6 thus moves away from the context of European unification by applying my understanding of the power of constructive memory in the aftermath of historical ruptures to other temporal and geographic contexts. I compare the generational crisis of leadership visible in the continental Euro-crisis to the American Civil War, the major crisis the United States experienced after the passing of the revolutionary generation that experienced its founding first-hand. Much like the United States seventy years after its creation, the EU will also have to find a way to preserve what their forefathers built after the passage of seven decades. US President Abraham Lincoln called the revolutionary cohort the 'pillars of the temple of liberty,' noting that after their passing 'that temple must fall unless we, their descendants, supply their places with other pillars.'[67] The same is true of the EU at a similar point in its own history. This brings my project into conversation with the broader debates on constitutional moments and the founding of political communities, allowing me to think about the broader theoretical implications of my argument.

In the book's concluding chapter I reflect on the ongoing issues facing Europe in the wake of the Brexit vote and the continued threat of right-wing populism. I focus in particular on the ways that populists leading the backlash against the constructive narrative of memory created in the aftermath of the European rupture of 1945 have drawn on older symbols, often associated with the fascist movements that dominated Europe's age of total war. While the experience of rupture enables the creation of constructive narratives out of the material of the past – as I argue in chapter 1 – collective memory can also function in destructive ways, as individuals and groups opposed to these projects are able to rehabilitate older narratives and symbols in times of crisis. A conception of European peoplehood that allows the EU to stand up to international pressures and resolve future problems by linking collective memories to future projects, the past to the future through the present, can hope to resolve the current European crisis.

In addition to bringing the book full circle by reflecting on the dangers of collective memory at the start of the third millennium, I also argue for the continued utility and applicability of the Frankfurt School's approach to social criticism. It is certainly possible to reconstruct the history of the past hundred years as part of a learning process resulting in large part from the world's experience of total war on the old continent. However, it is also true that many of the same problems – including prejudice, inequality, violence, and the increasing mechanisation of everyday life – that spurred the thinkers of the Frankfurt School to develop their distinctive approach to critical theory

Introduction

in the 1920s and 1930s still persist, albeit in slightly different guises. I argue that the Frankfurt School's approach to understanding the social pathologies of the present remains as critical for diagnosing the European crisis at the start of the twenty-first century as it was for understanding the rise of totalitarianism and the problems associated with instrumental reason in the interwar years.

Notes

1   K. Lowe, *Savage Continent: Europe in the Aftermath of World War II* (New York: St. Martin's Press, 2012); J. Habermas and J. Derrida, 'February 15, Or what Binds Europeans Together: A Plea for a Common Foreign Policy, Beginning in the Core of Europe,' *Constellations*, 10:3 (2003), 293. For more on total war, see J. Black, *The Age of Total War, 1860–1945* (Westport: Praeger Security International, 2006). My periodisation of the 'age of total war' differs slightly from Black's, as I focus on the twentieth century and the move towards total mobilisation of the whole of society for warfare over the course of two world wars.

2   P. Anderson, *The New Old World* (London: Verso, 2009), 132–133; R. Bellamy and D. Castiglione, 'Legitimizing the Euro-"polity" and its "Regime": The Normative Turn in EU Studies,' *European Journal of Political Theory*, 2:1 (2003), 7–34; U. Beck, 'The Cosmopolitan Condition: Why Methodological Nationalism Fails,' *Theory, Culture & Society*, 24:7–8 (2007); R. Falk, 'The Making of Global Citizenship,' in Bart van Steenbergen (ed), *The Condition of Citizenship* (London: Sage Publications, 1994), 136.

3   A. Ferrara, 'Europe as a "Special Area for Human Hope,"' *Constellations*, 14:3 (2007), 315–331; M. Loriaux, *European Union and the Deconstruction of the Rhineland Frontier* (Cambridge: Cambridge University Press, 2008), 1; H. Arendt, *The Human Condition* (Chicago: University of Chicago Press, 1998), 137.

4   M. J. Shapiro, 'The Moralized Economy in Hard Times,' *Theory & Event*, 14:4 (2011); C. Lapavitsas, 'Financialised Capitalism: Crisis and Financial Expropriation,' *Historical Materialism*, 17:2 (2009). On the democratic deficits of the EU, see J. Bohman, 'The European Union Democratic Deficit: Federalists, Skeptics, and Revisionists,' *European Journal of Political Theory*, 5:2 (2006); A. Moravcsik, 'In Defense of the "Democratic Deficit": Reassessing Legitimacy in the European Union,' *Journal of Common Market Studies*, 40:4 (2002); G. Majone, 'Europe's "Democratic Deficit": The Question of Standards,' *European Journal of Law*, 4:1 (March, 1998); K. Featherstone, 'Jean Monnet and the "Democratic Deficit" in the European Union,' *Journal of Common Market Studies*, 32:2 (1994); R. Bellamy and S. Kröger, 'Domesticating the Democratic Deficit? The Role of National Parliaments and Parties in the EU's System of Governance,' *Parliamentary Affairs*, 67:2 (2014).

5   E. Kaufmann, 'Brexit Voters: NOT the Left Behind,' *Fabian Review* (24 June 2016); S. Brakman, H. Garretsen, and T. Kohl, 'Consequences of Brexit and Options for a "Global Britain,"' *Papers in Regional Science*, 97:1 (2018); T. Fetzer, 'Did Austerity Cause Brexit?' *American Economic Review*, 109:11 (2019).

6   J. Rupnik, 'Surging Illiberalism in the East,' *Journal of Democracy*, 27:4 (2016); J.-W. Müller, 'Homo Orbánicus,' *New York Review of Books* (5 April 2018); P. J. Verovšek,

'Memory and Forgetting in Central Europe,' *Social Europe Journal* (20 December 2018), www.socialeurope.eu/migration-and-forgetting-in-central-europe (accessed 20 December 2018); S. Benhabib, 'The Return of Fascism,' *The New Republic* (29 September 2017).

7 Z. Bauman and C. Bordoni, *State of Crisis* (Cambridge: Polity, 2014), 7; R. J. Holton, 'The Idea of Crisis in Modern Society,' *The British Journal of Sociology*, 38:4 (1987), 504; S. N. Kalyvas, 'The Intellectual Impact of the Euro Crisis,' *European Politics and Society Newsletter*, Summer (2012), 11.

8 P. J. Verovšek, 'Critical Theory as Medicine? On the Diagnosis and Treatment of Social Pathology,' *Thesis Eleven*, 155:1 (2019).

9 M. Horkheimer, 'Notes on Science and the Crisis,' in *Critical Theory: Selected Essays*, trans. M. J. O'Connell (New York: Continuum Publishing Company, 1972), 7; S. Benhabib, *Critique, Norm, and Utopia: A Study of the Foundations of Critical Theory* (New York: Columbia University Press, 1986), 226.

10 P. M. R. Stirk, *Critical Theory, Politics and Society: An Introduction* (New York: Continuum, 2000), 127; Benhabib, *Critique, Norm, and Utopia*, 226; A. Mitscherlich, 'Die Krankheiten der Gesellschaft und die psychosomatische Medizin,' in T. Allert (ed), *Mitscherlich: Gesammelte Schriften II* (*Psychosomatik 2*) (Frankfurt am Main: Suhrkamp, 1983).

11 N. Fraser, 'Identity, Exclusion, and Critique: A Response to Four Critics,' *European Journal of Political Theory*, 6:3 (2007), 322; J. Habermas, *Knowledge and Human Interests*, trans. Jeremy J. Shapiro (Boston: Beacon Press, 1971).

12 K. R. McNamara, *The Politics of Everyday Europe: Constructing Authority in the European Union* (Oxford: Oxford University Press, 2015), 12.

13 J. Derrida, 'Force of Law: The Mystical Foundation of Authority,' in D. Cornell and M. Rosenfeld (eds), *Deconstruction and the Possibility of Justice* (New York: Routledge, 1992), 13. Within the history of the EU such discursive moments 'closed horizons, opened others, and forced the discursive representation of space in radically new directions,' Loriaux, *European Union and the Deconstruction of the Rhineland Frontier*, 15.

14 Loriaux, *European Union and the Deconstruction of the Rhineland Frontier*, 1; P. J. Verovšek, 'The Loss of European Memory,' *Social Europe Journal* (12 February 2019), www.socialeurope.eu/the-loss-of-european-memory (accessed 12 February 2019).

15 E. B. Haas, *The Uniting of Europe: Political, Social, and Economic Forces, 1950–1957* (Notre Dame, IN: University of Notre Dame Press, 2004), 16, emphasis in original.

16 C. Guisan, *A Political Theory of Identity in European Integration: Memory and Policies* (New York: Routledge, 2012), 1 and citations therein. For the best iterations of the existing scholarship, see E. B. Haas, *Beyond the Nation-State: Functionalism and International Organization* (Stanford: Stanford University Press, 1964); A. Moravcsik, *The Choice for Europe: Social Purpose and State Power from Messina to Maastricht* (Ithaca, NY: Cornell University Press, 1998); A. S. Milward, *The European Rescue of the Nation-State* (London: Routledge, 1992).

17 A. Pagden, 'Europe: Conceptualizing a Continent,' in A. Pagden (ed), *The Idea of Europe: From Antiquity to the European Union* (New York: Cambridge University Press, 2002), 45; O. Calligaro, *Negotiating Europe: EU Promotion of Europeanness since the 1950s* (New York: Palgrave Macmillan, 2013).

18 McNamara, *The Politics of Everyday Europe*, 3; B. F. Nelsen and J. L. Guth, *Religion and the Struggle for European Union: Confessional Culture and the Limits of Integration* (Washington, DC: Georgetown University Press, 2015), 4.

Introduction

19 J. Blustein, *The Moral Demands of Memory* (Cambridge: Cambridge University Press, 2008); Guisan, *A Political Theory of Identity in European Integration*, 1.

20 E. O. Eriksen, *The Unfinished Democratization of Europe* (Oxford: Oxford University Press, 2009), 1; R. N. Lebow, W. Kansteiner, and C. Fogu, *The Politics of Memory in Postwar Europe* (Durham, NC: Duke University Press, 2006); J. K. Olick, *The Politics of Regret: On Collective Memory and Historical Responsibility* (New York: Routledge, 2007); T. U. Berger, *War, Guilt, and World Politics After World War II* (Cambridge: Cambridge University Press, 2012).

21 *Convention Setting Up a European University Institute* (1972), www.eui.eu/Documents/ AboutEUI/Convention/English.pdf (accessed 12 November 2010), Art 2.1. The European Science Foundation also funds research into the key events of European unification.

22 Haas, *The Uniting of Europe*, 367. See also E. B. Haas, 'International Integration: The European and the Universal Process,' *International Organization*, 15:3 (1961).

23 This is the position of a group of scholars that gathered in Paris in 2006 to discuss the European memory of the Second World War. See 'Eben war ich noch ein Nationalheld. Rollenwechsel im Kollektivgedächtnis: In Paris erörtern Historiker Varianten der Erinnerung an den Zweiten Weltkrieg,' *Frankfurter Allgemeine Zeitung* (11 April 2006).

24 D. W. Blight, 'The Memory Boom: Why and Why Now?' in P. Boyer and J. V. Wertsch (eds), *Memory in Mind and Culture* (Cambridge: Cambridge University Press, 2009); R. Kagan, *Of Paradise and Power: America and Europe in the New World Order* (New York: Vintage Books, 2004), 55. See also T. Judt, 'The Past is another Country: Myth and Memory in Postwar Europe,' *Daedalus*, 121:4 (1992), 83–118; A. Assmann, 'Europe: A Community of Memory?' *GHI Bulletin*, 40 (2007), 11–25.

25 J. Derrida, *On Cosmopolitanism and Forgiveness*, trans. M. Dooley and M. Hughes (New York: Routledge, 2001), 28, emphasis in original. For a study of newspaper narratives, see C. Bottici, 'Europe, War and Remembrance,' in F. Cerutti and S. Lucarelli (eds), *The Search for a European Identity: Values, Policies and Legitimacy of the European Union* (London: Routledge, 2008), 45–58. For more on collective memory as a research paradigm, see P. J. Verovšek, 'Collective Memory, Politics, and the Influence of the Past: The Politics of Memory as a Research Paradigm,' *Politics, Groups, and Identities*, 4:3 (2016).

26 A. Sierp, *History, Memory, and Trans-European Identity: Unifying Divisions* (London: Routledge, 2017), 10, 12.

27 Guisan, *A Political Theory of Identity in European Integration*, 3, 2, 5. For more on the EU as an agent of peace, see R. G. Whitman and S. Wolff, *The European Union as a Global Conflict Manager* (London: Routledge, 2012); N. Tocci, *The EU and Conflict Resolution: Promoting Peace in the Backyard* (London: Routledge, 2007); T. Diez, M. Albert, and S. Stetter (eds), *The European Union and Border Conflicts: The Power of Integration and Association* (Cambridge: Cambridge University Press, 2008).

28 Guisan, *A Political Theory of Identity in European Integration*, 2.

29 See P. J. Verovšek, 'Unexpected Support for European Integration: Memory, Rupture and Totalitarianism in Arendt's Political Theory,' *The Review of Politics*, 76:3 (2014); P. J. Verovšek, 'Integration After Totalitarianism: Arendt and Habermas on the Postwar Imperatives of Memory,' *Journal of International Political Theory*, 16:1 (2020).

30 Sierp, *History, Memory, and Trans-European Identity*, 7, 3. See also T. Risse, *A Community of Europeans? Transnational Identities and Public Spheres* (Ithaca, NY: Cornell University

Press, 2010); T. Risse, 'A European Identity? Europeanization and the Evolution of Nation-State Identities,' in M. G. Cowles, J. Caporaso, and T. Risse (eds), *Transforming Europe: Europeanization and Domestic Change* (Ithaca, NY: Cornell University Press, 2001).

31 M. Foucault, *Language, Counter-Memory, Practice* (Ithaca, NY: Cornell University Press, 1977); E. J. Hobsbawm and T. O. Ranger, *The Invention of Tradition* (Cambridge: Cambridge University Press, 1992).

32 Sierp, *History, Memory, and Trans-European Identity*, 7; R. Brubaker, *Ethnicity without Groups* (Cambridge, MA: Harvard University Press, 2006), 162. See also J. K. Olick, 'Memory and the Nation: Continuities, Conflicts, and Transformations,' *Social Science History*, 22:4 (1998); J. Winter, 'The Generation of Memory: Reflections on the Memory Boom in Contemporary Historical Studies,' *Bulletin of the German Historical Institute* (2000); M. Schudson, 'The Present in the Past Versus the Past in the Present,' *Communication*, 11 (1989).

33 D. Leopold and M. Stears (eds), *Political Theory: Methods and Approaches* (Oxford: Oxford University Press, 2008), 2.

34 M. Horkheimer, *Sozialphilosophische Studien. Aufsätze, Reden und Vorträge 1930–1972* (Frankfurt am Main: Athenäum Fischer Taschenbuch Verlag, 1972), 33; T. W. Adorno, *Stichworte: Kritische Modelle 2*, vol. 347 (Frankfurt am Main: Suhrkamp, 1969), 174, translations mine; R. Celikates, *Kritik als soziale Praxis: gesellschaftliche Selbstverständigung und kritische Theorie* (Frankfurt am Main: Campus, 2009).

35 I. M. Young, *Justice and the Politics of Difference* (Princeton: Princeton University Press, 1990), 5.

36 M. Horkheimer, 'Vorwort,' *Zeitschrift für Sozialforschung*, 1 (1932), I; J. Habermas, *The Theory of Communicative Action*, trans. T. A. McCarthy (Boston: Beacon Press, 1984/87), vol. II, 403.

37 M. Cooke, *Re-Presenting the Good Society* (Cambridge, MA: MIT Press, 2006); L. Löwenthal, *An Unmastered Past* (Berkeley: University of California Press, 1987).

38 M. Jay, *The Dialectical Imagination: A History of the Frankfurt School and the Institute of Social Research, 1923–1950* (Boston: Little, Brown and Company, 1973), 221.

39 T. W. Adorno, 'Scientific Experiences of a European Scholar in America,' in D. Fleming and B. Bailyn (eds), *The Intellectual Migration: Europe and America, 1930–1960* (Cambridge, MA: Harvard University Press, 1969), 363; also Jay, *The Dialectical Imagination*, 251.

40 Benhabib, *Critique, Norm, and Utopia*, 226.

41 P. Strydom, *Contemporary Critical Theory and Methodology* (London: Routledge, 2013), 152.

42 M. Iser, *Empörung und Fortschritt: Grundlagen einer kritischen Theorie der Gesellschaft* (Frankfurt: Campus Verlag, 2008), 10.

43 H. Marcuse, *Soviet Marxism: A Critical Analysis* (Boston: Beacon Press, 1964), 106.

44 Fraser, 'Identity, Exclusion, and Critique,' 322.

45 M. Horkheimer, 'Traditional and Critical Theory,' *Critical Theory: Selected Essays*, trans. M. J. O'Connell (New York: Continuum, 1972), 220–221.

46 J. Bohman, 'Critical Theory and Democracy,' in D. M. Rasmussen (ed), *Handbook of Critical Theory* (Oxford: Blackwell, 1996), 190; Cooke, *Re-Presenting the Good Society*, 155. For more on the role of utopian thinking in critical theory – and political theory more generally – see P. J. Verovšek, 'Impure Theorizing in an Imperfect World: Politics, Utopophobia and Critical Theory in Geuss's Realism,' *Philosophy & Social Criticism* 45:3 (2019).

47   Benhabib, *Critique, Norm, and Utopia*, 226, 180; M. Postone, 'Political Theory and Historical Analysis,' in C. J. Calhoun (ed), *Habermas and the Public Sphere* (Cambridge, MA: MIT Press, 1992), 166–167.

48   M. Horkheimer and T. W. Adorno, *Dialektik der Aufklärung. Philosophische Fragmente* (Frankfurt am Main: Fischer Taschenbuch Verlag, 1944), 274, translation mine; H. Marcuse, *Eros and Civilization: A Philosophical Inquiry into Freud* (Boston: Beacon Press, 1966), 27–29.

49   D. Held, *Introduction to Critical Theory: Horkheimer to Habermas* (Berkeley: University of California Press, 1980), 34.

50   From this perspective, the move towards political community in Europe is unexpected, as it has occurred on a continent haunted by unprecedented bloodshed. See S. J. Kaufman, *Modern Hatreds: The Symbolic Politics of Ethnic War* (New York: Cornell University Press, 2001); S. N. Kalyvas, *The Logic of Violence in Civil War* (New York: Cambridge University Press, 2006), 401–411; J. J. Mearsheimer, 'Back to the Future: Instability in Europe After the Cold War,' *International Security*, 15:1 (1990), 5–56.

51   A. J. Zurcher, *The Struggle to Unite Europe, 1940–1958: An Historical Account of the Development of the Contemporary European Movement from its Origin in the Pan-European Union to the Drafting of the Treaties for Euratom and the European Common Market* (New York: New York University Press, 1958), x.

52   R. Geuss, *Philosophy and Real Politics* (Princeton: Princeton University Press, 2008), 1.

53   T. McCarthy, 'Response to Critics,' *Symposia on Gender, Race and Philosophy*, 8:1 (2012), 2.

54   This move is part of a general trend within studies of the EU, where 'the dividing line between historians and political scientists is less rigid than it once was.' D. Dinan, 'Introduction,' in D. Dinan (ed), *Origins and Evolution of the European Union* (Oxford: Oxford University Press, 2006), 6.

55   S. Hazareesingh and K. Nabulsi, 'Using Archival Sources to Theorize about Politics,' in D. Leopold and M. Stears, *Political Theory: Methods and Approaches* (Oxford: Oxford University Press, 2008), 152, 170.

56   Dinan, 'Introduction,' 5. Since many of the key source texts of European integration are readily available outside archives, I cite published sources where possible to make it easier for other researchers to locate and look up references.

57   Guisan, *A Political Theory of Identity in European Integration*, 6, 66, 2.

58   F. J. Fransen, *The Supranational Politics of Jean Monnet: Ideas and Origins of the European Community* (Westport: Greenwood Press, 2001), 134–135.

59   S. B. Wells, *Jean Monnet: Unconventional Statesman* (Boulder: Lynne Rienner, 2011), 157.

60   Chapter 2 is based on research conducted at a number of archives, including Monnet's papers at the Fondation Jean Monnet pour l'Europe in Lausanne, Switzerland, Schuman's archives in Lausanne and at the Archives départementales de la Moselle in Metz, France, and Adenauer's papers held at the Stiftung-Bundeskanzler-Adenauer-Haus in Rhöndorf, Germany.

61   Milward, *The European Rescue of the Nation-State*, 281; M. Joly, *Le mythe Jean Monnet: Contribution à une sociologie historique de la construction européenne* (Paris: CNRS Éditions, 2007). See also W. Kaiser, 'From Great Men to Ordinary Citizens? The Biographical Approach to Narrating European Integration in Museums,' *Culture Unbound: Journal of Current Cultural Research*, 3 (2011).

62   Nelsen and Guth, *Religion and the Struggle for European Union*, 187, 190, 189; P. Anderson, 'Under the Sign of the Interim,' *London Review of Books*, 18:1 (1996).

63   A. Littoz-Monnet, 'The EU Politics of Remembrance: Can Europeans Remember Together?' *West European Politics*, 35:5 (2012); H. Swoboda and J. M. Wiersma (eds), *Politics of the Past: The Use and Abuse of History* (Brussels: The Socialist Group in the European Parliament and the Renner Institute, 2009).

64   N. Fligstein, *Euro-Clash: The EU, European Identity, and the Future of Europe* (Oxford: Oxford University Press, 2008), vii.

65   Assmann, 'Europe: A Community of Memory?' 11–25.

66   Quoted in N. Tietze and U. Bielefeld, 'In Search of Europe: An Interview with Jacques Delors,' *Eurozine* (1 July 2011), www.eurozine.com/in-search-of-europe/ (accessed 2 July 2011).

67   A. Lincoln, 'Address before the Young Men's Lyceum of Springfield, Illinois,' speech, 27 January 1838, http://constitution.org/lincoln/lyceum.htm (accessed 2 February 2013).

Chapter 1

Collective memory as a resource for political change

The dreams of the future move in the temporal dimension of past life, fed by memory ... out of which all wishes and hopes are deduced.

Reinhart Koselleck, *Terror and Dream* (2004)

Critical theory and collective memory[1]

Over the course of the second half of the twentieth century, collective memory has become a central concept in the humanities and the social sciences.[2] Its surge in scholarly importance coincides with a number of broader social movements, most notably the student revolts of 1968, when the first generation that came of age in the postwar era sought to uncover the complicity of their parents and grandparents in the sufferings and atrocities of totalitarianism. The growing interest in collective remembrance that accompanied the fall of the dictatorships in Spain, Portugal, and Greece in the 1970s and 1980s was given further impetus by the events of 1989 and 'the resurfacing of suppressed national concerns among subjugated European peoples on both sides of the Iron Curtain,' which allowed issues of collective memory that had been repressed by the bipolar narrative of the Cold War to re-emerge.[3]

From its most pioneering early studies – such as Paul Fussell's pathbreaking work on the cultural impact of the Great War, to Henry Rousso's examination of Vichy France, and Annette Insdorf's study of cinematic representations of the Holocaust, to name just a few of the most prominent examples – collective memory studies, as well as the various social movements it has generated and responded to, has centred on the events that occurred between 1914 and 1945.[4] The increasing importance of remembrance to social and political life, combined with this relatively narrow temporal focus, shows how power-fully Europe's experience of total war 'retains its grip on memory and myth.' 1945 has become a crucial turning point, a *Stunde Null* (zero hour) that has replaced national dates and markers across the continent as the 'key to what lies both upstream and downstream.'[5] Given the prominence of the Holocaust in the origins and development of the broader interest in collective remem-brance, Germany is a central focus of collective memory studies as a research paradigm.[6]

Drawing on Friedrich Nietzsche's *Untimely Meditations* (1876) on the 'Use and Abuse of History,' the existing scholarship stresses how the past acts as a 'space' or 'site of contestation' and on the 'conflictual and divisive processes that memory mobilisation triggers.'[7] This emphasis has led to a focus on the 'sins of memory' that tie individuals and communities to the past through deterministic chains of cause and effect. On this dominant reading of the pol-itics of remembrance, memory and history are obstacles to conflict resolution at best; at worst they drive 'cycles of hatred' by passing historical grievances on to subsequent generations.[8] Despite its influence, I argue this understanding of collective memory is based on a one-sided reading of Nietzsche. Looking beyond the *Untimely Meditations* to the *Genealogy of Morals* (1887), Nietzsche himself acknowledges that neither individual identities nor the broader social order can exist without an awareness of the past. He concludes that humanity is faced with the 'paradoxical task' of having to remember, while not being trapped by the past.[9]

In contrast to this usual 'negative' reading of collective memory, I draw on the thinkers associated with the Institute for Social Research in Frankfurt to develop a critical theory of remembrance as a 'positive,' constructive resource for social and political transformation in the aftermath of broad historical ruptures.[10] In this sense, my work is part of a broader attempt to understand not only the problems and far-reaching consequences involved in historical injustice, but also the historical and contemporary responsibilities that it generates.[11] While collective memory can reduce the autonomy of both indi-viduals and communities in the present, the writings of the Frankfurt School show that these experiences can also be important resources for change in the aftermath of events that delegitimise existing narratives and make existing interpretations of the past untenable. Despite their differences and internal disagreements, Theodor Adorno, Max Horkheimer, Herbert Marcuse, Walter Benjamin, Jürgen Habermas, and the other critics associated with this intel-lectual tradition share an understanding of Europe's age of total war as a historical caesura, i.e. as a narrative break whose experience necessitates a fundamental rethinking of the meaning of the past.

Generalising from these insights, I argue that memory provides individuals and communities with important *cognitive*, *motivational*, and *justificatory* resources to rethink the meaning of the past in the aftermath of broad historical ruptures. During normal politics, narratives of collective memory serve established interests, as existing institutions, rules, habits, and traditions create forward-looking narratives that flow logically from previously established plotlines. In the course of everyday life, public understandings of the past therefore play a stabilising, conservative role.

In reflecting on their experience of Europe's bloody twentieth century, the members of the Frankfurt Circle realised that moments of crisis make paradigm shifts possible by breaking down existing causal chains. Harrowing events, particularly when they follow one upon the other, create a rupture in existing historical imaginaries, forcing individuals and communities to question received wisdom and rethink the meaning of the past. While historical events usually limit the range of possible plotlines, during 'Benjaminian moments' of crisis collective memory can also provide the resources necessary to think politics anew.[12]

By framing my theoretical contribution in this way, I both build on and depart from the small but increasingly important existing body of work on European integration and collective remembrance. Although I am interested in the EU's attempts to create shared understanding of the past and 'the wider question of whether or not it is possible to develop a European memory framework,' unlike Aline Sierp I do not focus on the development of the EU as a supranational arena 'where diverging memories can find their expression and be dealt with in a new way.' Similarly, while I also explore 'how participants in the European founding dealt with their historical memories of war, invasion and mutual exploitation,' in contrast to Catherine Guisan, who focuses on how the EU's approach the memory can serve as a model of peace and reconciliation, I do so in order to reflect on how collective memory can open space for new political thinking and new forms of political community in the aftermath of experiences that shatter existing narrative frameworks.[13]

The critical theory of rupture and collective memory that I present in this chapter is an exercise in theoretical development, not in hermeneutical interpretation. I therefore treat the thinkers of the Frankfurt School as part of a unified tradition that seeks to transmit 'a relatively coherent body of political thought and practice from one generation to the next.' This move is not meant to deny their disagreements. Despite their differences and internal squabbles, I argue that the members of the Frankfurt School all 'adopted some form of collective label and clearly believed that they were engaged in a common enterprise.'[14]

This is particularly true of their attempts to understand their experience of the rupture of 1945 as part of a broader diagnosis of the times (*Zeitdiagnose*). I use their insights to better understand the role of collective memory as a constructive resource for social innovation following events that break apart existing communal understandings of the past. Even though my conclusions diverge from the explicit positions held by certain members of the Frankfurt Circle, my project shares the basic theoretical orientation and emancipatory goals of the tradition of critical theory.

For example, in reconstructing the concept of rupture I draw heavily on a Benjaminian reading of history that Horkheimer opposed. In his early writings on history and memory, Benjamin argues that the past has to remain open and incomplete so that the survivors can – potentially at least – satisfy their moral debt to victims in the present. In a letter from March 1937 Horkheimer disagrees vehemently with this approach, arguing that Benjamin's ideas are an affront to the sufferings of the victims of atrocity: 'Past injustice has occurred and is completed. The slain are really slain.' Responding to this critique, Benjamin writes, 'The corrective to this line of thinking may be found in the consideration that history is not simply a science but also and not least a form of remembrance <*Eingedenken*>. What science has "determined," remembrance can modify.'[15] Despite Horkheimer's explicit objections, I argue that by preserving the force of memory's critical content for the present, Benjamin's perspective on history better exemplifies the emancipatory mission of critical theory than the position Horkheimer outlines in his letter.[16]

This theoretical chapter starts by defining collective memory and clarifying the connection between the personal recollections of individuals and collective remembrance. I then turn to the thinkers associated with the Frankfurt School to show how crises create a break in the narrative fabric of the past, allowing collective memory to be redeployed as a form of social criticism. The section after that considers the differences between the narrative breaks that occur in the private lives of individuals and the communal caesurae that count as broad historical ruptures for the generations that share an experience of them. This is followed by an explication of my critical theory of memory, which shows how remembrance can function as a *cognitive, motivational,* and *justificatory* resource in the aftermath of historical ruptures. The chapter concludes by examining the important role political leaders play in interpreting collective narratives of the past. In so doing, I also tie these theoretical insights back to European integration.

History, memory, and narrative

On a conceptual level, memory and history can be differentiated in a number of ways. Whereas history is defined by the study of external data, especially archival texts, memory is experienced as something that comes from within. It is an affective connection, 'a felt knowledge of recent events' created by formative experiences in the life of the individual or community. In contrast to history, remembrance is not defined by the chronology of linear time. Instead, memory 'makes the past "reappear" and live again in the present,' refusing 'to keep the past in the past, to draw the line, as it were, that is constitutive of the modern enterprise of historiography.'[17]

The concept of collective memory (*mémoire collective*) originates in the work of the French sociologist Maurice Halbwachs. While he was not a member of the Institute for Social Research, Halbwachs had direct personal and intellectual connections to the Frankfurt School. In 1933 he helped Horkheimer move the Institute from Frankfurt to Geneva, where it was reincorporated as the Société internationale de recherches sociales (International Society of Social Research). Halbwachs also intervened to ensure Walter Benjamin's release from the Vichy internment camp at Nevers in 1940 before his own arrest and deportation to Buchenwald, where he died of dysentery shortly before the camp's liberation in 1945.[18]

Halbwachs's observations of European society in the aftermath of the First World War show that it is impossible to separate individual memories from collective remembrance, since personal life histories are always created through interaction with others and with society as a whole. In his masterwork, *On Collective Memory* (*Les cadres sociaux de la mémoire*, 1925), Halbwachs argues that individual identities are not only socially rediscovered (*retrouvée*); they are also socially reconstructed (*reconstruite*). Individual remembrance does not exist independently of society, since, 'It is in society that people normally acquire their memories. It is also in society that they recall, recognise, and localise their memories.'[19]

Halbwachs demonstrates that social frameworks are necessary to give meaning to recalled events. In addition to helping individuals form stable identities and connecting them to other members of their community, existing institutions and traditions link them to their ancestors as well as to posterity by giving the community a vertical, temporal dimension to go with the horizontal, social dimension of daily life. These reference points also provide individuals with a historical imaginary that shapes their selection and interpretation of formative occurrences. As a result, individual life histories and communal narratives of the past do not give equal weight to all events. On the contrary, collective remembrance is marked by a distinctive temporality. Unlike linear time, memory is multilevelled and subject to different rates of acceleration and deceleration. It endows certain events with particular and repeated meaning while silencing or forgetting others.[20]

The thinkers of the Frankfurt School were quick to pick up on Halbwachs's concept of collective memory and his insights into the socially constructed structure of the past. The work of Walter Benjamin is particularly important in this regard. Building on Halbwachs's ideas, Benjamin distinguishes between two types of experience: socially integrated 'authentic experiences' (*Erfahrungen*) and atomistic 'everyday events' (*Erlebnisse*). Whereas *Erlebnisse* are the building blocks that make up the minutiae of the daily life, he argues that *Erfahrungen* change the individuals who experience them at a fundamental level.

Unlike everyday events, authentic experiences are incorporated into narratives of identity, which help individuals link their communal experiences of the past to shared visions of the future. For Benjamin, 'Experience is indeed a matter of tradition, in collective existence as well as private life. It is less the product of facts firmly anchored in memory than of a convergence in memory of accumulated and frequently unconscious data.'[21] Authentic experiences are thus always defined within communal frameworks or 'experience rooted in tradition.'[22]

Despite its importance, memory is a singularly unreliable faculty. The fragility of recall highlights the distinction between what Aleida Assmann calls 'communicative and cultural memory' (*kommunikatives und kulturelles Gedächtnis*).[23] Both forms are socially mediated and relate to group identity, but in contrast to cultural memory, communicative remembrance has a limited temporal horizon. It depends on oral retelling, which is sporadic and difficult to maintain, especially when the memories conveyed run counter to the dominant social frameworks of collective remembrance. At the phenomenological level of social experience, institutions work in concert with social norms and traditions to give collective memories greater permanence. Both of these mechanisms legitimise community by linking political authority to the joint action of citizens. Halbwachs observes that 'social organization gives a persistent framework into which all detailed recall must fit, and it very power-fully influences both the manner and matter of recall.' As the primary loca-tion for the deployment of constructive memory, communal institutions are crucial.[24]

Informal mechanisms also play an important role. In contrast to individual and communicative memory, the social norms and traditions of cultural memory have been reified and bound to artefacts within the world of human experience. This objectification is achieved through the use of symbols, texts, rituals, and the creation of other 'social facts' (Durkheim). Unlike the shifting horizon of communicative memory, the fateful actions and objects of cultural memory become fixed points in the historical memory of a community. These enacted norms and traditions become part of what Adorno calls 'unconscious memory' (*unbewußte Erinnerung*).[25]

My brief reconstruction of remembrance has shown how narratives of the past help individuals and communities maintain stable, coherent identities. However, collective memory can also limit freedom of thought and action. While it creates stable points of reference, established societal pathways of recall can also turn narrative frameworks of the past into iron cages that imprison individuals and communities within certain repeated, fixed patterns of thought and action.

Rupture and collective memory as critique

The ability of the past to limit the present autonomy of individuals and inhibit critique was particularly worrying to the members of the Frankfurt School given their commitment to the possibility of radical social change and political emancipation. On one hand, critical theory recognises that collective memory enables critique by helping individuals to question the normally implicit authority of tradition by providing them with an outside perspective which shows that change is possible. Without tradition, Adorno notes that 'nothing could even be questioned.' On the other hand, its loss would quickly lead to the decay of a society that had lost all common points of reference tied to the past. Adorno sums up this paradox by observing, 'No timely tradition exists to be summoned, but if all tradition is lost, then the march into inhumanity begins.'[26]

The problem with relying on tradition is that it usually remains unthematised. It restricts thought and action in the present precisely because its effects are masked by social taboos and historical inertia. Within normal politics, collective narratives of the past stabilise societal structures by ordering human experience through time. Collective remembrance is typically a conservative force, taking account of custom and the way things have been done since time out of mind. However, during paradigm shifts crucial experiences 'unfolding within an irreversible linear time, [are] absorbed into cyclical, liturgical memory' that repeatedly revisit and reinterpret these events to construct new narratives in the present.[27]

The desire to break the narrative bonds of tradition while maintaining the ability to learn from experience led critical theory to develop the concept of historical rupture (*Bruch*). This idea has its origins in the experiences of the first generation of the Frankfurt School during Europe's age of total war, which allowed them to ascribe an 'epoch-forming significance to the developments in Nazi Germany.'[28] Based on their personal experiences of suffering and exile during Europe's age of total war, the members of the Institute came to argue that the experience of events that delegitimise the existing structures of historical time can also free collective remembrance from its normal, stabilising role, allowing it to act as a resource for social critique and innovation. A rupture can thus be defined as 'an epoch-creating occurrence' (*ein epochemachendes Ereignis*) in which '[a]ll relations appear to be ordered in another way and to be joined to new forms.'[29]

Using Habermas's terminology, a caesura (*Zäsur*) can be understood as disrupting the 'more or less diffuse, always unproblematic, background conditions' that underlie the unthematised lifeworlds (*Lebenswelten*) of individuals in society. It allows new processes of communication, socialisation, and cultural differentiation based on novel reconstructions of the past to come to the fore. Such ruptures spawn new 'memories in which earlier experiences break through to the centre point of our lives and reveal new and dangerous insights for the present.'[30] Building on these ideas, Adorno advocates for an active 'working through of the past' (*Aufarbeitung der Vergangenheit*) that is achieved by maintaining 'a critical relationship towards tradition as the medium of its preservation.'[31]

These insights regarding the critical potential of collective memory build on Benjamin's enigmatic but influential 'Theses on the Philosophy of History' (1940). In these posthumously published reflections, Benjamin seeks to understand how freedom can be saved from teleological conceptions of cause and effect. He argues that historical ruptures shatter existing norms and customary forms of behaviour, allowing individuals to 'wrest tradition away from a conformism that is about to overpower it' (Thesis IV). Benjamin points out that such breaks are necessarily violent. Traumatic historical ruptures destroy existing narrative frameworks, leaving only fragments of the past behind. While this frees the present from teleological philosophies of history, it also tears the narrative webs that had previously supported the identities of individuals and communities asunder. Benjamin notes that revolutionary moments make 'the continuum of history explode' by developing new temporal understandings (Thesis XV).[32]

Benjamin's reflections are haunted by the rise of totalitarianism over the course of the interwar years. In a particularly poignant image of the traumatic power of collective memory, he describes the European crisis of the 1920s and 30s and the rise of totalitarianism as an experience that rips the future out of the fabric of historical time. In contrast to the usual image of the future as forward-looking and progressive, Benjamin argues that ruptures are backward-looking. They force individuals and communities to confront the authentic experiences of the past that make old narratives untenable.[33] Invoking the image of the 'Angel of History,' Benjamin writes after a rupture,

> His face is turned towards the past. Where we perceive a chain of events, he sees one single catastrophe which keeps piling wreckage upon wreckage and hurls it in front of his feet. [… A] storm is blowing from Paradise, it has got caught in his wings with such violence that the angel can no longer close them. This storm irresistibly propels him into the future to which his back is turned, while the pile of debris before him grows skyward. The storm is what we call progress. (Thesis IX)[34]

This passage identifies two important characteristics of rupture. First, Benjamin makes clear that such fractures in historical time are the result of 'a chain of events,' not a single experience. While individual events can weaken the fabric of historical time, only the accumulated pressure of multiple experiences can shatter it completely. Second, ruptures force individuals and communities to question their previously unthematised ideas about the past. Assumptions of progress turn out to be a violent storm as the 'pile of debris before [the Angel of History] grows skyward.' Benjamin's reflections are echoed in Daniel Diner's concept of 'civilisational breaks' (*Zivilizationsbrüche*). Such ruptures – Auschwitz is the paradigmatic example for Diner and many other thinkers – act as 'harrowing events … [that] generate serious and often catastrophic challenges to communal self-understandings.'[35]

Despite the violent imagery of the Angel of History, unlike the dominant 'negative' reading of collective memory, Benjamin also emphasises that historical ruptures have the potential to bring about positive political change. Crisis frees individuals and communities from existing traditions and the spell of existing chains of cause and effect. In Hegel's terms, ruptures make it impossible to simply remain 'in a state of unthinking inertia.' Without erasing the past, the experience of a historical caesura allows individuals to treat the past as a 'repertoire of the imagination' or a 'treasury of possibilities.'[36]

Hannah Arendt, who saved the original manuscript of the 'Theses on the Philosophy of History' and ensured their publication after Benjamin's death, uses his reflections to argue that ruptures free individuals to reconfigure the past in ways that point to a different future. She invokes the image of a pearl diver, who searches the depths for bits of the past that have '"undergone a sea-change" and survive in new crystallised forms and shapes that remain immune to the elements, as though they waited only for the pearl diver ... [to] bring them up into the world of the living.'[37] Thus freed from the narrative constraints of established institutions and traditions, collective memory can become an important resource for change. This process of transformation not only involves the rearranging and reinterpreting of formative, genuine experiences; it is also a process of rediscovery, as events that were previously forgotten are reinvigorated and given new meaning. As a result, Marcuse observes, 'The *recherche du temps perdu* becomes a vehicle of future liberation.'[38] However, in order to truly function as historical ruptures, the community as a whole must share such traumatic events.

Individual breaks and communal ruptures

I have argued that ruptures have the power to unleash the critical potential of collective memory by breaking apart pre-existing, unthematised narratives of the past. While individuals may experience traumatic events as important turning points in their private lives, societal ruptures must have broad meaning for the community as a whole. These disruptions must enter their collective remembrance as a single break, not merely as a series of smaller, individually traumatic experiences. It is not enough for harrowing events to cause certain individuals to rethink their life histories; these experiences must challenge broader communal self-understandings of the past. The rupture itself must become part of collective memory, transferring memories to individuals through the social frameworks theorised by Halbwachs. In ruptures the past presents itself to individuals as a task, spurring thought and action.

34

Collective memory and political change

The relationship between individual breaks and communal ruptures can clearly be seen in the European age of total war, which is emphasised by all of the theorists of the Frankfurt School. The experience of the interwar years – and of his own persecution after the Nazis took power in Germany – was enough to trigger a rupture for Benjamin. By contrast, the Holocaust and the image of Auschwitz were central to the historical break as understood by Adorno, Horkheimer, and Habermas. In 1947 Horkheimer noted: 'The anonymous martyrs of the concentration camps are the symbols of the humanity that is striving to be born. The task of philosophy is to translate what they have done into language that will be heard even though their finite voices have been silenced by tyranny.'[39] This emphasis on the Holocaust is reflected in much of the broader literature, which focuses on the industrial slaughter of the gas chambers as the central experience driving the politics of memory.[40]

Regardless of their analysis of the substantive trigger of rupture, the thinkers of the Frankfurt School all saw the industrialised slaughter of millions and the rationalised control that was exercised over all aspects of life under National Socialism as having 'created a "gap" between past and future of such a magnitude that the past, while still present, is fragmented and can no longer be told as a unified narrative.'[41] Given Benjamin's insistence that a 'chain of events' is necessary to create a rupture, the Frankfurters realised that the single shock of the First World War was not enough to transform European narratives of the past. The so-called Great War was indeed followed by a 'utopian moment' highlighted by the founding of the League of Nations, the writing of a liberal-democratic constitution of the Weimar Republic and the signing Kellogg-Briand Pact outlawing war. There were even some nascent calls for European unification, including Richard von Coudenhove-Kalergi's Pan-European movement. However, by the mid-1930s all of these initiatives had failed.[42]

Despite its importance in twentieth-century history, the need for the historical break to be broadly and collectively shared across society explains why 1918 is not a rupture. The unprecedented death toll of the Great War was certainly shocking and had tremendous consequences. However, only certain segments of European society, such as the monarchists in Weimar Germany, experienced the shameful peace and the Treaty of Versailles as a rupture. For the continent and its politics more broadly, the First World War was a false start, a possible break that failed. Instead of enabling a fundamental rethinking of basic institutions and traditions, its aftermath strengthened the most dangerous aspects of politics, fuelling renewed cycles of hatred. Attempts to change fundamental aspects of the system failed to make a difference. Despite the internationalist rhetoric of the time, states soon reverted to the 'time-honoured core of international diplomacy.' Nations continued to tell nationalist narratives and individuals returned to traditional practices of memory.[43]

The Second World War was not merely a repeat of the horrors of the Great War as it involved death and destruction on a far greater scale. It also brought about the industrial production of corpses at Auschwitz and the other Nazi extermination camps. In line with the double structure of rupture I identified in Benjamin's work, 1945 was not only violent enough to rip the fabric of historical time; it was also the second occurrence within a broader 'chain of events'. In contrast to the return to tradition following the Great War, the Second World War marks the end of the 'heroic age' of national history.[44] The old narratives glorifying the nation's exploits became stale; the old traditions linking experience and expectation had been pulled apart.

The necessarily communal nature of historical rupture points to the importance of historical generations. On a basic level, the members of such temporal cohorts are defined by the fact that they share 'forms of knowledge [that] become available to us only as a result of certain historical experiences.'[45] Although generations never present a homogeneous interpretation of the key events of their lives, they are defined by their search for an answer to common questions that arise from the genuine experiences (*Erfahrungen*) of their time.

Even with this caveat, the concept of experience remains vague.[46] In trying to come to terms with the generational dynamics in interwar Germany, Karl Mannheim develops a framework for understanding both the objective and subjective dimensions of generational experience by focusing on how and why they arise in the first place. Mannheim's analysis thus combines the insights of the French positivists with those of the German romantics. On one hand, the temporal and spatial location of birth is an objective fact, which predisposes individuals to 'a certain characteristic mode of thought and experience, and a characteristic type of historical action.'[47] While many interpretations are possible, they are constrained by the structural limits of the situation. On the other, social facts do not guarantee the formation of a self-conscious generation. The relevant genuine experiences become salient when socially, politically, and intellectually relevant individuals thematise them as such. Thus, 'A generation exists if and only if a number of birth

cohorts share a historical experience that creates a community of perception ... Generations and memories are mutually constitutive ... because of
experiential commonalities and resultant similarities in individual memories
of historical events.'[48]

The period from 1914 to 1945 struck deeply into the continent's collective
memory, raising fundamental questions about European political, social,
and cultural life. By providing what Mannheim calls 'fundamental integra-
tive attitudes and formative principles,' the critical theorists of the Frankfurt
School pushed individuals to interpret the events of the interwar years
and the Second World War as a historical rupture.[49] Using the theoretical
tools provided by Benjamin, Adorno, Marcuse, and Habermas, subsequent
generations were more likely to see the events of the early twentieth century
as a 'Benjaminian moment' of rupture.

The resources of collective remembrance

Although none of the Frankfurters formulated an explicit critical theory of
collective memory – a fully-fledged 'theory of storms' – based on Benjamin's
reflections, an understanding of the past as a resource with a clear 'practical, emancipatory interest' emerges from their writings.[50] As Marcuse notes,
'Critical theory has engaged with the past in such unheard of dimensions
precisely because it cares about the future.'[51] I draw on these reflections to formulate a critical theory of memory that acts as a *cognitive, motivational,* and *justificatory* resource for social transformation in the aftermath of historical ruptures.
My basic thesis is that the resources of collective remembrance created by the
rupture of 1945 produced the necessary conditions for the foundation and
subsequent development of European integration as a new form of politics
in the postwar years. These categories are central to my historical analysis of
the crucial role that collective memory and the rupture of 1945 played in the
origins and development of European integration in Part I.

As a *cognitive resource* memory gives individuals and communities a perspective from which they can critically engage with the present. It enables them
to exist on an alternate temporal plane, providing inspiration for creative
solutions to old problems. Benjamin points out that in this situation, 'History
[becomes] the subject of a structure whose site is not homogeneous, empty
time, but time filled by the presence of the now [*Jetztzeit*]' (Thesis XIV).[52] The
need to reinterpret the past thus helps individuals conceive of new solutions
by giving them a critical perspective on the present. Marcuse notes that 'the

restoration of memory goes hand in hand with the restoration of the cognitive content of the imagination [*Phantasie*].'[53] Despite the horrors of the past, hope for the future exists because of the faculty of human imagination. Once unleashed, the ability to imagine a different future can help individuals create new forms of communal life. Although the content of the politics of memory is rooted in past events, the desired communicative effect of this discourse is clearly directed by contemporary events.

From this perspective, memory is a threat to existing traditions despite the fact that it draws upon them. In Marcuse's words, 'Remembrance of the past may give rise to dangerous insights, and the established society seems to be apprehensive of the subversive contents of memory. Remembrance is a mode of dissociation … which breaks, for short moments, the omnipresent power of the given facts.'[54] Collective memory therefore allows individuals to think beyond the limits imposed by present institutions, empowering them to realise Marx's dictum by 'making their own history.'

Following ruptures in historical time, collective remembrance not only frees individuals to rethink and reinterpret their own experience; it also allows them to retell communal narratives by drawing on their 'imagination of history.'[55] By tying these together in the present, the observer not only brings these different elements into contact with each other, but is also able to reveal in them an altogether different meaning than what they stood for in the original context. Following experiences of rupture, 'The rediscovered past supplies the critical criteria whose application is condemned and repudiated in the present.'[56] The ability of the past to expand the imaginary scope of individuals in the present is crucial to understanding its importance for postwar Europe.

I identify two ways that collective memory can act as a cognitive resource for political change. First, ruptures help to expand the imaginary scope of individuals. Reflecting on the past helps them push the boundaries of the thinkable, allowing them to consider ideas that would previously have been dismissed. In speaking about the influence of the Second World War on his thought, Habermas notes that the experience of Nazism expanded his imaginary scope by giving him a critical perspective on society and its practices.[57] By thematising institutions and traditions that had previously been taken for granted, the past helps to expand perceptions of the possible.

Second, shared memories set the context for new political action, providing individuals with a common starting point that helps them define important issues as shared problems. The difficulty in translating experience into expectation highlights the importance of generations, since being able to draw on communal 'modes of thought and experience' can help groups of individuals to cognitively bridge the gulf between experience and expectation.[58] While people approach problems in different ways, a common starting point can open a space for discussion that would not otherwise be possible. Individuals who share experiences, even if they interpret them differently, are thus able to enter into expectation and constitute it collectively because they apply significance to the same events. Representatives of the same generation often hold similar views precisely because they are drawing on the same events to construct their cognitive repertoire through collective memory.

Any theory of change, whether on the individual or the communal level, must not only provide an account of the cognitive origins of transformation; it must also give insight into the motivational background that pushes changes through against the tide of the status quo. The question of motivation is crucial for the Frankfurt School, since their critical theory of society not only seeks to provide the cognitive resources for emancipation within an alternative form of life, but also to ensure that this critique is motivationally effective.[59] A critical theory of memory must therefore also conceive of remembrance as a motivational resource that pushes individuals to act on their cognitive engagement with alternative possibilities.

As a *motivational resource* memory also builds on the experience of rupture. The events that cause such breaks damage and erode the customary prompts for action, spurring what Habermas describes as 'a discrepancy between the need for motives that the state and the occupational system announce and the supply of motivation offered by the sociocultural system.'[60] Such demands for implicit reasons to justify certain actions and ideas cannot be met once the build-up of traumatic events has made traditional understandings of the past untenable. Seyla Benhabib notes that historical ruptures, such as those brought about by the experience of 'National Socialism and totalitarianism in our century, were precisely instances when the intersubjectivity constitutive of the social world was so disrupted and damaged that … the capacity of individuals to engage in enlarged thought disappeared.'[61]

Despite the destruction wrought by such breaks, following ruptures collective memory not only reengages the cognitive capacity for enlarged thought; it also helps reactivate the motivational basis for the transformation of communal life through participation in the public realm.[62] The traumatic experience of a caesura in traditional narrative frameworks is precisely what spurs individuals and communities to change the foundations of communal life. As Raymond

Geuss points out, 'The experience of pain and frustration is what gives the agents addressed motivation to ... change their social arrangements.'[63]

In my critical theory of memory, the past acts as a motivational resource in two distinct ways. First, as an emotional connection to lived experience, collective memory helps to motivate action, even when this involves significant sacrifices and risk. The emotional reaction they inspire is what makes these experiences crucial and preserves their importance in memory. Habermas notes that critical theory's interest in the trajectory of postwar Europe was 'spurred by ... [a] concern with the past.' This anxiety draws on the emotional 'fear of a political relapse.' For the Frankfurters, their shared memories of Nazism served a 'negative point of reference' that expanded their cognitive capacities and motivated them to pursue change.[64]

Second, as a motivational resource collective memory also helps agents place problems into the broader context by defining the stakes of revision and of remaining within the status quo. Although it can be paralysing like the storm that 'irresistibly propels' Benjamin's Angel of History into the future, an awareness of the crises of the past and the fear it provokes in the present can also help to place quotidian problems into a new context. Narrative breaks such as the caesura of 1945 are 'eye-opening experiences' that change the orientations of individuals and communities, forcing them to reconsider their basic values and giving them the impetus to pursue change, reordering their priorities. Voicing a sentiment shared by the rest of the Frankfurt School, Habermas observes, 'After the revelations concerning Auschwitz, nothing could be taken at face value.'[65]

In addition to its cognitive and motivational aspects, a critical understanding of memory also provides individuals with the *justificatory resources* necessary to endow new understandings of the past – and the practices that they entail – with sufficient discursive legitimacy. Within the Frankfurt School, critique does not only have the negative function of exposing unjustified social arrangements; it must also be able to act in a positive, affirmative, or justificatory role.[66] By demonstrating the inability of existing institutions and traditions to maintain stable communal relations, historical ruptures also create what Habermas refers to as 'legitimation crises.'

The seemingly endemic disasters leading up to a caesura in prevailing understandings of the past result in 'an erosion of belief in the system ... the inchoate feeling that "things" are not what they should be and that certain "forces" have put the operation of the system beyond our control.' A crisis of legitimacy undermines the implicit justification for existing forms of life based on their ability to provide a stable social order. As a result, 'new and increased demands for legitimation arise.'[67]

As a justificatory resource, collective memory is crucial in helping communities to endow new norms and new traditions with meaning following historical ruptures. Collective remembrance helps individuals construct persuasive stories that generate communal support for social transformations. The cognitive and motivation basis generated by memory must also be deployed through justificatory arguments that can persuade society with reasons (*Gründe*) that establish a ground (*Grund*) upon which their post-rupture beliefs and actions can 'stand.' These reasons have to be able to withstand public challenges and relevant criticism in order to gain credibility – they cannot simply be accepted at face value.[68] While norms and traditions are usually unthematised, changes to the social order have to withstand active debate before they can once again fade into the background of the lifeworld. Following broad historical ruptures, the need for justification is usually posed not only in terms of action, but also as a question about the values and ideals of the community. Collective memories and individual experiences do not constitute powerful discursive reasons in and of themselves. In order to stand up to social criticism, collective memories have to be shaped into a narrative or story. Only then can they truly become part of a post-rupture 'justificatory strategy.'[69]

My understanding of memory as a justificatory resource highlights the importance of the persuasive, reason-giving power of the past to political action in two ways. First, collective remembrance serves as a justificatory resource in the very formulation and serious consideration of alternatives. Second, memory is an important resource within public discussions regarding the changes necessitated by the experience of rupture. New narratives based on the salient experiences of the recent past can help rally support, legitimising the creation of new institutions and traditions. This latter dimension of collective memory as a justificatory resource is especially important in democratic contexts, where citizens can demand reasons and vote on the changes they wish to make to their communal structures.[70]

This critical account of memory as a *cognitive, motivational*, and *justificatory* resource for social change in the aftermath of historical ruptures shows how remembrance can help to overcome the 'negative' effects individuals experience when they feel 'trapped' in the past. While it is true that historical events can paralyse individuals, 'the gaze upon disaster reveals a certain fascination' that can also 'serv[e] as legitimation for escape' from dangerous forms of existing social praxis.[71] In this way collective memory can overcome its negative, Nietzschean reading and become a positive, constructive resource for social innovation. It can thus help to create 'an image of the future which springs indeed from a deep understanding of the present ... even in periods when the course of events seems to be leading far away from such a future.'[72]

Conclusion

This chapter has developed a narrative conception of collective memory where ruptures within established narratives of the past free actors to rethink the foundations of political life. I started by distinguishing a constructive, critical understanding of remembrance that stresses the ability of historical ruptures to expand the imaginary scope of individuals from a more negative view of the past as a source of conflict. Whereas the former is usually attributed to Adorno, the latter has its roots in Nietzsche, However, as I point out, the association of positive and negative views of collective memory with Adorno and Nietzsche as the paradigmatic spokesmen for each approach is overly simplistic.[73]

Just as Nietzsche acknowledges the necessity of memory, Adorno also recognises the usefulness of forgetting and the pitfalls of memory. In 'What does Coming to Terms with the Past Mean?' (1959), Adorno notes the need to step out of the long shadow of Nazism, if one ever wanted to escape the vicious circle of violence and guilt.[74] There is no such thing as perfect memory; anyone who remembered everything would be overwhelmed by sensory data. It is just as impossible to completely forget important experiences, as the ever-increasing rise of psychotherapy makes clear.

In a given situation, collective memory can operate both in positive and negative ways. While certain aspects of the past can be deployed constructively, others have more destructive consequences and are better silenced or forgotten. In other words, it is not a question of remembering *or* forgetting, but of remembering *and* forgetting. While individuals and the communities they form must be able to remember, they must also develop the ability to create boundaries separating the 'past in the present,' which helps set 'horizons of expectations' for the future, from the simply past.[75] There are times to remember and times to forget; events to remember and events to forget.

All peoples depend on and are the products of narrative structures that help them to define who they *are* at least in part by who they *are not*. While all members of a community participate in the interplay between individual and collective memory, influence over the predominant narrative frameworks of the past is unevenly divided. Although European integration was long defined by a 'permissive consensus' among the peoples of Europe that built on the new narratives of collective memory that formed after the rupture of 1945, it was politicians who took these cognitive, motivational, and justificatory resources and used them to create and develop the EU. Joining with historians, writers, and other cultural elites, political leaders play a key role in mobilising society around certain understandings and interpretations of the past. They use the past to define the boundaries of the thinkable, making use of 'narratives [as] formidable instruments of politics.' In this way, 'elite actors hammer out and validate the politically acceptable memory regime, the public transcript of memory.'[76]

In periods of normal politics leaders are inclined towards established narratives because the existing storylines legitimise their position in society. In contrast to this establishment bias, in times of crisis following the experience of a communal rupture in the fabric of historical time, elites are more likely to establish new visions to legitimise new practices and institutions. Because genuine experiences have destroyed the institutions and traditions that individuals and the community had previously depended on, they are able to practice a 'fragmentary historiography' that reassembles the shattered pieces of the past into new narratives.[77]

Given the physical, moral, and political destruction of Europe's period of total war, many of the prewar narrative frameworks were shattered beyond repair. These background conditions created favourable circumstances for the construction of new 'stories of peoplehood'. The creation of the supranational European Communities after the end of Europe's age of total war shows how crisis can lead to a fundamental rethinking of politics. The new narratives enabled by this historical breach served as the impetus for the move away from national sovereignty and self-determination towards integration and collective action. However, as the difficulties that Europe faces as a result of the fragmentation and loss of this shared foundation in collective memory at the start of the twenty-first century show, these postwar narratives have not yet rooted themselves deeply enough in the self-conceptions of the European peoples to be able to survive the passing away of the generations of experience and the moral authority of their personal memories of total war.

Following the two-stage model of the Frankfurt School, a historical explanation of the normative roots of the European project is necessary to properly diagnose the existing pathologies of the EU. Only then can critique move on to its second 'anticipatory-utopian' stage. In the next section, which comprises three chapters, I thus conduct an 'explanatory-diagnostic' analysis of the history of the EU, which illustrates the important role that collective memory played as a cognitive, motivational, and justificatory resource for integration in the aftermath of the rupture of 1945. Part I also shows how the loss of the normative orientation provided by the authentic experience of this caesura has contributed to the EU's problems as the generations that shared these experiences have passed away and have been replaced by new cohorts that view the European project through a purely economic lens. Part II then builds on this diagnosis of the pathologies of the present and suggests paths that could make the European project into a source of future emancipation.

Notes

1 Parts of this chapter have previously been published as P. J. Verovšek, 'Memory, Narrative, and Rupture: The Power of the Past as a Resource for Political Change,' *Memory Studies*, 13:2 (2020).

2 K. L. Klein, 'On the Emergence of Memory in Historical Discourse,' *Representations. Special Issue: Grounds for Remembering*, 69 (2000), 127–150; J. K. Olick, V. Vinitzky-Seroussi, and D. Levy (eds), *The Collective Memory Reader* (Oxford: Oxford University Press, 2011).

3 J. R. Resina (ed), *Disremembering the Dictatorship: The Politics of Memory in the Spanish Transition to Democracy* (Atlanta: Rodopi, 2000), 1.

4 See P. Fussell, *The Great War and Modern Memory* (Oxford: Oxford University Press, 1975); H. Rousso, *The Vichy Syndrome: History and Memory in France since 1944* (Cambridge, MA: Harvard University Press, 1991); A. Insdorf, *Indelible Shadows: Film and the Holocaust* (Cambridge: Cambridge University Press, 1983). See also P. Nora, *Les Lieux De Mémoire* (Paris: Gallimard, 1984); J. Winter, *Sites of Memory, Sites of Mourning: The Great War in European Cultural History* (New York: Cambridge University Press, 1995); P. Finney, 'The Ubiquitous Presence of the Past? Collective Memory and International History,' *The International History Review*, 36:3 (2014), 443–472.

5 D. Reynolds, 'World War II and Modern Meanings,' *Diplomatic History*, 25:3 (2001), 469; F. Furet, *Interpreting the French Revolution* (Cambridge: Cambridge University Press, 1981), 3, see also 5.

6 W. Kansteiner, 'Losing the War, Winning the Memory Battle: The Legacy of Nazism, World War II, and the Holocaust in the Federal Republic of Germany,' in R. N. Lebow, W. Kansteiner, and C. Fogu (eds), *The Politics of Memory in Postwar Europe*, trans. T. Appleton and E. Lebow (Durham, NC: Duke University Press, 2006); W. Kansteiner, 'Between Politics and Memory: The Historikerstreit and the West German Historical Culture of the 1980s,' in R. J. Golsan (ed), *Fascism's Return: Scandal, Revision, Ideology* (Lincoln: University of Nebraska Press, 1998); J. K. Olick and D. Levy, 'Collective Memory and Cultural Constraint: Holocaust Myth and Rationality in German Politics,' *American Sociological Review*, 62:6 (1997); J. K. Olick, 'What does it Mean to Normalize the Past? Official Memory in German Politics since 1989,' *Social Science History*, 22–4 (1998); J. Herf, *Divided Memory: The Nazi Past in the Two Germanys*

(Cambridge, MA: Harvard University Press, 1997). On memory studies as a research paradigm, see P. J. Verovšek, 'Collective Memory, Politics, and the Influence of the Past: The Politics of Memory as a Research Paradigm,' *Politics, Groups, and Identities*, 4–3 (2016), 529–543; Lebow *et al.*, *The Politics of Memory in Postwar Europe*; J. Müller, *Memory and Power in Post-War Europe: Studies in the Presence of the Past* (New York: Cambridge University Press, 2002).

7 J. V. Wertsch and H. L. Roediger, 'Collective Memory: Conceptual Foundations and Theoretical Approaches,' *Memory*, 16:3 (2008), 319; C. McGrattan and S. Hopkins, 'Memory in Post-Conflict Societies: From Contention to Integration?' *Ethnopolitics*, 16:5 (2017), 488.

8 M. Minow (ed), *Breaking the Cycles of Hatred: Memory, Law, and Repair* (Princeton: Princeton University Press, 2002); C. S. Maier, 'A Surfeit of Memory? Reflections on History, Melancholy and Denial,' *History & Memory*, 5:2 (1993), 140; D. L. Schacter, *The Seven Sins of Memory: How the Mind Forgets and Remembers* (Boston: Houghton Mifflin, 2001).

9 F. Nietzsche, *On the Genealogy of Morals; Ecce Homo*, ed. W. Kaufmann (New York: Vintage Books, 1989), 57.

10 H. König, *Politik und Gedächtnis* (Weilerswist: Velbrück Wissenschaft, 2008), 23–31.

11 See A. Nuti, *Injustice and the Reproduction of History: Structural Inequalities, Gender and Redress* (Cambridge: Cambridge University Press, 2019); O. Bakiner, *Truth Commissions: Memory, Power, and Legitimacy* (Philadelphia: University of Pennsylvania Press, 2016).

12 S. Benhabib, 'Arendt and Adorno: The Elusiveness of the Particular and the Benjaminian Moment,' in L. Rensmann and S. Gandesha (eds), *Understanding Political Modernity: Comparative Perspectives on Adorno and Arendt* (Stanford: Stanford University Press, 2012).

13 A. Sierp, *History, Memory, and Trans-European Identity: Unifying Divisions* (London: Routledge, 2017), 2–3; C. Guisan, *A Political Theory of Identity in European Integration: Memory and Policies* (New York: Routledge, 2012), 1.

14 S. Hazareesingh and K. Nabulsi, 'Using Archival Sources to Theorize about Politics,' in D. Leopold and M. Stears (eds), *Political Theory: Methods and Approaches* (Oxford: Oxford University Press, 2008), 153; P. M. R. Stirk, *Critical Theory, Politics and Society: An Introduction* (New York: Continuum, 2000), 3.

15 Horkheimer's letter and Benjamin's reply are both in W. Benjamin, *The Arcades Project* (Cambridge, MA: Belknap Press, 1999), 471.

16 M. Horkheimer, *Critical Theory: Selected Essays*, trans. M. J. O'Connell (New York: Continuum Publishing Company, 1972), 188–243.

17 G. Kateb, 'Foreword,' in J. N. Shklar (ed), *Political Thought and Political Thinkers* (Chicago: Chicago University Press, 1998), viii; G. M. Spiegel, 'Memory and History: Liturgical Time and Historical Time,' *History and Theory*, 41:2 (2002), 162.

18 M. Jay, *The Dialectical Imagination: A History of the Frankfurt School and the Institute of Social Research, 1923–1950* (Boston: Little, Brown and Company, 1973), 30, 38, 197–198.

19 M. Halbwachs, *On Collective Memory*, trans. L. A. Coser (Chicago: University of Chicago Press, 1992), 38.

20 König, *Politik und Gedächtnis*, 165–166.

21 W. Benjamin, *Illuminations: Essays and Reflections*, ed. H. Arendt, trans. H. Zohn (New York: Schocken Books, 1977), 159. I have retranslated *Erlebnis* and *Erfahrung* as event and experience to emphasise the personal import of the latter over the mere occurrence of the former. Interestingly, Hans-Georg Gadamer draws a similar

distinction. See H.-G. Gadamer, *Truth and Method*, trans. J. Weinsheimer and D. G. Marshall (London: Continuum, 2004), 86, 278.

22 Jay, *The Dialectical Imagination*, 210.

23 See A. Assmann, J. Assmann, and C. Hardmeier (eds), *Schrift und Gedächtnis: Beiträge zur Archäologie der literarischen Kommunikation* (Munich: W. Fink, 1983).

24 M. Halbwachs, *The Collective Memory*, trans. F. J. Ditter Jr. and V. Yazdi Ditter (New York: Harper & Row, 1980), 296; Verovšek, 'Unexpected Support for European Integration.'

25 T. W. Adorno, 'Negative Dialektik,' in *Gesammelte Schriften*, Band 6 (Frankfurt am Main: Suhrkamp Verlag, 1966), 63, translations mine.

26 *Ibid.*, 63; T. W. Adorno, *Kulturkritik und Gesellschaft. Prismen. Ohne Leitbild*, Gesammelte Schriften Band 10 (Darmstadt: Wissenschaftliche Buchgesellschaft, 1998), 315, translations mine.

27 Spiegel, 'Memory and History,' 152.

28 Stirk, *Critical Theory, Politics and Society*, 100.

29 H.-G. Gadamer, 'Concerning Empty and Ful-filled Time,' *Southern Journal of Philosophy*, 8:4 (1970), 350.

30 J. Habermas, *The Theory of Communicative Action, Volume One: Reason and the Rationalization of Society*, trans. T. A. McCarthy (Boston: Beacon Press, 1984), 70; J. B. Metz, *Faith in History and Society: Toward a Practical Fundamental Theology* (New York: Seabury Press, 1980), 8; also M. Pensky, 'Solidarity with the Past and the Work of Translation: Reflections on Memory Politics and the Postsecular,' in C. J. Calhoun, E. Mendieta, and J. VanAntwerpen (eds), *Habermas and Religion* (Cambridge: Polity, 2013), 316.

31 Adorno, *Kulturkritik und Gesellschaft*, 318.

32 Benjamin, *Illuminations*, 261–262.

33 See P. J. Verovšek, 'Historical Criticism without Progress: Memory as an Emancipatory Resource for Critical Theory,' *Constellations* (2018).

34 Benjamin, 'Theses on the Philosophy of History,' in Benjamin, *Illuminations*, 257–8.

35 D. Diner, *Zivilisationsbruch: Denken nach Auschwitz* (Berlin: Fischer Taschenbuch, 1988); D. Bell, *Memory, Trauma and World Politics: Reflections on the Relationship between Past and Present* (New York: Palgrave Macmillan, 2006), 5.

36 G. W. F. Hegel, *Phenomenology of Spirit*, ed. John Niemeyer Findlay, trans. A. V. Miller (Oxford: Clarendon Press, 1977), 51; A. Muschg, 'Europa – Identität und Andenken,' in H. König, J. Schmidt, and M. Sickling (eds), *Europas Gedächtnis: Das neue Europa zwischen nationalen Erinnerungen und gemeinsamer Identität* (Bielefeld: Transcript Verlag, 2008), 111, translations mine.

37 Benjamin, *Illuminations*, 51; Verovšek, 'Unexpected Support for European Integration,' 401–402.

38 H. Marcuse, *Triebstruktur und Gesellschaft. Ein philosophischer Beitrag zu Sigmund Freud* (Frankfurt am Main: Bibliothek Suhrkamp, 1955), 24ff., translation mine.

39 M. Horkheimer, *Eclipse of Reason* (New York: Oxford University Press, 1947), 161.

40 See Olick and Levy, 'Collective Memory and Cultural Constraint'; A. Becker, 'Building Up a Memory: Austria, Switzerland, and Europe Face the Holocaust,' in E. Langenbacher and Y. Shain (eds), *Power and the Past: Collective Memory and International Relations* (Washington, DC: Georgetown University Press, 2010); W. Kansteiner, 'Losing the War, Winning the Memory Battle: The Legacy of Nazism, World War II, and the Holocaust in the Federal Republic of Germany,' in Lebow *et al.*, *The Politics of Memory in Postwar Europe*; J. B. Wolf, *Harnessing the Holocaust: The Politics of Memory*

in France (Stanford: Stanford University Press, 2004); J. Resnik, '"Sites of Memory" of the Holocaust: Shaping National Memory in the Education System in Israel,' *Nations and Nationalism*, 9–2 (2003); D. Levy and N. Sznaider, 'Memory Unbound: The Holocaust and the Formation of Cosmopolitan Memory,' *European Journal of Social Theory*, 5:1 (2002); N. G. Finkelstein, *The Holocaust Industry: Reflection on the Exploitation of Jewish Suffering* (New York: Verso, 2000).

41 S. Benhabib, *The Reluctant Modernism of Hannah Arendt* (Lanham: Rowman & Littlefield, 2003), 92.

42 J. Winter, *Dreams of Peace and Freedom: Utopian Moments in the Twentieth Century* (New Haven: Yale University Press, 2006).

43 Winter, *Sites of Memory, Sites of Mourning*, 49.

44 N. Frei, 'Deutschlands Vergangenheit und Europas Gedächtnis,' in König *et al.*, *Europas Gedächtnis*, 81.

45 S. Benhabib, *The Claims of Culture: Equality and Diversity in the Global Era* (Princeton: Princeton University Press, 2002), 135.

46 M. Jay, *Songs of Experience: Modern American and European Variations on a Universal Theme* (Berkeley: University of California Press, 2005); H. Jaeger, 'Generationen in der Geschichte. Überlegungen zu einer umstrittenen Konzeption,' *Geschichte und Gesellschaft*, 3:4 (1977), 444.

47 K. Mannheim, *Essays on the Sociology of Knowledge* (London: Routledge & Paul, 1952), 291.

48 J. K. Olick, *The Politics of Regret: On Collective Memory and Historical Responsibility* (New York: Routledge, 2007), 25.

49 Mannheim, *Essays on the Sociology of Knowledge*, 305. Cf. Benjamin, *Illuminations*, 165; Jay, *The Dialectical Imagination*, 208.

50 M. Pensky, 'Contributions toward a Theory of Storms: Historical Knowing and Historical Progress in Kant and Benjamin,' *The Philosophical Forum*, 41:1–2 (2010); N. Fraser, 'Identity, Exclusion, and Critique: A Response to Four Critics,' *European Journal of Political Theory*, 6:3 (2007), 322.

51 H. Marcuse, 'Philosophie Und Kritische Theorie,' in *Kultur und Gesellschaft I* (Frankfurt am Main: Suhrkamp Verlag, 1970), 126, translation mine.

52 Benjamin, 'Theses on the Philosophy of History,' 261.

53 Marcuse, *Triebstruktur und Gesellschaft*, 24ff., translation mine.

54 H. Marcuse, *One-Dimensional Man: Studies in the Ideology of Advanced Industrial Society* (New York: Routledge Classics, 1964), 101–102.

55 M. Merleau-Ponty, *Les aventures de la dialectique* (Paris: Gallimard, 1955), 2.

56 Marcuse, *Triebstruktur und Gesellschaft*, 24.

57 J. Habermas, *Between Naturalism and Religion*, trans. C. Cronin (London: Polity, 2008), 18.

58 Mannheim, *Essays on the Sociology of Knowledge*, 291.

59 T. W. Adorno, *Gesammelte Schriften, Band 8: Soziologische Schriften 1* (Frankfurt am Main: Suhrkamp Verlag, 1972), 481–482; also A. Kauppinen, 'Reason, Recognition, and Internal Critique,' *Inquiry*, 45:4 (2002), 479; M. Cooke, *Re-Presenting the Good Society* (Cambridge, MA: MIT Press, 2006), 38, 43.

60 J. Habermas, 'What does Crisis Mean Today? Legitimation Problems in Late Capitalism,' *Social Research*, 51:1/2 (1984), 56.

61 Benhabib, *The Reluctant Modernism of Hannah Arendt*, 193.

62 W. P. Forster, 'Administration and the Crisis in Legitimacy: A Review of Habermasian Thought,' *Harvard Educational Review*, 50:4 (1980), 501–502.

63 R. Geuss, *The Idea of a Critical Theory: Habermas and the Frankfurt School* (Cambridge: Cambridge University Press, 1981), 80.

64 J. Habermas, 'Public Space and Political Public Sphere: The Biographical Roots of Two Motifs in My Thought,' in *Between Naturalism and Religion* (London: Polity, 2008), 17, 21.

65 *Ibid.*, 18.

66 D. Couzens Hoy and T. A. McCarthy, *Critical Theory* (Oxford: Blackwell, 1994); P. Strydom, *Contemporary Critical Theory and Methodology* (London: Routledge, 2013), 122.

67 Forster, 'Administration and the Crisis in Legitimacy,' 500; Habermas, 'What does Crisis Mean Today?' 63; J. Habermas, *Legitimation Crisis* (Boston: Beacon Press, 1975).

68 R. Forst, *The Right to Justification: Elements of a Constructivist Theory of Justice*, trans. J. Flynn (New York: Columbia University Press, 2012); 13, 15–16, 62–78; J. Neyer, *The Justification of Europe: A Political Theory of Supranational Integration* (Oxford: Oxford University Press, 2012).

69 R. M. Smith, *Stories of Peoplehood: The Politics and Morals of Political Membership* (New York: Cambridge University Press, 2003), 19–65; Cooke, *Re-Presenting the Good Society*, 55–57.

70 J. Habermas, *Zur Verfassung Europas: Ein Essay* (Berlin: Suhrkamp Verlag, 2011), 72.

71 Z. Tarr, *The Frankfurt School: The Critical Theories of Max Horkheimer and Theodor W. Adorno* (New Brunswick: Transaction Publishers, 2011), 152.

72 Horkheimer, *Critical Theory*, 220.

73 König, *Politik und Gedächtnis*, 23, 29.

74 T. W. Adorno, 'What does Coming to Terms with the Past Mean?' in G. H. Hartman (ed), trans. T. Bahti and T. W. Adorno, *Bitburg in Moral and Political Perspective* (Bloomington: Indiana University Press, 1986).

75 R. Koselleck, *Futures Past: On the Semantics of Historical Time*, trans. K. Tribe (Cambridge, MA: MIT Press, 1985), 2, 255–275.

76 S. Kotkin, '1991 and the Russian Revolution: Sources, Conceptual Categories, Analytical Frameworks,' *The Journal of Modern History*, 70:2 (1998), 403; E. Langenbacher, 'Collective Memory as a Factor in Political Culture and International Relations,' in Langenbacher and Shain, *Power and the Past*, 31. For a critical theory perspective, also Benhabib, *The Claims of Culture*, 16.

77 Benhabib, *The Reluctant Modernism of Hannah Arendt*, 94.

Part I

Origins and crisis diagnosis

Chapter 2

Choosing integration based on the community model: memory, leadership, and the first phase of integration (1945–58)

> One must know the past [*das Gestern*], one must *also think about the past*, if one is to successfully and durably shape the future [*das Morgen*].
>
> Konrad Adenauer, speech at the University of Frankfurt (1952)

Memory and the founding of Europe

In the introductory section I argued that ruptures in historical time allow communities to reshape how they link the past to the future through the present by drawing on collective memory as a *cognitive, motivational,* and *justificatory* resource for social transformation. This chapter begins to apply this theoretical framework to the EU. It starts the 'explanatory-diagnostic' phase of this volume by examining the origins of European integration in the foundation of the first European Communities in the 1950s. This period represents what I refer to as the 'first phase of integration' (1945–58). In addition to showing the role that shared collective memory played in creation of the first community-based European institutions, it also serves as a case study for my broader theoretical argument by demonstrating how the constructive resources of the past can lead to fundamental political changes in the immediate aftermath of a historical rupture.

In this chapter I focus on the key individuals involved in the creation of the first institution of European integration, the ECSC, in 1951. I argue that three leaders played a particularly important and possibly irreplaceable role in founding the coal and steel community: its institutional architect and the primary visionary of integration based on the community method, the French technocrat Jean Monnet; French Foreign Minister Robert Schuman, who took up these ideas despite France's long tradition of defending its sovereignty;

and German Chancellor Konrad Adenauer, who sacrificed both the Federal Republic's short-term economic interests and immediate unification with East Germany in order to ensure peace and unity west of the Iron Curtain. I demonstrate that their experiences of rupture – and the resources of collective memory they gained as a result – allowed them to act as 'promoters of Europe … rally[ing] a broad-based political clientele.' My basic thesis is that their shared generational experiences imparted these three 'fathers of Europe' with 'a certain characteristic mode of thought and experience, and a characteristic type of historical action' that formed the basis for their cooperation.[1]

As I noted in the introduction to this volume, paying attention to individual leaders – an approach that is often dismissively caricatured as focusing on 'the lives and teachings of the European saints' – is hardly uncontroversial in the history of European integration. However, it is much more common within collective memory studies and intellectual history, as well as in studies of the founding of political communities, particularly within American political development. These fields emphasise the difference that individuals can make as concrete carriers of specific political ideas, who are able to bring about political change by fighting to have their conceptions accepted within the broader public sphere, as well as within the institutions they lead.[2]

While it is true that it is difficult to generalise from studies of agents who operate in specific contexts, this deeply contextual approach demonstrates the important role that leaders play by revealing 'how individual political actors changed their own minds, [and] how they persuaded others to change their minds in order to pursue their worldly objectives.' In this sense, this book is also an argument for treating individuals as important – if somewhat contingent – players that can make a difference in politics alongside the kinds of economic and structural factors that political scientists and social historians usually tend to address. I argue that leaders are especially pivotal in moments of rupture, thus reinforcing the notion that political life 'is a matter of human, and not merely mechanical, interaction between individuals, institutions, or groups.'[3]

This kind of individualised approach is especially well-suited to studies of political foundings, which focus on how a political tradition is inagurated 'in the texts of the Republic's actors.' Given that the creation of the EU represents what is quite possibly the most important innovation in political governance since the founding of the United States, I follow Catherine Guisan in applying this approach, which is 'quite common in the study of American political roots,' to European integration.[4] More specifically, I argue that while the

Choosing integration on the community model

ECSC may never have come into existence without Monnet, Schuman, and Adenauer, it most certainly would not have taken the supranational form that it did without them. I do so by showing that at key points in the creation of the ECSC the resources of the past led these three leaders to support, fight for, and defend supranational solutions to European integration that gave these institutions independent decision-making powers outside of the constitutional architecture of its member-states. As the creators of a Europe based on the community model of pooled sovereignty, Monnet, Schuman, and Adenauer set the institutional foundations of the European project.

The idea of unifying Europe has a long history. While previous initiatives gained little traction, the rupture of 1945 made the European movement part of the continent's postwar *Zeitgeist*. However, despite its newfound popularity, in the early postwar period the shape that this new Europe would take was still open. As Craig Parsons points out, 'The massive environmental changes of World War II made "Europeanist" ideas broadly salient by 1945–6, but the real political battle over the format of European cooperation only emerged with the outbreak of the cold war.'[5]

Building a union of European peoples based on community institutions with autonomous decision-making powers was not the only solution to Europe's problems after the Second World War. Both the traditional approach of dismembering Germany and a confederal model, which sought to weave Germany into the fabric of international society through intergovernmental institutions like the interwar League of Nations, had greater historical precedence and were more in line with traditional diplomatic practice. Although the community-based approach was in many ways the least likely to succeed – because it was both unprecedented and required the greatest changes to the structure of international politics in Europe – it still won out over other proposals with the foundation of the ECSC in 1952.

Drawing on archival evidence and other primary sources, I attribute the victory of these community-based solutions to the collective memories created by the European rupture of 1945. I demonstrate that the experience of two world wars – one following so closely on the other – gave postwar European leaders who had lived through these events the specific cognitive, motivational, and justificatory resources that led them to endorse the creation of the first European *community*, which was not merely an international organisation or confederation. My basic conclusion is that the development of the ECSC proceeded on this model, 'Only because certain leaders ... chose "community" projects.' The supranational character of the EU – in the sense that it is able to make decisions independently of its member-states – is the result of the 'aggressive leadership of some ideological champions of supranationality, whose episodic control of national policy-making allowed them to bind all their compatriots into their European vision.'[6]

The first two sections of the chapter start by examining the experiences of these three leaders during the two world wars. While the events of the Great War were traumatic, I argue that the Second World War – following so soon after the First – acted as a historical rupture requiring a fundamental rethinking of the foundations of European political life. The next three sections recount the origins and early history of the ECSC in order to demonstrate the role the constructive resources of the past played in helping Monnet, Schuman, and Adenauer to imagine, stick with, and argue for a supranational European community.

The failed rupture of the Great War

In the previous chapter I argued that while the First World War was a calamity that shook European society, it was not a rupture that destroyed the existing narrative threads of the past. Instead of enabling a rethinking of the continent's basic institutions and traditions, particularly the grounding of politics on the idea of nationalism and the institution of the nation-state, attempts at change quickly failed. US President Woodrow Wilson's Fourteen Points and the minority treaties created to protect non-state peoples in the nation-states that were born from the rubble of the Habsburg, Ottoman, and Russian Empires actually represented a retrenchment to the principle of nationalism and national self-determination. Following the Great War world leaders did not rethink the foundations of political life; instead, they returned to old ideas, seeking to implement the principles of nationalism more consistently.[7]

This observation applies to the constellation of leaders who would push for the foundation of the ECSC after 1945 as well. Jean Monnet (1888), Robert Schuman (1886), and Konrad Adenauer (1876) were all born and grew up in the late nineteenth-century world of traditional European politics. While all three experienced the Great War as a shock, it was only the second, repeated experience of yet another world war that created a rupture or break in their thinking, allowing new ideas to come to the fore of their thinking. Although Monnet, Schuman, and Adenauer all later built on their experiences during the Great War, the evidence I muster in this chapter demonstrates that they only realised its importance after the rupture of the Second World War.

Monnet's work during the First World War clearly played into his later political convictions. Early in the war Monnet had already become convinced that Britain and France were damaging their ability to stand against Germany by bidding against each other for foodstuffs in international markets.[8] Since Britain and France were allies, it seemed obvious to Monnet that they should pool their resources and bargain collectively to obtain the additional materials they needed. This conviction led Monnet to set up a transnational resource-sharing system between the members of the *Entente* in London.[9] The experiment started with wheat and eventually led to the creation of the Allied Maritime Transport Executive (AMTE) to pool resources among France, Great Britain, and Italy. Although the AMTE was able to affect national decision-making, its formal powers were limited. Necessity was its driving force.

The weakness of the commitment to international cooperation and the return to traditional ideas of sovereign self-sufficiency after the war quickly showed that the experience of 1914 through 1918 was not enough to constitute a rupture. As Monnet himself admitted, '[A]t the time I did not see the pooling of sovereignty as a way of solving international problems. Nobody did, even if their words seem to imply an appeal to some authority that would be above nations.'[10]

While the events of the Great War had a large effect on Robert Schuman as well, they did not constitute a caesura for him either. What they did do was open his path into political life. At the end of the Great War the territory of Alsace-Lorraine was reincorporated into France after it had been annexed by Germany in the wake of the Franco-Prussian War of 1871. Reintegrating this borderland into France posed many cultural, linguistic, legal, and political challenges. The repeated requests of the Catholic and German-speaking communities of Alsace-Lorraine convinced Schuman to make his 'involuntary entry into politics'; he was elected as a *député* to the French Assemblée nationale in 1919.[11]

Schuman's experience working to integrate Alsace-Lorraine back into France demonstrated that the integration of two different cultures within the same political community was possible, even without the total assimilation of one to the other.[12] In a newspaper article entitled '*Notre législation future*,' Schuman stressed the need for the region to maintain its regional traditions and legal identity: 'That is what regionalism in fact means … We do not want to be a state within a state. What we want is for the law and administration to take into account, as far as possible, our particularisms.'[13]

While Schuman's ideas about regionalism would play an important role in his commitment to Europe after 1945, the Great War did not lead him away from traditional ideas of sovereignty or nationalism. On the contrary, his experiences as an *attaché* to a medical division of the German army did not cause him to question nationalism as such; instead they made him sceptical of nationalism in what he saw as its militaristic Prussian form. In a letter to his cousin Albert Duren, Schuman noted, 'It was the events of 1914 through 1918 that forced me to choose.' He described visiting Messancy in Belgium after the German invasion on 2 November 1914: 'I will never forget that evening, when I saw opened before me the abyss that would forever separate me internally from Germany, from her regime, her national character, her principles.'[14] Instead of serving as a rupture that allowed new thinking, the Great War merely led Schuman to switch his national allegiance from Germany to France.

In a similar fashion to Monnet and Schuman, Adenauer's work rationing supplies in Cologne set the stage for his later career, as he was elected mayor of the city in 1917, shortly before the end of the Great War. Like Schuman, Adenauer was also committed to regionalism. He suggested that postwar Germany be organised upon federalist lines around a Rhenish state: 'By virtue of its size and economic significance this Western German Republic would play an important role in the new German Reich and ... the domination of Germany by the spirit militaristic spirit of the east would become impossible.' This would ensure peace in Europe, because 'Prussia, which is understandably feared, would no longer exist.'[15]

The economic dimension of Adenauer's thinking and his sympathies for the 'organic interweaving' (*Verflechtung*) of Germany's industry with its neighbours also emerge at this point. Although the word 'integration' did not enter his vocabulary until after the Second World War, Adenauer's experiences in Cologne gave him an appreciation for the importance of coal and steel and the extent to which these industries depended on trade with Germany's western neighbours, especially France.[16] However, in the interwar years Adenauer's commitment to economic cooperation with the west and to the reconciliation of France and Germany seem to have been mainly rhetorical. Despite the fact that the basic themes of Adenauer's political thought began to emerge in the interwar period, he was not yet prepared to act upon his ideas in the aftermath of the Great War.

While Monnet, Schuman, and Adenauer had begun to think of alternatives, they all accepted the return to traditional politics and diplomacy after the failure of the 'utopian moment' following the end of the Great War in 1919.[17]

Hans-Peter Schwarz notes, 'Though they were affected by the crises of the First World War and the post-war period, the men of the 1870s and 1880s did not feel the need for radical political change.'[18] Although they gained important cognitive resources from the Great War, this experience was not enough to convince Monnet, Schuman, and Adenauer to abandon existing political structures, either in their thought or in their actions. It did not motivate them to actually pursue their embryonic ideas, nor did it give them the justificatory resources necessary to do so.

The rupture of 1945

It was the repeated crisis brought on by the rise of National Socialism and the Second World War that convinced Monnet, Schuman, and Adenauer of the necessity of breaking with politics in its traditional, nationalist form; all three experienced the Second World War as a historical rupture. It was this experience – and the shared collective memories of it that they carried for the rest of their lives – that gave them the resources necessary to imagine, pursue, and argue for radical change in the form of supranational integration.

In Monnet's case, the Second World War provided him with another opportunity to test his ideas regarding the benefits of independent economic coordination above the level of the nation-state. Although he left the public sector after serving as an under-secretary at the League of Nations in the early 1920s, Monnet reprised his old role soon after the Nazi invasion of Poland, as he was named the chairman of the Anglo-French Coordinating Committee in November 1939. This new institution built on the lessons of resource-sharing Monnet had learned at the AMTE during the First World War. Made up of individuals with technical expertise, it went farther than the informal powers granted to Monnet in 1917 by investing its members with their own independent authority. Their task was to act directly in the common interest, bypassing national mechanisms of decision-making.[19]

After the Committee was disbanded following the fall of France to the Nazis, Monnet set out to mobilise the US war effort through what came to be called the Victory Program. Monnet's central insight was that the Allies would only be successful if they learned the 'concrete lessons' of their experience coordinating resources during the Great War.[20] Underlining these words on his typewriter, he emphasised that this approach must be based on 'the inter-dependence of allied forces in virtually every sector of the world.'[21] While the Anglo-French Coordinating Committee had failed to save France, Monnet's efforts bore fruit in mobilising the American war effort. Robert Nathan, the chairman of the War Production Board's Planning Committee, sang his praises: 'Monnet may have been the most important single person in terms of the American victory in World War II.' John Maynard Keynes even credited Monnet's work for having shortened the war by a year.[22]

This repeated experience of the success of resource-sharing solidified Monnet's belief in the necessity of independent decision-making outside the institutional framework of the nation-state. His successes in both world wars gave him the cognitive, motivational, and justificatory resources to include an independent High Authority (HA) in his proposal for a new European community and to ensure that it was not removed during the subsequent negotiations, even though some members were staunchly opposed to the idea of including any supranational structures in this new entity. His experiences during the Second World War also helped him identify coal and steel as the key sectors where such resource-sharing could succeed.

With the Victory Program in place, Monnet travelled to Algiers in 1943 to help form the Comité français de la libération nationale (CFLN). During the debates surrounding the creation of the CFLN, Monnet began 'attempting to find the golden mean between national sovereignty and supranational authority' in the organisation of postwar Europe.[23] He was already concentrating on the coal and steel industries based in the Ruhr and the Saar as the key issues that postwar Europe needed to resolve. Monnet observed that all of the continent's problems in the first half of the twentieth century had come from the heavy industry in this border region where France and Germany had 'forged the instruments of war.' He argued that 'we must take these territories away from the states that possess them and make war impossible.'[24]

In a private *note de réflexion* penned to organise his own thoughts, Monnet concluded that after the Great War the *Entente* had 'lost the peace because we imposed the law of the victors on the defeated. We have to ... imagine a community in which the enemies of today rediscover themselves as partners, working together on the basis of equality.' He argued for a unified Europe, 'a single economic entity with free trade.' He suggested removing coal and steel from national economies and placing production under a common international authority. To overcome the dangers of national sovereignty Monnet envisioned the creation of 'a Europe of the West.'[25] As a result of the rupture of 1945, his thinking had changed and his view of the need for international cooperation that rooted decision-making in institutions over and above the nation-state was firmly rooted in his memories of total war in Europe.

The experience of a second, deadlier world war also provided Robert Schuman with important resources of memory and put him in a position to implement them. Although he had spent the interwar years as a little-known *député* in the Assemblée nationale, the outbreak of the Second World War thrust the unassuming Schuman onto the grand stage of government. Immediately following the German invasion of France in May 1940, Prime Minister Paul Reynaud appointed Schuman as the new Under-Secretary of State for Refugees. As a representative of the borderlands that were being invaded, this position allowed Schuman to do what he could for his compatriots in Alsace-Lorraine.

The key advances in Schuman's thinking occurred after the Nazis arrested him on 14 September 1940. During his incarceration he began to think seriously about Europe's problems and the changes that would be necessary after a second devastating war. He came to see that '[t]here is only one salvation [*Rettung*] for Europe – that is the United States of Europe.' Georges Ditsch, an old university friend, recalls Schuman arguing that '[t]his time we cannot repeat the mistakes of the First World War … We have to find the path to the unification of Europe through peaceful cooperation.'[26] These thoughts only became stronger after Schuman escaped from house arrest in 1942, after which he went into hiding in monasteries and other Roman Catholic institutions.

Despite the fact that the war was not over and he could not yet act upon his convictions, the events of the Second World War convinced Schuman that it was time to abandon the ways of the past and set a new beginning for Europe. His experience of the rupture of 1945 thus allowed him to question existing narratives of the past. In a letter from 13 April 1942, Schuman wrote, 'Tradition gives us inexhaustible vigour and is poles apart from regretful moaning and crippling scepticism. I remain anchored in the past, without closing myself off to the building of the new. I feel compelled to be able to plant new roots in the ground.'[27] After the war he was finally able to act upon these newfound convictions rooted in his own experiences and remembrance of war.

Much like Schuman, Adenauer spent periods of particular tension in self-described exile, hiding out in Roman Catholic institutions. While he had contact with the resistance, his brief detention between 30 June and 2 July 1934 made him loath to participate in any overtly anti-regime activities. However, despite his caution, towards the end of the war Adenauer's wife was arrested and he was sent to a concentration camp. He was even condemned to die, but the American advance prevented the Gestapo from carrying out the sentence.[28]

These experiences cemented Adenauer's antimilitarism, his political Catholicism, his fear of the excesses of nationalism, and his rejection of the totalitarian tendencies 'of the east.' As part of his two Germanys thesis, Adenauer incorporated a historical narrative of the west as unified *Abendland* ('evening' or 'western country'). The idea of a Christian west, whose mission was to rebuild a shattered world, was attractive to him because it blamed Germany's sufferings on the Prussian Protestants that had dominated the old Reich.[29] The image of the *Abendland* also located powerful resources in the past that were not associated with the nationalistic militarism that had led Germany into two world wars. This rejection of nationalism led Adenauer back to an earlier ecclesiastical tradition of internationalism, a perspective he shared with Schuman, who was also a devout Catholic.[30]

After the failure of 1919, Monnet, Schuman, and Adenauer all abandoned their revolutionary ideas and settled into the interwar European order, with its traditional reliance on national sovereignty and balance of power politics. Europe had experienced a shattering event, but had retrenched to old ideas. It was not until after the rise of National Socialism and the experience of a Second World War had ruptured European understandings of the past that radical changes in political organisation became possible. As a result, Monnet, Schuman, and Adenauer had the cognitive, motivational, and justificatory resources to move away from the nation-state as the basic building block of international politics in Europe.

Imagining a European community

After their shared experience of rupture Monnet, Schuman, and Adenauer had the opportunity to fill the vacuum left by the breakdown of existing narratives to tell a new European story based on the rupture of 1945 that centred on the integration of the continent (at least its western half). Their transnationally shared collective memories provided them with the cognitive resources to look beyond traditional balance of power and confederal solutions towards approaches that began to question the principle of national sovereignty as the basis of international political organisation. However, although the events of 1914–45 had created an Arendtian 'gap' in existing narratives of the past, these three leaders still had to devise a new path for Europe and see it through the many political obstacles that awaited. By cooperating with each other they settled on the *grande idée* of a coal and steel community that pooled decision-making powers over key resources within shared institutions.

Jean Monnet came out of the Second World War convinced that 'European cooperation … depends on the settlement of the German problem' and believed that France would have to 'take the initiative on this point.'[31] Building on his reflections in Algiers, he noted in 1947: 'The objective is on the one hand, to ensure that the Ruhr can never again be used as an instrument of aggression, and, on the other, that access to the products of the Ruhr shall not be at the exclusive will of Germany, as in the past.'[32] In order to deal with the situation Monnet believed that 'something new [is] required.' In particular, he honed in on the need for a 'Western European Federation' that included 'decisive action on sovereignty.'[33] Although Monnet led the French national recovery effort for five years as the leader of the *Plan de modernisation et d'équipement*, he was convinced that 'the idea that 16 sovereign countries can cooperate effectively is an illusion. I believe that only the creation of a <u>Federation</u> … will give us the time we need to solve our problems and finally prevent war.'[34]

Monnet's conviction of the need for both resource-sharing and going beyond the nation-state by providing joint mechanisms of decision-making formed the backbone of his proposal for the ECSC. The plan Monnet drew up envisioned creating a European 'metallurgical state' (*état métallurgique*) based on a common market for coal and steel.[35] This approach sought 'to solve many problems at once: the control of German coal and steel, Franco-German reconciliation, the creation of a European entity, the development of economic prosperity in Europe, [and] an initiative for peace on the international level.'[36]

In itself, creating such a shared market was hardly revolutionary. However, the idea of bypassing traditional diplomacy and national sovereignty by creating a 'common High Authority' was both novel and timely.[37] In addition to the HA, the coal and steel community would also have an assembly made up of national representatives and a common court, both of which would check the power of the Authority. In formulating his ideas, Monnet made sure that the references to the community as 'the first step toward a European federation' were vague enough to take advantage of pro-European sentiment without prompting immediate opposition.

Now that he had a plan, Monnet needed 'to find someone who had the power, and the courage to use it to trigger a transformation in standard political practice. Robert Schuman … [was] the ideal man to do so.'[38] Schuman, who had been propelled to the upper echelons of French politics after the war, was already predisposed to Monnet's ideas. Speaking to the National Assembly in December 1948 Schuman noted that his primary goal was 'to prepare for [German] admission into a peaceful and democratic organisation of European nations.'[39] He believed that bringing Germany into 'the community of nations' was the only way to prevent her from 'retaking an independent political course, which is ultimately harmful to the security of the continent.'[40] Echoing Adenauer's ideas of *Westbindung*, Schuman noted his desire to integrate Germany into the west in the hopes that this would 'detox Germany.'[41]

As a result of his wartime reflections, Schuman quickly connected his experiences of the potential of regionalism in Alsace-Lorraine to the need to integrate Germany back into international society through transnational institutions. Under Schuman's leadership, the French Foreign Ministry had come to the view that 'a European union ... [was] the only possible formula capable of bringing a solution to a great number of European problems, in particular the problem of Germany.' In his words, the goal of such a union was to 'present to the German political imagination a continental system where Germany has a part and a role.'[42] This would give Germany the hope necessary to combat a rebirth of nationalism after the fall of the Third Reich.

By the spring of 1950 Schuman was under increasing pressure to come up with a proposal to resolve the so-called 'German problem.' At the second meeting of the Foreign Ministers of the western occupying powers after the signature of the North Atlantic Treaty, US Secretary of State Dean Acheson charged Schuman with proposing a common Allied policy vis-à-vis Germany by their next session on 11 May 1950.[43] Schuman received the text of Monnet's plan for the ECSC less than two weeks before that date. What 'captivated' Schuman about Monnet's initiative was the fact that it explicitly sought to build on the lessons of the failure of 1919 by going beyond intergovernmentalism or a customs union. Although the cognitive resources he had gained did not lead him to share Monnet's deep faith in the power of supranationalism, he accepted 'the principle of renouncing sovereign rights ... as a necessity, as the only means with which we can overcome national egoisms, antagonisms and the narrowness that is killing us.'[44]

Getting Schuman on board was not only important in terms of French domestic politics; it was also critical in securing German support for the plan that ultimately came to bear Schuman's name. Schuman and Adenauer already knew each other personally as a result of the former's visit to Bonn shortly after the latter was elected chancellor in 1949. Aside from the fact that they literally spoke the same language, Adenauer's trust in Schuman was also rooted in their common Catholic faith.[45]

Given his personal memories of the war, Adenauer was already predisposed to support Monnet's proposal. However, one of the few things that gave him pause after the proposal of the Schuman Plan was the involvement of Monnet. Adenauer's reservations were based primarily on Monnet's role in the creation of the French *Plan de modernisation et d'équipement*, which he saw as an attempt to rob Germany of its industrial infrastructure. During a visit to Bonn in late May 1950 Monnet managed to overcome Adenauer's initial misgivings.[46] It turned out that both men had drawn many of the same lessons from their shared, collective memories of Europe's age of total war. Both also felt that Europe had to unite to make a moral contribution to the development of the modern, increasingly interdependent world. Monnet noted that '[Adenauer] was in agreement with my most basic convictions,' while Adenauer came to see Monnet as 'a man endowed with a very great talent for economic organisation, a real man of peace.'[47]

In addition to these personal issues, the community-based aspects of Monnet's plan also posed difficulties. Integration through the kinds of independent institutions proposed by Schuman in 1950 was very different from the economic 'interweaving' (*Verflechtung*) that Adenauer had considered in the aftermath of the First World War. Most notably, none of Adenauer's reflections on Europe before the Second World War involved giving up any aspects of national sovereignty.[48] Moving beyond this point required Adenauer to draw on all the cognitive resources he had gained from the rupture of 1945 so that he could rethink the basis of politics on the German continent.

Moving forward with the ECSC was risky for all three of these political leaders. Following the rupture of 1945, the cognitive resources Monnet, Schuman, and Adenauer had gained as a result of their collective remembrance of the two world wars led them to act as Arendtian pearl-divers, searching the depths for bits of the past that have '"undergone a sea-change" and survive in new crystallised forms and shapes.' While the ECSC clearly built on the past, it was also 'a leap into the unknown' ('*un saut dans l'unconnu*'), as Schuman described it at his press conference announcing the Schuman Plan on 9 May 1950. Ensuring the success of this leap would require all three to draw on the motivational and justificatory resources of the past as well.

Persevering through opposition

Founding a European community based on coal and steel not only required a proposal; it also required the solutions it suggested to be negotiated, ratified, and implemented. Monnet's supranational ideas aroused the intense opposition of certain segments of the political elite, who still believed in national sovereignty and favoured either the traditional approach of dismembering Germany or tying it into the fabric of European society based on the confederal model. This opposition required Monnet, Schuman, and Adenauer to draw on their transnationally shared collective memory of the recent past as a motivational resource that would allow them to persevere and place the costs of integration on a supranational basis into perspective.

In the days leading up to the official announcement of the Plan, Schuman and Monnet had proceeded with great secrecy. While they were confident that their ideas would gain popular support, both feared that powerful forces within the French bureaucracy would try to scuttle the ECSC before it could be announced.[49] Speaking in broad terms, Schuman managed to secure the approval of the French cabinet immediately before lunch during their meeting on 8 May 1950. The project had cleared a crucial hurdle.[50]

On the evening of the next day Schuman publicly announced the plan that now bore his name. Despite their euphoria, Monnet, Schuman, and Adenauer still had to conduct the negotiations to hammer out a concrete agreement based on the Schuman Plan, ensure its ratification in all the participating states, and successfully implement their experiment. In order to achieve these goals, they would have to draw heavily on the motivational resources provided by Europe's collective memory of total war.

Due to his experiences with the impotent League of Nations, 'Monnet was uncompromising on the question of sovereignty for the institutions he was creating.'[51] His insistence on the importance of permanent structures was based on his personal memories of how the lessons of wartime cooperation had been forgotten in 1919 and on his fear that these insights would again be neglected after 1945. He knew that the only way these experiences could be reified and passed on to future generations was if they were grounded within institutions that had their own autonomous powers.

Unlike Monnet, Schuman had to overcome the powerful force of the French traditional emphasis on the importance of state sovereignty contained in the works of thinkers like Jean Bodin. Accepting the principle of shared decision-making was even harder given that this power would be shared with

Germany. Schuman's memories of the 'deep abyss' of German militarism gave him plenty of reason to fear France's eastern neighbour. However, his resources of memory convinced him to pursue a different policy vis-à-vis Germany after 1945. Even then, there were clear limits to how far he was prepared to go. For Schuman the idea of 'doing Europe' (*'faire l'Europe'*) was not a question of destroying national boundaries, but rather of changing their significance. The goal of integration was 'to unite that which is divided and separated, but not necessarily to fuse that which remains distinct.'[52]

Adenauer also had to deploy the motivational resources he drew from his own memories to remind himself of what was at stake during the difficult negotiations at the Schuman Plan Conference. During the interwar period, Adenauer had jealously guarded German sovereignty, arguing that national self-determination was the only possible basis for political authority. His proposals for the interweaving of Germany's economies with those of her neighbours developed during the interwar years were based on the idea of a customs union in which the governments retained their sovereignty. Even after his experiences during the war, Adenauer was loath to go beyond a Europe of states.[53] While Adenauer was not particularly excited about the prospect of giving up any of the authority he had managed to win back for postwar West Germany to the ECSC, he saw this as a necessary step to ensure a better settle-ment than had been possible at Versailles after the Great War.[54] Following Schuman's invitation in May 1950, Adenauer committed himself fully. For him the contents of the plan were secondary – action on a concrete, if limited, proposal for integration had been secured.[55]

In the following months Monnet, Schuman, and Adenauer's joint commitment to 'the principle of supranationality [as] the essential basis of the Schuman Plan' would be severely tested.[56] Their steadfast support for the creation of the HA with autonomous decision-making powers did not mean that the other four participating states – Italy, the Netherlands, Luxembourg, and Belgium – were equally comfortable delegating sovereignty to an insti-tution outside of their domestic constitutional architecture.[57] The Dutch negotiators in particular worked hard to limit the supranationality of the pro-posal, insisting on the creation of a committee of ministers empowered to give orders to the HA based on majority voting.

Monnet's intransigence was made possible by the constant support he received from Schuman, who actively defended the principle both at the meetings at the conference and in the Assemblée nationale. Speaking before parliament, Schuman noted, 'Our shared preoccupation is, above all, to make national hegemony impossible through the High Authority.'[58] Walter Hallstein, the head of the German delegation, also played an important role, ensuring that the key players at the conference presented a unified front regarding supranationality. Although Monnet ultimately agreed to quarterly meetings of a Council of Ministers, he thwarted further efforts to water down the HA by ensuring that the Authority did not have to ask for the agreement of government ministers before taking action.[59] Monnet's perseverance paid off on 20 July, when he reported 'that the Dutch delegate can affirm that his government has really rallied to the fundamental principle which is the supranational character of the High Authority.'[60]

In Germany, Adenauer also faced significant pressures at home that tested the strength of his own convictions. He drew on the past to place the proposal for the ECSC in its proper perspective by arguing for the priority of politics over economics and of European integration with the west over the unification of East and West Germany, at least in the short term. Although Hallstein strongly supported the project and its supranational principles, this was not true of all high-ranking German officials.[61] Most notably, the Minister of Economics and future Chancellor of the Federal Republic, Ludwig Erhard, was not well disposed to the plan, objecting to both the supranational qualities of the HA and to the *dirigiste* elements of planning reflected in very idea of regulated resource-sharing, which offended his ordoliberal economic principles. In December 1950 Erhard recommended to Adenauer that Germany leave the negotiations at the Schuman Plan Conference on economic grounds.

Despite his own reservations, Adenauer was able to resist the pressure placed upon him by his Minister of Economics by drawing on the collective memory of the rupture of 1945 that he shared with Monnet and Schuman to remind himself of the bigger picture. The motivational resources Adenauer had gained from the past helped him to identify 'questions of secondary importance' and to recognise when sacrifices should 'grudgingly be accepted in the interest of higher aims.'[62] The stakes – 'the security of the free world against the threat from the east and the building of a European and Atlantic community including Germany that works together amicably' – were too high for the west to quarrel over 'side questions' such as the economic issues with which Erhard was obsessed.[63]

The rupture of the Second World War was also crucial to Adenauer's prioritisation of *Westbindung* over German reunification. Without this commitment the creation of the ECSC would not have been possible. Just months after the war, Adenauer had already resigned himself to the fact that the eastern part of Germany had been 'lost for a time that cannot be estimated.' In contrast to his unwillingness to break with Prussia in 1919, Adenauer was prepared to let the socialist east go in order to integrate the western part of Germany within the ECSC.[64] This prioritisation of *Westbindung* over reunification was not merely rhetorical. In a diplomatic note on 10 March 1952, Joseph Stalin offered Germany the chance to reunify with almost complete sovereignty. His only condition was that Germany not be allowed to enter into 'any organisations inimical to democracy' or 'any kind of coalition or military alliance directed against any power which took part … in war against Germany.'[65]

Adenauer immediately saw this as a ploy designed to prevent European integration. He rejected it out of hand: 'Under no circumstances must we arouse suspicion that we are wavering in our policy.'[66] Not all Germans were willing to let go of the eastern half of their country in exchange for integration. Although Kurt Schumacher, the leader of the Social Democratic Party (SPD) supported the idea of binding Germany to a federation of democratic states, he objected to Adenauer's pursuit of this goal over and above reunification. Sticking with his commitment to the ECSC in the face of this politically dangerous nationalist opposition required Adenauer to draw on all of the motivational resources he had gained in the past to persevere and place the importance of the European project in proper perspective.

As a motivational resource, their collective memories of the rupture of 1945 helped Monnet, Schuman, and Adenauer to turn their new ideas into action. More specifically, this shared remembrance helped to remind them that their pursuit of integration was about avoiding a reversion to past practices of violence by going beyond the traditional political practices of sovereign nation-states. However, in order to succeed in the democratic context of postwar Western Europe, all three leaders also needed to convince their constituents of the validity of their convictions. As a result, they also had to draw on the reconfigued, post-rupture frameworks of collective memory to provide them with the justificatory resources necessary to argue for their ideas and defend their reasoning in public.

Arguing for community

In justifying their turn to community principles and shared control over the key resources of coal and steel, Monnet, Schuman, and Adenauer took advantage of the fact that in 1950, 'Europe [enjoyed] a general though not very alert sympathy in public opinion.'[67] Despite broad agreement on the need to create a European entity based on the principle of supranationality, the big question was how this could be done. While pro-European sentiment made it somewhat easier to formulate arguments, they still had to choose specific reasons on which to ground their justifications for a supranational, community-style Europe.[68]

The geopolitical situation of the nascent Cold War, the need for economic reconstruction, and the Marshall Plan had an impact on public opinion, making the economic justification of sectoral integration relatively easy. This argument built on broadly shared cognitive resources resulting from the war, when both the Vichy regime and the *Résistance*, to say nothing of the Nazis and their close coordination of industry, advocated forms of economic planning.[69] Since the belief in planning was widespread, Monnet and his partners made sure to stress that while the common market in coal and steel would benefit producers and the overall economy, it would also 'improve the living conditions of the 1,500,000 workers who are employed in the mines and factories of the Community.'[70]

In his attempts to 'liberate [Europeans] from their history' and the traditions that bound them to pre-rupture nationalist narratives of the past, Monnet drew heavily on images of the past and collective memories of suffering to justify the creation of supranational institutions. Speaking to the opening session of the ECSC Common Assembly in September 1952, Monnet noted, 'When one looks back a little on the past fifty, seventy-five or hundred years, and one sees the extraordinary disaster the Europeans have brought upon themselves, one is literally aghast.' Something had to change. Europe had to 'learn the lessons of its past failures to recognise that progress has become inevitable.'

He argued that the only way to do so was through the creation of common institutions: 'Good will comes and goes, only common institutions could guarantee the permanence of concord and give people confidence that it would last.'[71] While Monnet ultimately gave in to the Dutch insistence on a Council of Ministers, which gave national interests a direct voice in the ECSC, he noted that 'there is one point on which there will be no turning back: these institutions are supranational and, let us not shrink from the word, federal.' As Monnet pointed out in an interview, 'The operation of the Community will scramble the eggs and once they are scrambled it will be difficult to unscramble them.'[72]

In addition to public speeches and articles published in the popular press, accounts of the origins of the Schuman Plan and of integration in general in the form of memoirs were an important way the founders of the ECSC could affect societal narratives of integration. Monnet's and Adenauer's respective memoirs were particularly influential. By contrast, instead of writing an account of his own recollections, Schuman instead compiled his thoughts on Europe from various speeches he had delivered into a short handbook entitled *For Europe* (*Pour l'Europe*, 1963), which presented his justifications for the European project.[73] This demonstrates that he was aware of the importance of rallying public support for the project of unification on a community basis.

In his public defences of integration, Schuman always downplayed the economic aspects of integration. For him, European unification was first and foremost a political project. Reflecting back on the foundation of the ECSC in 1953, he argued, 'We were moved much less by economic considerations than by political ones: to detoxify relations between France and Germany, assure peace, creating a climate of cooperation throughout Europe – this was our objective above all others.'[74]

While the passions of nationalism had obscured this essential truth, Schuman looked back to the older, more cosmopolitan traditions of unified Christendom as a model, a Benjaminian 'pearl' that postwar Europeans could bring back to the surface after 1945. Schuman hoped that 'the follies of the past' would not obscure 'what Christian Europe had in common.' In this sense, a supranational Europe was not something completely new, but a return to an older, pre-nationalist trope of European history. For him, 'The Europe that we have founded will be thus, not a bold construction of the imagination, but the hopefully enduring return to perennial tradition which a momentary aberration had succeeded in making us forget.'[75]

Adenauer's experiences and interpretations of the past played an important role in his public justifications of Europe as well. Due to his commitments and international fears about German militarism Adenauer had to find a way to create horizontal bonds with the citizens of Germany without relying on the ideology of nationalism.[76] In order to build a collective identity that was not contaminated by Nazi rhetoric, he turned to the constructive resources contained in the suffering of two world wars and the lessons of the National Socialism's rise in Germany. Instead of neutralisation and demilitarisation, which would leave Germany vulnerable to the east and repeat the mistakes of 1918, Adenauer counselled the creation of a new European military culture that would not be vulnerable to the aggressive nationalist excesses of the previous century.[77] When it came to giving up sovereignty, he also called on the past. Adenauer often noted that the fragmentation of Europe had become 'a relic' (*ein Relikt*) of the previous era. 'Sovereignty is of great value to us, but we are now ready to yield it to a supranational community of European peoples.' Adenauer also observed that 'the dismantling of anachronisms was among the most necessary but also the most difficult things in politics.'[78]

The attempts of Monnet, Schuman, and Adenauer to justify the European project as a response to the European rupture that followed the Second World War were largely successful. For many on the continent, 'The inevitable moment of choice had arrived.'[79] At the time of its creation in 1951, the ECSC was supported by a 'permissive consensus' that built on the broadly shared experience of 1945 as a caesura. It was these shared constructive resources that helped leaders like Monnet, Schuman, and Adenauer to convince the national parliaments of the six original member-states – and through them also the peoples of Europe more generally – that community-based institutions with clear economic goals could succeed in inaugurating a new form of European politics that could avoid the mistakes of the past.

Conclusion

Looking back at the European postwar context and at how far the EU has come it is easy to forget how revolutionary the ECSC was at the time. Certainly the actors involved in its creation, most notably Monnet, Schuman, and Adenauer, saw it as such. They had to draw extensively on the cognitive, motivational, and justificatory resources provided by their experience of the rupture of 1914 through 1945 to get their minds around the idea of going beyond the nation-state, motivate themselves to see the project through and justify it to their constituents. Far from being inevitable, 'Europe took the supranational path only because aggressively integrationist leaders used a series of *faits accomplis* to resolve a wider battle over alternatives to Europe.'[80]

The successful passage of the ECSC and its entry into force in 1952 started the first phase of European unification. Despite the new thinking made possible by the rupture resulting from the two world wars, traditional ideas were still powerful. This was particularly true in defence and military affairs. Due to the efforts of Monnet, Schuman, and Adenauer, the proposal for the European Defence Community (EDC), an attempt follow on the heels of the ECSC by unifying Europe's military forces, was signed by the Six in 1952. However, it failed to win ratification in the French parliament two years later. Opposition came from both right and left, but was most vociferous among the partisans of

General Charles de Gaulle, who believed that 'the soul and fate of the nation were constantly reflected in the mirror of the Army.'[81]

While this setback disappointed Monnet, Schuman, and Adenauer, it was only temporary. By 1958, Europe had experienced a *relance* with the ratification of the Treaties of Rome. This agreement created two new European communities: the European Atomic Energy Community (Euratom) to oversee the continent's supply of nuclear material, as well as the EEC, which aimed to create a common market in beyond the sectors of coal and steel. This 'relaunch' represented a significant institutional deepening of the European project into new areas of political life. However, due to the rise of leaders like Charles de Gaulle, who denied that the European rupture of 1945 necessitated new thinking, integration stagnated in the 1960s and 1970s. This period of Eurosclerosis was highlighted by the attempt to change the European Communities into a 'Europe of the nation-states.'

This return to more traditional modes of politics was followed by what I call the 'second phase of integration' (1985–2003), which was driven by a new constellation of leaders that mirrored Monnet, Schuman, and Adenauer in their commitment to the community method based on transnationally shared collective memories of the rupture of 1945. Jacques Delors, the President of the European Commission, French President François Mitterrand, and German Chancellor Helmut Kohl once again sought to build on the constructive resources of the past. The result was that 'economic governance in Europe went through its deepest transformation since the end of World War II, leading to the emergence of a distinctive European model of political economy.'[82] It is these two periods to which I now turn.

Notes

1 N. Jabko, *Playing the Market: A Political Strategy for Uniting Europe, 1985–2005* (Ithaca, NY: Cornell University Press, 2006), 2; Mannheim, *Essays on the Sociology of Knowledge*, 291.

2 Milward, 'The Lives and Teachings of the European Saints,' in *The European Rescue of the Nation-State*, 284–303; Kaiser, 'From Great Men to Ordinary Citizens?'; Anderson, 'Under the Sign of the Interim.'

3 Guisan, *A Political Theory of Identity in European Integration*, 6; Geuss, *Philosophy and Real Politics*, 1.

4 Guisan, *A Political Theory of Identity in European Integration*, 66, 2.

5 C. Parsons, 'The Triumph of Community Europe,' in D. Dinan (ed), *Origins and Evolution of the European Union* (Oxford: Oxford University Press, 2006), 109.

6 C. Parsons, *A Certain Idea of Europe* (Ithaca, NY: Cornell University Press, 2003), 1; Parsons, 'The Triumph of Community Europe,' 124.

7 For an analysis of this period, see H. Arendt, *The Origins of Totalitarianism* (New York: Brace Harcourt, 1951), 267–302.

8 F. J. Fransen, *The Supranational Politics of Jean Monnet: Ideas and Origins of the European Community* (Westport: Greenwood Press, 2001), 24.

9 Fondation Jean Monnet pour l'Europe, Lausanne, Switzerland (hereafter FJM), AMB 1/1/13, 'Note de Jean Monnet à R. Fillioux,' 18 September 2015.

10 FJM, AMB 1/1/127, '"Note au Président Wilson." Télégramme, de Jean Monnet à R. Fillioux,' 18 December 1928, translation mine; FJM, AMB 1/1/97, 'Télégramme, de Jean Monnet à R. Fillioux,' 18 November 1925, translation mine; J. Monnet, *Memoirs* (London: Collins, 1978), 80.

11 Lettre de Robert Schuman à Henri Eschbach, 1 January 1919. Cited in F. Roth, *Robert Schuman, 1886–1963: Du Lorrain des frontières au père de l'Europe* (Paris: Fayard, 2008), 95–6, translation mine.

12 H. Brugmans, *Le message européen de Robert Schuman* (Lausanne: Fondation Jean Monnet pour l'Europe, 1965), 12.

13 *Le Courrier du Metz* (14 November 1919), translation mine.

14 Lettre de Schuman à Albert Duren, 10 August 1920. Cited in C. Pennera, *Robert Schuman: La jeunesse et les débuts politiques d'un grand européen de 1886 à 1924* (Paris: Editions Pierron, 1985), 82–83, translation mine.

15 Versammlung der linksrheinischen Abgeordneten zur Nationalversammlung und zur preußischen Landesversammlung sowie der Oberbürgermeister der besetzten rheinischen Städte in Köln am 1. Februar 1919. Niederschrift o.D. (HAStK 2/253/I. Erstschrift), published in K. D. Erdmann, *Adenauer in der Rheinlandpolitik nach dem ersten Weltkrieg* (Stuttgart: E. Klett Verlag, 1966), 212–234.

16 P. Weymar, *Konrad Adenauer. Die autorisierte Biographie* (Munich: Kindler, 1955), 94.

17 Winter, *Dreams of Peace and Freedom*.

18 H.-P. Schwarz, *Konrad Adenauer: A German Politician and Statesman in a Period of War, Revolution, and Reconstruction, Vol. 1: From the German Empire to the Federal Republic, 1876–1952* (Providence: Berghahn Books, 1995), 93. One of Schuman's biographers makes a similar point. 'As is the case for many future Europeanists, it was the experience of the Second World War that was crucial for Robert Schuman.' M.-T. Bitsch, *Robert Schuman, apôtre de l'Europe, 1953–1963* (Brussels: P.I.E. Peter Lang, 2010), 20, translation mine.

19 FJM, AME 4/1/4, 'Note on the allied executives' (40.04.29), Caisse de Londres.

20 FJM, AME 14/1/4, '[Basic summary of the basic conditions...],' notes, de J.M. (41.11), manuscrit.

21 FJM, AME 14/1/8, 'Experience, both in World War I and since 1939...,' de [J.M.] (41.12.17), emphasis in original.

22 FJM, Washington, DC, 'Interview Robert Nathan' (with Leonard Tennyson), 18 December 1981.

23 Fransen, *The Supranational Politics of Jean Monnet*, 88.

24 É. Hirsch, 'Il y a dans les affairs humaines une mare montante... (Shakespeare),' in H. Rieben, B. Clappier, and É. Hirsch, *Une Mémoire vivante* (Lausanne: Fondation Jean Monnet pour l'Europe, 1986), 65–66, 78–79, translation mine.

25 FJM, AME 56/1/1, '[Le but ultime est une organization du monde qui permette le développement maximum de ses ressources...],' Note, manuscrit., translation mine.

26 Quoted in H. A. Lücker and J. Seitlinger, *Robert Schuman und die Einigung Europas* (Luxemburg: Editions Saint-Paul, 2000), 37–38, translation mine.

27 *Ibid.*, 39, translation mine.

28 W. Conze, E. Kosthorst, and E. Nebgen, *Jakob Kaiser. Der Widerstandskämpfer* (Stuttgart: Kohlhammer, 1970), 60; Adenauer an Hertha Kraus (10.4.45), published in Konrad Adenauer, *Briefe über Deutschland, 1945–1951*, ed. Hans Peter Mensing (Berlin: Corso, 1983b), 13.

29 G. Müller and V. Plichta, 'Zwischen Rhein und Donau. Abendländisches Denken zwischen Deutsch-Französischen Verständigungsinitiativen und Konservativ-Katholischen Integrationsmodellen 1923–1957,' *Journal of European Integration History*, 5:2 (1999), 17–47; R. J. Granieri, *The Ambivalent Alliance: Konrad Adenauer, the CDU/CSU, and the West, 1949–1966* (New York: Berghahn Books, 2003), 15–18.

30 P. J. Verovšek, 'Habermas's Theological Turn and European Integration,' *The European Legacy*, 22:5 (2017).

31 FJM, AMF 14/1/6, 'Mémorandum remis à monsieur G. Bidault par monsieur Monnet … sur la question des crédits Marshall,' 24 July 1947.

32 FJM, AMG 20/2/10, 'Préambule,' texte en anglais (incompet?).

33 FJM, AMF22/1/3c, 'JM's statement to J.P.D. Wisconsin,' 8 April 1948.

34 FJM, AMF 22/1/6c, 'Lettre de J.M. à G. Bidault,' Texte dactylographié avec début, fin et corrections de la main de J.M., 18 April 1948, translation mine, emphasis in typewritten original.

35 FJM, AME 33/2/14, 'L'organisation politique et économique de l'Europe occidentale,' Avec des corrections manuscrites; É. Hirsch, *Ainsi va la vie* (Lausanne: Fondation Jean Monnet pour l'Europe, 1988), 78–79.

36 P. Gerbet, *La genèse du plan Schuman* (Lausanne: Fondation Jean Monnet pour l'Europe, 1962), 20, translation mine.

37 'There was no precedent in European tradition' for an institution like the HA. See J. Gillingham, 'Jean Monnet and the European Coal and Steel Community: A Preliminary Appraisal' in D. Brinkley and C. P. Hackett (eds), *Jean Monnet: The Path to European Unity* (Houndmills: Macmillan, 1991), 140; cf. also D. Dinan, *Europe Recast: A History of European Union* (Boulder: Lynne Rienner, 2004), 38. It was only in the fourth draft of his proposal, that Monnet replaced an 'international authority' with a 'common High Authority' based on 'supranational' principles. FJM, AMG 1/2/4, '4e projet du 26.4.1950,' avec notes J.M.

38 Monnet, *Memoirs*, 298.

39 R. Lejeune, *Robert Schuman: Une âme pour l'Europe* (Paris: Editions Saint-Paul, 1986), 111.

40 Note des Affaires étrangères, direction d'Europe, 23 octobre 1948, généralités, t. 11, quoted in R. Poidevin, *Robert Schuman: Homme d'état, 1886–1963* (Paris: Impr. nationale, 1986), 220.

41 *Cahiers de Bruges*, December 1953.

42 Note d'Affaires étrangères, direction d'Europe, 22 octobre 1948, généralités, t. II, quoted in Poidevin, *Robert Schuman*, 220; Robert Schuman à ambassadeur Londres (Massigli), 7 octobre 1948, généralités, t. 10, quoted in Poidevin, *Robert Schuman*, 221.

43 United States Department of State, *Foreign Relations of the United States, 1949*, vol. III: 'Council of Ministers; Germany and Austria' (Washington, DC: US Government Printing Office, 1974), 610, 623.

44 D. Christnacker, *Les interventions de Robert Schuman du Conseil de l'Europe (1949–1951)* (Strasbourg: Mémoire IEP, 1975), 37ff.

45 R. Lejeune, *Robert Schuman (1886–1963), père de l'Europe: La politique, chemin de sainteté* (Paris: Fayard, 2000), 45.

46   Diary entry by Schäffer, 3 June 1950, in Klaus Schwabe, 'Konrad Adenauer und der Schuman Plan. Ein Quellenzeugnis,' in K. Schwabe (ed), *Die Anfänge des Schuman-Plans, 1950/51: Beiträge des Kolloquiums in Aachen, 28.-30. Mai 1986 = the Beginnings of the Schuman-Plan: Contributions to the Symposium in Aachen, may 28–30, 1986* (Baden-Baden: Nomos, 1988), 131–140. Monnet was aware of Adenauer's suspicions, see Monnet, *Memoirs*, 309.

47   FJM, AML 239, 'Déclaration de J.M. à propos du chancelier Adenauer pour le Rheinische Merkur,' 11 October 1963; K. Adenauer, *Memoirs 1945–53*, trans. B. Ruhm von Oppen (Chicago: Henry Regnery Company, 1966), 263. For Monnet's full report on their initial conversation, see FJM, AMG 2/3/11, 'C.R. de l'entrevue J.M. – K. Adenauer,' published in *L'Europe: Une Longue Marche* (Lausanne: Fondation Jean Monnet pour l'Europe, 1985), 81–88.

48   The idea was controversial even in Christian Democratic circles. See P. Pulzer, 'Nationalism and Internationalism in European Christian Democracy,' in M. Gehler and W. Kaiser (eds), *Christian Democracy in Europe since 1945* (London: Routledge, 2004), 21–23; U. Lappenküper, 'Between Concentration Movement and People's Party: The Christian Democratic Union in Germany,' in Gehler and Kaiser, *Christian Democracy in Europe since 1945*, 28; W. Kaiser, 'Transnational Christian Democracy: From the Nouvelles Equipes Internationales to the European People's Party,' in Gehler and Kaiser, *Christian Democracy in Europe since 1945*, 231.

49   G. Bossuat, 'La Politique Française de libération des échanges en Europe et le Plan Schuman (1950–1951),' in Schwabe, *Die Anfänge des Schuman-Plans, 1950/51*, 319–332; A. Deighton, *Building Postwar Europe: National Decision-Makers and European Institutions, 1948–63* (New York: St. Martin's Press, 1995), 21–37.

50   R. Rochefort, *Robert Schuman* (Paris: Les Éditions du Cerf, 1968), 225.

51   M. Bromberger and S. Bromberger, *Jean Monnet and the United States of Europe* (New York: Coward-McCann, 1969), 131.

52   R. Schuman, 'Comment le Français d'aujourd'hui peut-il concevoir l'Europe?' 2 March 1951, speech in Paris, Maison Robert Schuman (MRS), published in and translated by A. P. Fimister, *Robert Schuman: Neo-Scholastic Humanism and the Reunification of Europe* (Brussels: Peter Lang, 2008), 220.

53   Anlage zum Schreiben an Weitz: 'Meine Einstellung zur außenpolitischen Lage,' 31 October 1945, published in Konrad Adenauer, *Briefe 1945–1947*, ed Rudolf Morsey and Hans Peter Mensing (Berlin: Siedler Verlag, 1983), 130.

54   H. Blankenhorn, *Verständnis und Verständigung: Blätter eines politischen Tagebuchs, 1949 bis 1979* (Frankfurt am Main: Propyläen Verlag, 1980), 71–72 (3 October 1949); H. Köhler, *Adenauer: Eine politische Biographie* (Frankfurt am Main: Propyläen, 1994), 567–573; T. A. Schwartz, *America's Germany: John J. McCloy and the Federal Republic of Germany* (Cambridge, MA: Harvard University Press, 1991), 75.

55   K. Adenauer and Th. Heuss, *Unter vier Augen: Gespräche aus den Gründerjahren 1949–1959*, ed. H. P. Mensing (Berlin: Siedler Verlag, 1997), 55 (2 March 1951).

56   FJM, AMG 23/3/15, 'Annexe. Mémorandum JM sur les rapports entre les institutions prévues par le Plan Schuman et le Conseil de l'Europe,' 14 August 1950, Copie dactylographiée, translation mine. Published in J. Monnet and R. Schuman, *Jean Monnet, Robert Schuman: Correspondance, 1947–1953* (Lausanne: Fondation Jean Monnet pour l'Europe, 1986), 49.

57   FJM, AMG 22/2/1, 'Note relative aux effets du Plan Schuman sur les industries du charbon et de l'acier en France,' 12 September 1950.

58 *Année politique*, 1951, 500ff, translation mine.

59 H. J. Küsters, 'Jean Monnet and the European Union: Idea and Reality of the Integration Process,' in G. Majone, E. Noël and P. van den Bossche (eds), *Jean Monnet et l'Europe d'aujourd'hui* (Baden-Baden: Nomos, 1989), 84.

60 'Conversations sur le plan Schuman: Réunion du comité des chefs de délégation sur les questions institutionnelles,' 20 July 1950, 81/AJ/132, AN, quoted and translated by Fransen, *The Supranational Politics of Jean Monnet*, 107–108.

61 FJM, AMG 2/3/11, 'C.R. de l'entrevue J.M. – K. Adenauer,' in *L'Europe: une longue marche*, 87.

62 Anlage zum Schreiben an Weitz: 'Meine Einstellung zur außenpolitischen Lage,' 31 October 1945, published in Adenauer, *Briefe 1945–1947*, 124.

63 Adenauer an den Hohen Kommissar des Vereinigten Königreiches, Sir Ivone Kirkpatrick, 24 January 1952, published in Adenauer, *Briefe, 1953–1955*, 171, translation mine.

64 Aktennotiz über ein Gespräch mit ausländischen Pressevertretern, 9 October 1945, published in Adenauer, *Briefe 1945–1947*, 124; Adeanuer an Oberbürgermeister Dr. Karl Scharnagl, 21 August 1945, published in *ibid.*, 78; N. G. Annan, *Changing Enemies: The Defeat and Regeneration of Germany* (New York: W. W. Norton & Co., 1996), 224.

65 United States Department of State, *Foreign Relations of the United States, 1952–1954. Germany and Austria. Vol. 7, Part 1*, ed. William Z. Slany (Washington, DC: US Government Printing Office, 1952–54), 169–172.

66 O. Lenz, *Im Zentrum der Macht: Das Tagebuch von Staatssekretär Lenz, 1951–1953*, ed K. Gotto, H.-O. Kleinmann, and R. Schreiner (Düsseldorf: Droste, 1989), 273 (11 March 1952), 276–277 (14 March 1952); Blankenhorn, *Verständnis und Verständigung*, 132–133 (10 March 1952); H. Booms (ed), *Die Kabinettsprotokolle der Bundesregierung, Band 7, 1954* (Boppard am Rhein: Harald Boldt Verlag, 1993), 217. Adenauer believed, 'Any connection between West Germany and East Germany would, as long as East Germany remains nothing more than a satellite of Soviet Russia, only strengthen the position of the Soviets in Germany.' Adenauer to Dannie N. Heineman (12 June 1949), published in Adenauer, *Briefe, 1949–1951*, 33.

67 H. W. Ehrmann, *Organized Business in France* (Princeton: Princeton University Press, 1957), 411; also H. Rieben, *Des guerres européennes à l'Union de l'Europe* (Lausanne: Fondation Jean Monnet pour l'Europe, 1987), 118.

68 Forst, *The Right to Justification*, 13.

69 S. Hoffmann, 'The Effects of World War II on French Society and Politics,' *French Historical Studies*, 2:1 (1961), 30–31; P. Mioche, 'L'Invention du Plan Monnet,' in B.Cayes and P. Mioche (eds), *Modernisation ou décadence* (Aix-en-Provence: Publications de l'Université de Provence, 1990), 15–24.

70 J. Monnet, *Speeches Delivered by Jean Monnet, President of the High Authority at the Inauguration of the High Authority on August 10th, 1952 [and] at the Opening Session of the Assembly on Sept 11th, 1952* (Strasbourg: European Coal and Steel Community, 1952), 21. Also FJM, AMG 49/1/3, 'Jean Monnet Interview,' *Radio Free Europe*, Series 4, program 22, 4.51.

71 Monnet, *Speeches Delivered by Jean Monnet*, 25, 20; FJM, AMG 49/2/14, 'Projet d'allocution de M. Monnet à l'occasion du cinquantenaire de l'Alliance française aux Etats-unis. – Texte revisé, 3,' 10 April 1952, translation mine; FJM, AML 352/11, 'France at War,' Article de J.M. in 'United States at War,' *Army & Navy Journal*,

7 December 1942; FJM, AML 171/10, 'Outline for Article "Ferment of Change,"' 1 April 1961.

72 Monnet, *Speeches Delivered by Jean Monnet*, 8–9. For more on institutions, cf. 20. FJM, AMG 10/1/la, 'Note générale sur le Plan Schuman,' [Paris] 4 December 1950, Annexe, Copie dactylographiée, published in Monnet and Schuman, *Jean Monnet, Robert Schuman*, 76–89; FJM, AMG 49/1/37, 'Suggested questions and answers on the Schuman Plan,' Texte dactylographié sans notes manuscrites.

73 This book was finally translated into English in the following edition, Robert Schuman, *For Europe*, ed. Foundation Robert Schuman (Paris: Nagel Editions SA, 2010).

74 *Cahiers de Bruges*, décembre 1953, translation mine.

75 R. Schuman, 'Ce que signifie la Communauté européenne pour le Chrétien?' Abbaye de Fleury, August 1958, ADM 34J38. Translated by Fimister, *Robert Schuman*, 200.

76 U. Frevert, 'Die Sprache des Volkes und die Rhetorik der Nation: Identitätssplitter in der Deutschen Nachkriegszeit,' in A. Bauerkämper, M. Sabrow, and B. Störver (eds), *Doppelte Zeitgeschichte: Deutsch-Deutsche Beziehungen 1945–1990* (Bonn: Dietz, 1998), 18–31.

77 Besprechung der drei Hohen Kommissare mit dem Bundeskanzler (17 August 1950), published in H. Booms (ed), *Die Kabinettsprotokolle der Bundesregierung, Band 3, 1950, Wortprotokolle* (Boppard am Rhein: Harald Boldt Verlag, 1986), 84; Lenz, *Im Zentrum der Macht*, 289 (1 April 1952), 363 (15 June 1952); Adenauer, *Memoirs 1945–53*, 68, 267–269.

78 'Ansprache über den SFB am 5.5.1955,' *Bulletin*, 85/55, 702; Adenauer, *Memoirs 1945–53*, 334, 363, translation mine.

79 A. S. Milward, *The Reconstruction of Western Europe, 1945–51* (Berkeley: University of California Press, 1984), 157.

80 Parsons, 'The Triumph of Community Europe,' 108, emphasis in original.

81 C. de Gaulle, *Complete War Memoirs of Charles de Gaulle* (New York: Simon & Schuster, 1967), p. 27; N. Beloff, *The General Says No: Britain's Exclusion from Europe* (Baltimore: Penguin Books, 1963), 65.

82 Jabko, *Playing the Market*, 2.

Chapter 3

Counter-memory and generational change: Eurosclerosis (1959–84) and the second phase of integration (1985–2003)

A bellicose past entangled all European nations in bloody conflicts. They drew a conclusion from that military and spiritual mobilisation ... the imperative of developing new, supranational forms of cooperation after the Second World War.
Jürgen Habermas and Jacques Derrida, *Frankfurter Allgemeine Zeitung* (2003)

The classic narrative of integration

In the previous chapter I showed how Monnet, Schuman, and Adenauer drew on the resources of collective memory they had obtained as a result of the narrative break of 1945 to imagine, motivate, and justify the creation of the first European community. The experience of total war and the legacy of bloody nationalism was front of mind for these 'founding fathers' of integration whenever they considered the future of Europe. Interestingly, given its central place in what I call 'the classic narrative of integration,' the original arguments in favour of European unification did not mention the Holocaust. Instead, while collective memories of war and suffering played an important role, the initial unification of Europe was also the product of 'vital forgetting.'[1]

Following the end of the Second World War the complicity of large segments of society in Germany as well as the rest of the Six – most notably the French Vichy regime and Mussolini's Italy – inclined postwar governments in Western Europe towards silence regarding their collaboration with the crimes they had committed during the Second World War. Across Europe politicians decided that bringing attention to domestic war crimes and the Holocaust more generally would be counterproductive, as it would result in purges of the bureaucrats, police, judges, and other officials whose expertise was needed for reconstruction. Since these postwar governments had to recreate functioning democracies while simultaneously dealing with the geopolitical problems engendered by the emerging Cold War, working through the past was not their top priority: 'Economic recovery and political legitimacy, not additional purges, were the proper medicine. Democratic renewal went hand in hand with silence.'[2]

A mere twenty years after the end of the Second World War, all of this had changed. The silence of the late 1940s and 1950s was followed by an explosive confrontation with the wartime past that culminated in the student protests of 1968. The so-called 'sixty-eighters,' who had no personal memories of the Second World War, reacted against the silence of the previous generation. They brought the Holocaust and the image of Auschwitz to the fore as a 'type of distancing and purification ritual in relation to the sins of [their] fathers.'[3] As a result of this activism, 'the deterrent horror of Auschwitz' came to be seen as one of 'the forces that impelled Europe's unprecedented integration in the second half of the twentieth-century.' The sixty-eighters changed European memory culture by forcing individuals and the discourses of remembrance in the west to confront the atrocities of industrially organised slaughter.[4]

Despite their influence on domestic politics and on the narrative of European integration, the activism of the 1960s and 1970s coincided with the institutional stagnation of the European project. By this period, Monnet, Schuman, Adenauer and much of the rest of the *Erfahrungsgeneration* (the 'generation of experience'), who were born in the late nineteenth century and had lived through the *fin de siècle* and both world wars, had left the political stage. While students protested in the streets, the development of the European Communities stalled after the Treaty of Rome. During this time, 'the Six concerned themselves with such prosaic matters as import quotas, product safety standards and agricultural prices.' Although these activities had a positive economic effect, they did not spur further integration. On the contrary, 'The 1970s had taught that the Community could not stand up to stiff headwinds.'[5]

In addition to outside factors, including an economic recession and the global oil crisis, this institutional sojourn was reinforced by a pushback against community-based solutions by leaders who had not experienced Europe's age of total war as proof of the obsolescence of the Westphalian state. Foremost among these champions of traditional, state-based approaches was French President Charles de Gaulle, who maintained a view of international politics as a Hobbesian world where states confronted each other in 'the posture of Gladiators.'[6] Although he had lived through the same events as Monnet, Schuman, and Adenauer, de Gaulle had not experienced 1945 as a rupture and thus did not share the same cognitive, motivational, and justificatory resources of collective memory as these founders of the European project. On the contrary, as a supporter of a 'Europe of nation-states' ('*l'Europe des patries*'), de Gaulle stridently opposed *la méthode Monnet*. In 1964 he sought to prove the pre-eminence of the member-states and national leaders in community affairs by withdrawing all French representatives from community institutions in the 'empty chair crisis.'

De Gaulle's resistance was reinforced by the first expansion of the European Communities. When the United Kingdom, Denmark, and Ireland were finally allowed to join the European Communities in 1973, the anti-community movement de Gaulle had spurred gained further allies who viewed the European project through a decidedly economic lens. This was especially true of the British, who did not share the collective memory of Nazi occupation with continental Europe. As a result of these differences, leaders in the UK were thus more willing to continue to believe in the traditional politics of national sovereignty. With the support of Eurosceptics in other member-states, Britain was able to resist the expansion of the powers and prerogatives of community institutions, a role that it continued to play all the way up to the Brexit referendum in 2016.

The institutional gridlock of the 1960s and 1970s was broken in the mid-1980s by the political leadership of the 'forty-fivers,' who had had experienced the end of the Second World War as young men between the ages of fifteen and thirty, a key period for the development of generational memories.[7] Led by Jacques Delors, François Mitterrand, and Helmut Kohl, this new constellation of leaders expanded on the foundation provided by Monnet, Schuman, and Adenauer. The second phase of integration (1985–2003) represents the culmination of the classic narrative, as these leaders built on the lessons of the past to complete the CM, turning the European Communities into the EU.

The argument of this chapter is organised chronologically. I divide the postwar period between the *relance* of 1958, which completed the first phase of integration, and the culmination of the classical narrative in 2003 into two parts: Eurosclerosis (1959–84) and what I call the 'second phase of integration' (1985–2003). In addition to the economic difficulties of the 1970s, which caused the member-states to look inward, the former period is associated with the resistance of de Gaulle and the accession of the UK. The second half of the chapter focuses on how the rise of a new generation of leaders who shared community ideas based on their memories of the past once again led to the institutional deepening of the European project and the creation of the EU.

De Gaulle and the denial of rupture (1958–84)

Growing up in a modest Catholic family that traced its roots to the aristocracy, de Gaulle's views of life were deeply rooted in the glory of the French state. The pre-First World War France of his childhood was defined by a nationalist revival that sought to recover the nation's status and honour. While these values were present across the political spectrum, they were especially strong in the social milieu of de Gaulle's parents and his Jesuit teachers.[8] In the opening lines of his memoirs, the General observed, 'All my life I have had a certain idea of France. This is inspired as much by sentiment as by reason ... France cannot be France without greatness.'[9]

As an army officer de Gaulle was well positioned to experience the rupture of 1945. However, unlike Monnet, Schuman, and Adenauer, who turned to new ideas in the aftermath of the Second World War, de Gaulle instead sought to return to the past. This posture led Hannah Arendt to accord the General 'a special position' among the postwar leaders of Europe, observing that he 'represents not the forces of yesterday but is, rather, a solitary reminder of the forces of the day before yesterday ... [H]e alone truly represents patriotism and nationalism in the old sense.'[10]

Many of de Gaulle's contemporaries observed that he 'rarely absorbs ideas produced after the First World War.'[11] On the contrary, de Gaulle looked to France under Louis XIV, a France of *grandeur* with leaders that 'strove incessantly to increase their territory, to support their allies and to weaken their rivals, but ... avoided the great jolts, ruptures of the equilibrium and upheavals.' It was this romantic vision of his *patrie* that led Stanley Hoffman to describe de Gaulle as 'the saviour of France, knight-errant for her grandeur, believer in the cultural values embodied in a national tradition.'

In addition to this '*certaine idée de la France*,' the General also admired the old European balance of power, which eschewed the 'inexpiable hatreds' that 'poison the relations between nations and menace the order of the world.'[12] This admiration for traditional geopolitics made de Gaulle critical of the utopian moment that followed the Great War. He railed against the 'dreams' and 'pieties' of a new international system epitomised by the Kellogg-Briand Pact, which ignored the 'egoism of nations' in its naïve attempt to outlaw war and 'efface the power of the sword from History.' Even after 1945, when so many others questioned nationalism and the Westphalian order, de Gaulle still lauded the 'mystique of the nation-state as the supreme repository of human endeavour.'[13]

The General's distinctive understanding of twentieth-century European history led him to conclude that the Second World War 'may have been the result of a crisis of civilisation.' In his estimation the west 'tends essentially towards the freedom and development of the individual.'[14] De Gaulle saw what he called the 'new Thirty Years War' ('*la nouvelle guerre de Trente Ans*') as rooted not in bloody nationalism, but in totalitarianism's attack on liberalism and the basic dignity of the individual, which he argued was best preserved in the European nation-states. He construed both communism and National Socialism as part of 'a movement which admits no rights save those of the racial or national collectivity; a movement which denies the individual the right to think, judge, or act as he sees fit.'[15]

As a result of these reflections de Gaulle 'was never in any doubt as to his duty to confront the challenge thrown down by totalitarianism.' It was this conviction, and his commitment to preserving the 'treasure of French sover-eignty which for fourteen centuries had never been surrendered' that led to his condemnation of the Vichy regime's armistice with Nazi Germany. For de Gaulle it was inconceivable that a great nation like France could simply cease to exist. Instead, it was crucial that she preserve her sovereignty, so that she could continue her traditions and eventually return to greatness.[16]

These considerations underlie de Gaulle's famous appeal on the BBC following the news that France had officially requested an armistice with Germany on 18 June 1940. In it, he claimed to be the personification of the French resistance and called on the remaining French forces to rally to him. In saying the words '*nous sommes la France*' the General meant it literally: 'in his view Free France *was* France, and he was the head of a sovereign French government.' Thus de Gaulle's policy was based on a three-fold fiction: 'the armistice was null and void; France had never quit fighting; and the Vichy government had not a speck of political or moral legitimacy.'[17]

It was in the context of the Nazi *Blitzkrieg* that de Gaulle and Jean Monnet first crossed paths. In the days following the German invasion of France Monnet began to work on a radical proposal for Franco-British union. It was 'a dramatic call for unity,' suggesting a joint cabinet to run the war, mixed sessions of parliament, and a commitment to joint reconstruction.[18] On the morning of 16 June 1940, Monnet presented the General with this scheme.

He focused on the need to rescue European culture from 'the onslaught of barbarism has already shattered the mould in which separate nations of free men have ... fashioned their distinctive culture and traditions.' Despite its radical ideas, de Gaulle saw Monnet's scheme as the only way to safeguard French sovereignty so that it could not be used to portray Nazi occupation as an expression of 'the unity of Europe.'[19] The General agreed to try and persuade Churchill to support Monnet's plan based on his belief that 'France herself as a sovereign entity must be brought back into the war.'[20]

While Churchill was sceptical, he agreed to let the cabinet vote on the scheme. To his amazement, the declaration was approved almost exactly as drafted by Monnet.[21] De Gaulle immediately called French Prime Minister Paul Reynaud in Bordeaux. After reading him the text word for word, he handed the receiver to Churchill, who assured Reynaud that the proposal was meant in earnest. However, the French cabinet, fearing that Britain wanted to turn France into a dominion, rejected the offer.[22]

De Gaulle and Monnet next encountered each other again in Algiers in 1943, where both were involved in the debates surrounding the creation of the CFLN. At this point, Monnet and de Gaulle found themselves on opposite sides of the debate. Monnet argued for the creation of 'a Europe of the West' that would act as 'a single economic entity with free trade.'[23] By contrast, de Gaulle was stridently opposed to turning over sovereignty to international authorities. Instead, he favoured a loose economic union of France with the Benelux. He argued, 'After a war such as this, it is hard to see French and Germans belonging together to an economic union.'[24]

These differences continued after the war. On one side, Monnet did not see any contradiction between the greatness of France, a united Europe, and a strong Atlantic partnership with the United States. On the contrary, he believed that France could and should *'faire l'Europe sans défaire la France.'*[25] By contrast, de Gaulle, who referred to Monnet derogatorily as *'l'inspirateur,'* believed that the nation-states of Europe must be preserved as a bulwark against fascism, communism, and the homogenising tendencies of modern economic life. He argued that Europe could only maintain its identity through the cultural, linguistic, and political diversity provided by the national state:

> I do not believe that Europe can be a living reality if it does not contain France with its French, Germany with its Germans, Italy with its Italians and so forth. Dante, Goëthe, Châteaubriand belong to Europe as a whole precisely because they were first and foremost Italian, German and French. They would not have

meant so much to Europe if they had been people without a fatherland and had thought and written in some kind of 'integrated' Esperanto or Volapük.[26]

As this remark makes clear, for de Gaulle the nation and the state were the enduring realities of political life. While he believed in constructing Europe, he argued for an intergovernmental *Europe des patries* that built on the historic-ally rooted idea of the nation-state. In this sense, 'de Gaulle's European vision was conservative. He wished to conserve amidst change and to adjust older institutions that had served the peoples of Europe well.' Unlike Monnet and the rest of the postrupture constellation of political leaders, de Gaulle truly believed it when he told US President Richard Nixon, 'Things have been the same since the world has been the world.'[27]

The only area where Monnet and de Gaulle were able to find common ground after the war was on the need to reconstruct the French economy. It was the General's support in this endeavour after 1945 that helped Monnet secure American loans leading to the creation of the *Plan de modernisation et d'équipement de la France*. Although they both agreed on the need to unify Europe, de Gaulle opposed all of Monnet's attempts to do so on a supranational basis.[28]

As a result of these considerations, it is clear that if de Gaulle had 'not inherited the EEC, nothing would have pushed him to anything like it.'[29] However, despite his animosity to supranationalism – and his statement to his aides in 1957 that he would 'destroy' the EEC and Euratom if he ever came back to power – he did not do so after taking over the French presidency in 1958. In fact, de Gaulle seemed to appreciate the EC's economic benefits. However, he was still stridently opposed its supranationalism and worried about the influence the United States exercised over Europe.[30]

The relative geopolitical calm of the early 1960s gave de Gaulle the oppor-tunity to realise his vision of Europe. His first attempt to do so came in the form of the Fouchet Plan. Named for its French chairman, Christian Fouchet, this 1961 proposal aimed to further integration through the development of a common foreign and security policy. The plan appealed to de Gaulle not only because it sought to assert Europe's military power independently of the United States and the North Atlantic Treaty Organisation (NATO), but also because it sought to do so on a confederal basis through regularly scheduled consultations between the ministers and heads of state of the Six.[31] As such, it was an attempt to replace Monnet's supranational vision with a 'Union of States' that balanced a rise in the community's competencies by increasing the control of the member-states over it.[32]

The idea of binding the member-states participating in the CM together in a political union had been in the air since de Gaulle's first meetings with Adenauer in 1958. De Gaulle had slowly built a relationship of trust with the Chancellor, leading to German support of this initiative.[33] However, Adenauer's agreement proved to be insufficient. The Dutch and Belgian governments vetoed the Plan because they saw its intergovernmental characteristics as a threat to the influence of the smaller member-states and objected to de Gaulle's exclusion of Great Britain from the talks.

Despite this setback, de Gaulle was undeterred. At a press conference on following their vetoes, he reaffirmed his beliefs: 'It is only the states that are valid, legitimate and capable of achievement. I have already said, and I repeat, that at the present time there cannot be any other Europe than a Europe of states.'[34] If he could not change the EEC with a new political initiative, he would do so by attacking the parts of the existing Treaty of Rome (1958) that he did not like, i.e. the provisions that 'set it apart most sharply from traditional international organisations.'[35]

De Gaulle's opportunity came in the summer of 1965. Starting in January 1966, the Treaty specified that majority voting would replace consensus in the Council of Ministers within a number of different sectors of community business, including the setting of agricultural prices, trade policy, transport, and capital movements. The President of the European Commission, Walter Hallstein (who had previously served as the head of the German delegation to the Schuman Plan Conference), sought to take advantage of this opportunity to set a new stage of supranational integration in motion. When the issue of the Common Agricultural Policy (CAP) – a crucial issue for rural France – came up, he departed from the usual procedure by informing the European Parliament (EP) before sending the proposal to the Council of Ministers.

De Gaulle's reaction was based on two simultaneous sentiments: rage at this attempt to further supranationalism, which he opposed, and fear that involving the EP would adversely affect France on the CAP and the other issues subjected to majority voting. In a move drawn directly from the playbook of traditional bilateral diplomacy, de Gaulle recalled France's ambassador to the Communities and announced that France would no longer participate in the ministerial meetings of the European Council. After this, 'The conflict lay where de Gaulle wanted it from the start: between the states.' This became known as the 'empty chair' policy.[36]

Despite de Gaulle's pragmatic fears regarding the CAP and his dislike of Hallstein, the crisis was constitutional in nature. He sought to limit the influence of the community institutions through mechanisms of intergovern-mental cooperation, 'which would leave the national states as leaders in the field and would not create dangerous supranational powers by appropriating part of the states' sovereignty.'[37] As such, it should be seen as a continuance of de Gaulle's attempt to move the EEC in a confederal direct with the Fouchet Plan. As he later noted, 'The crisis was inevitable, sooner or later.'[38]

After six months, these issues were resolved with a pragmatic agreement to disagree. In the 'Luxembourg Compromise,' France agreed to participate in community institutions and to allow majority voting to go forward as planned in the Treaty of Rome, with the proviso that the remaining members would not even call a vote if any of the states announced that 'a very important issue' was at stake.[39] The community's legal order was thus preserved, while respecting France's insistence on a *de facto* veto over important issues. Following the compromise, a report from the Central Intelligence Agency predicted that the EEC was 'likely to be a system of government by "permanent crisis"' as a result of the empty chair.[40] Indeed, these words are an apt description of the situation of Eurosclerosis that followed in the late 1960s and 1970s. Despite de Gaulle's personal opposition to the further expansion of the European Communities, his view of Europe gained new allies with the accession of new member-states in the 1970s and 1980s.

New members, new memories (1973, 1981–86)[41]

In the aftermath of the sclerosis brought about by de Gaulle's rejection of Europe as a community-based project, the EEC sought to reinvigorate itself and to institutionalise the lessons of the rupture of 1945 by expanding its membership for the first time. Britain, which many on the continent had hoped would join the ECSC in 1952, was the key player in these negotiations. While its experience of total war differed greatly from those on the con-tinent, collective memories of the two world wars had also reshaped attitudes across the English Channel. In contrast to the UK's traditional scepticism towards involvement in continental affairs, after 1945 many in the British Isles concluded that they could not afford to ignore events on the continent. As a result, 'Britain decided to reorient its traditional, essentially maritime, defence policy and to commit itself, in political and strategic terms, more closely to its West European allies than ever before in peacetime.'[42] However, this was done with the understanding that increased commitments in Europe were only pos-sible with the involvement of the United States as well.

Despite this fact, for many in Britain the experience of war did not point to the need for greater commitment to continental allies, but to the joys of a 'splendid isolationism.'[43] Unlike 'the Six,' who had fought on their own soil and experienced Nazi rule first-hand, the war between the UK and Germany was fought *over* Britain, not *on* it. Since it did not experience the humiliating loss of sovereignty that came with occupation, collective memories of the conflict in the UK did not have the same tragic quality. Hoffman observes that despite the Kingdom's internal problems and her tottering postwar Empire, the British could at least 'bitterly [savour] the memories of its past glories and "finest hour."'[44]

Immediately following the end of the war Churchill gave pro-European speeches in the United States and Switzerland. His experiences had convinced him of the need to unify the continent by reconciling France and Germany. However, he also made clear that 'our attitude is that we help, we dedicate, we participate, but we do not merge and we do not forfeit our insular or Commonwealth character.'[45] The pre-existing tendency of the British to perceive Europe as a 'friendly other' combined with its different experience of the war, led Churchill to reject participation in the ECSC. Many 'Tory Strassbourgers' like future Prime Minister Harold Macmillan interpreted this refusal as a 'betrayal' of Europe.[46] In this sense, differing collective memories of the war – which did not include defeat or occupation – distinguished the British cognitive, motivational, and justificatory lessons most Britons drew from the past compared to 'the Six.'

Despite this decision, Britain maintained an interest in the success of Franco-German rapprochement. Over time, the success of Europe made the UK's refusal increasingly costly. Ernst Haas observes, 'Britain's continued efforts to penetrate the Six testify to the reality of the spillover as experienced by the trade and defence partners of the Community countries.' It was not until after the Suez Crisis (1956) had made Britain's inability to continue to rely on the Commonwealth for economic and political success clear that the UK seriously began to consider joining Europe. In retrospect, it seems that successive British governments overestimated their ability to maintain effective foreign and economic policies outside of the new Europe.[47]

This change of tack coincided with Harold Macmillan's return to office. His wartime experiences as the Parliamentary Secretary to the Minister of Supply and as the Minister Resident in the Mediterranean gave him the cognitive resources to see the benefits of integration and the motivational mettle to pursue it. In August 1961, the UK formally applied for membership in the European Community, along with its economic satellites, Denmark, and Ireland.

Despite Macmillan's 'extraordinary act of leadership,' de Gaulle vetoed the British application.[48] Against the backdrop of an agreement for the United States to supply Polaris missiles to its allies, which Britain had negotiated and presented to France as a *fait accompli*, de Gaulle seemed to be sending the message that the British could have their special relationship with the United States or be part of Europe, but not both. Macmillan was aghast at this narrow interpretation of his nation's self-interest, noting that the French President 'wants to be the cock on a small dunghill instead of having two cocks on a larger one.' Despite this flippant interpretation, de Gaulle's veto – which was to be followed by a second in 1967 – shook Macmillan deeply. He noted in his private diary, 'It is the end … to everything for which I have worked for many years. All our policies at home and abroad are in ruins.'[49]

The accession of the UK, Denmark, and Ireland finally took place in 1973. After de Gaulle's death, his successor Georges Pompidou made it clear that he would welcome British accession. His counterpart Edward Heath was 'unambiguously and enthusiastically in favour of joining his nation's fate to that of its continental neighbours.' Heath had served as a major commanding a battery unit on the continent during the Second World War. He drew on the collective memories of combat he shared with many other leaders of Europe at the time as a resource to justify the benefits of integration to the British public by reinterpreting the UK's remembrance of the war as sign that European affairs were British affairs. Heath's leadership in bringing the UK into Europe was confirmed at a popular level when the people of Britain resoundingly approved a referendum on membership called by the new Labour government in 1974.[50]

In spite of these changes, Britain's accession to the European Communities did not eliminate the great differences between the memory cultures on the British Isles compared to those on the mainland, which resulted in differing commitments to European unification. While many continental Europeans build their commitment to integration on the normative resources of the past, support for the EU in Britain – which was always weaker than on the continent to begin with – has traditionally been based more on economic cost–benefit calculations. It is precisely this economic, calculating approach that most frustrates continental supporters of the European project.

De Gaulle's desire for a *Europe des patries* based on a more traditional, intergovernmental approach makes his two vetoes of British membership all the more puzzling. After all, 'Bringing in three similarly-minded states, particularly the UK given its comparable economic and political status to France and West Germany, could only push the EEC further along an intergovernmental path.'[51] However, despite de Gaulle's desire for 'a British Europe without the British,' what followed his death could be called a British Europe with the British.[52]

The first expansion of the European Communities north to the UK, Denmark, and Ireland, all of which were sceptical of supranationalism, solidified the movement towards a 'Europe of the states' and expanded the number of members in the 'Luxembourg Compromise club,' who were committed to upholding their right to block proposals in the Council from majority voting.[53] The second expansion south into Greece and the Iberian peninsula (1981 and 1986) further challenged the approach taken by Europe's founding fathers. Due to their more recent experiences of authoritarian rule, these three members did not share the same wartime memories with the rest of the western states.

Unlike Spain and Portugal, Greece had at least participated in the Second World War. However, in the decades since 1945 it had been wracked by civil conflict and social unrest. Much like Spain, whose experience of civil war was followed by Franco's military dictatorship, the army also played an important role Greece. In April 1967 a group of right-wing army officers staged a coup in Athens that resulted in Greece's expulsion from the Council of Europe in 1969. Similarly, although Portugal did not share a legacy of civil war with Spain and Greece, it was also an authoritarian regime. Like Spain, the Portugal of António de Oliveira Salazar had sat out the Second World War. An economist by training, Salazar was obsessed with debt avoidance and assiduously balanced every budget. A fanatical mercantilist, he kept high gold reserves and did not seek to stimulate either investment or imports since he saw Portugal's economic stagnation as the key to its stability.

While the rest of Europe was experiencing an unprecedented postwar economic miracle, Greece, Spain, and Portugal had all been isolated, dictatorial, and economically underdeveloped. Despite these difficulties, the Commission was determined to proceed with their integration, concluding that 'the three countries have entrusted the Community with a political responsibility which it cannot refuse.'[54] For large majorities within Greece, Spain, and Portugal, Europe functioned as a beacon of freedom, prosperity, and modernity. As Spanish supporters of accession put it, they would prefer Spain to be 'the last wagon in Europe, rather than the locomotive of a Spanish America.'[55]

Among the three candidates from southern Europe, Greece had a number of historical advantages: (1) it had taken part in the fight against Hitler during the Second World War as part of the western alliance and thus shared the European narrative of integration; (2) unlike Spain and Portugal it had been a member of NATO since 1952; and (3) Greece had successfully acquired associate status in the EEC in 1962 before its democratic government was overthrown. Unfortunately, the military coup of 1967 negated many of these benefits. It was only after the end of the junta that Greece was able to continue on its path to Europe. Konstantinos Karamanlis, who had negotiated and signed Greece's Treaty of Association (1961) during his precoup tenure as prime minister, was able to pick up where he left off after being re-elected in 1974. One of his first actions after his return to office was to deliver an *aide-mémoire* to Brussels stating his intention to seek full membership.

While Karamanlis acknowledged his economic motives, he also stated that he would have pursued membership in the EEC even if there were no financial benefits. As an MP in the Greek legislature since 1936, he saw membership as part of 'Greece's European destiny.'[56] He believed that it would help stabilise the country by tying Greece to the democratic political culture of the west. He also highlighted Greece's desire to participate in the project of creating a unified democratic Europe powerful enough to confront the problems of the new global order.[57] Although he did not get to oversee Greece's entry into the EEC – that honour fell to his successor George Rallis – Karamanlis's leadership was crucial.

Spain lacked many of the direct experiential and political advantages of Greece. However, the Catholic *Opus Dei* ministers installed by Franco believed 'the solution to all of Spain's problems lay in its full integration into Western capitalism.'[58] These religious technocrats began to push Spain towards Europe in economic matters even before the fall of the Franco regime and its transition to democracy. Franco's death in 1975 allowed these elites, who had already sought membership in the European Communities in March 1962, to make a pacted transition from the previous regime, thus securing accession to Europe.[59] Within this process, 'Memories of high numbers of victims on both sides of the Civil War acted as an incentive for moderation.' Despite his anti-capitalist rhetoric, long-time Prime Minister Felipe González saw Spain's future as located firmly in Europe. Like many other Spaniards born in the aftermath of the civil war and raised under Franco, González associated being European with modernity.[60]

In contrast to the Spanish consensual approach, Portugal's conflict-ridden transition represented a clear historical caesura.[61] The Portuguese transition was initiated by a popular military coup on 25 April 1974. A period of instability followed until Mário Soares formed a democratically elected government in July of 1976. Born in 1924 to an anti-fascist republican activist, Soares's political sympathies were evident from an early age. After being exiled in 1970, he settled in France and helped create the Socialist Party out of the Portuguese Social Action movement under the umbrella of Willy Brandt's SPD.[62] During his second stint in office in the early 1980s, Soares helped convince the Portuguese public that its future lay in Europe. For him, membership in the EEC was 'one of the most significant events in contemporary Portuguese history,' representing a 'fundamental choice for a progressive and modern future.'[63]

In their transitions to democracy, all three states looked to what they percieved as 'modern Europe' as a way of breaking with an anachronistic, dictatorial past. Despite their different memorial cultures, which were defined by important experiences and historical breaks after 1945, Greece, Spain, and Portugal all had long-standing historic ties with Western Europe, which the narrative break of the democratic transition allowed them to exploit. These regimes in also shared the basic anti-communist orientation of the Atlantic alliance, which was reflected in the fact that their foreign policies had been compatible with the EEC and NATO after the war. The transition to democracy from authoritarian forms of government fit well within the existing European narrative of overcoming Nazism.[64]

The second phase of integration (1985–2003)

Although the events of the 1960s and 1970s contributed to the classic narrative of integration, endowing it with the central image of Auschwitz, this was a period of institutional paralysis. The Commission gradually lost influence, as its technical expertise failed to resolve political or economic crises, including the empty chair of the mid-1960s and the oil shocks of the 1970s. As Europe expanded and the number of states committed to supranationality diminished, 'The Commission was forced back into the position of subservient bureaucracy.'[65]

Integration had stagnated since the *relance* of 1958 due to both the absence of leaders with community-based ideals and the sensitive Cold War geopolitics of détente.[66] However, in the mid-1980s and 1990s, 'In less than two decades, economic governance in Europe went through its deepest transformation since the end of World War II, leading to the emergence of a distinctive

European model of political economy.'[67] In addition to these political changes brought about by the leadership of Jacques Delors, François Mitterrand, and Helmut Kohl, this period also represents the culmination of the classical narrative of integration.

The institutions needed to address these challenges and to allow the practice of solidarity beyond state borders began to emerge in the Treaty of Maastricht (1992). Officially known as the Treaty on European Union, this agreement paved the way for the expansion of the CM and granted the nationals of the member-states European citizenship. As citizens of the newly created European *Union* (previously Community), individuals from the member-states were allowed to work anywhere in Europe and were granted voting rights in that country's local as well European parliamentary elections. Nicolas Jabko points out that 'it was obvious at the time of the Maastricht treaty that the idea of European unity had become more powerful than at any time since the early steps of the European Coal and Steel Community in the 1950s.'[68]

The idea of a monetary union and a single European currency go back to the origins of the European project. As a result of his interwar experience as a businessman and financier, Monnet was well aware of the advantages of monetary integration at the beginning of the European *projet*. However, especially after the failure of the EDC in 1954, he accepted that existing economic and political realities prevented the pursuit of this project.[69]

The first serious attempt at monetary integration date back to a 1969 call by the Commission for 'greater co-ordination of economic policies and monetary cooperation.'[70] Although this initiative had no direct effect at the time, it set the groundwork for Delors to reignite the debate on EMU in 1988. The following year, the 'Delors Report' laid out a three-stage plan for monetary union, which ultimately resulted in the creation of the European Central Bank (ECB, 1998) and the common currency, the euro (introduced on financial markets in 1999 and into broader circulation in 2002).[71]

The Treaty of Amsterdam (1997) continued the institutional makeover of the EU. In addition to creating a high representative for foreign policy, putting greater emphasis on individual rights, and laying the foundation for a Europe without internal borders, it also expanded the powers of the EP. Most notably, the treaty subjected most legislation to the consultation of Europe's legislature through the principle of co-decision. It also gave the EP the responsibility of approving the individuals selected to serve in the Commission.

Most economic accounts of this second European '*relance*' stress international pressures to stabilise exchange rates between France and Germany.

By contrast, structural explanations focus on the geopolitical situation and the need for the rest of Europe to balance the *Ostpolitik* (Eastern policy) of a soon-to-be-reunified Germany with fuller cooperation with the west.[72] However, it would be wrong to ignore the role of leadership in precipitating the renewed focus on integration. Led by Delors, Mitterrand, and Kohl, a new generation of leaders with community ideals expanded on the foundation provided by Monnet, Schuman, and Adenauer. 'It was a change in leadership, not objective pressures,' that brought about the second major phase of institutional integration on the continent in the 1980s and 1990s.[73]

The idea to 'play the market' in order to rally support for the combined logic of globalisation and further integration came from the European Commission under the leadership of Delors. Within this constellation, 'In essence, the market served as a conveniently broad repertoire of justifications.'[74] Although this process began with a push for 'negative' integration through the removal of trade barriers on the continent, it was soon combined with the 'positive' integration involved in creating new institutional mechanisms for closer cooperation.

Delors, who served as the president of the European Commission for a decade from 1985 to 1995, was a self-avowed student of *la méthode Monnet*. Much like his idol, Delors had also experienced the war directly, albeit as a young man. During the conflict he was active in a number of religiously-based social and political groups. He entered the French administration as a trainee at the Bank of France in 1944 and even worked at the postwar French *Plan de modernisation et d'équipement*, which had been created by Monnet in 1945.[75] Like Monnet, Delors formed a close group of collaborators, who sought to institutionalise the supranational structure of Europe by increasing the competences of European institutions, especially the Commission.[76]

In 1984, leading up to his appointment as President of the Commission, Delors embarked on a tour of the capitals of Europe in search of a 'big idea' that would elicit the support of member governments. Although he was already thinking about monetary union, which had long been his pet project, Delors settled on the idea of creating a single market without borders as a way to get the ball rolling.[77] In order to justify his ideas to the member-states, Delors played on the economic fears of globalisation that had begun to swirl by the mid to late 1980s by presenting his plans as an attempt to fashion Europe into an 'organised space' centred on a single market.[78] Like Monnet, Delors proved adept at harnessing the spirit of the times to develop ideas that governments across Europe were able to agree to. However, he was also dependent on the presence of political leaders in Germany and France, who would be willing take risks and accept political responsibility for his ideas. In Mitterrand and Kohl, Delors, the self-professed follower of Monnet, found his Schuman and his Adenauer.

Given the crucial role French President François Mitterrand played in ensuring Delors's appointment as Commission President, the close cooperation between the two is hardly surprising. Mitterrand's strong belief in a community-based model of Europe also help to explain his support of Delors. Although he had briefly collaborated with the Vichy regime during the Second World War, Mitterrand quickly rejected the right-wing nationalism of Marshall Pétain. He moved to the left and joined the *Résistance*, where he was exposed to the European ideas he would espouse in his future career as a politician.

After turning around Socialist electoral fortunes in 1972, Mitterrand fought to prevent a reversion to the left's traditional opposition to integration. The threat of his resignation in 1973 forced traditionalists within the Socialist Party to accept that for the foreseeable future – at least as long as Mitterrand led the party – French socialism and community-style integration would proceed in tandem.[79] Once again, the presence of specific leaders proved crucial in furthering pro-community ideas in Europe: 'The French pursuit of full EMU was decided personally by Mitterrand, over objections from some of his closest allies and advisors.'[80]

After convincing his party to pursue integration as a key part of the socialist agenda, Mitterrand turned his attention to the French public. Although his push for greater integration pre-dated the *Wende* of 1989 and French fears of a reunified Germany, these events undoubtedly bolstered the force of his arguments in favour of the EMU and further integration generally as a way of binding Germany to France and the rest of her European partners. In an acknowledgement of traditional socialist fears of the power of neoliberal economics to dominate political decision-making, Mitterrand also argued for integration by pointing out that 'only Europe allows politics to restore its power' vis-à-vis market forces.[81]

In order to succeed in relaunching Europe for a second time, the French tandem of Delors and Mitterrand needed the support of the German leadership, just as Monnet and Schuman had needed Adenauer's backing in the 1950s. Luckily for them, German Chancellor 'Helmut Kohl, self-styled as Adenauer's last great disciple, turned out to be the man in the wings.'[82] Like his predecessor in the immediate postwar years, Kohl shared the conviction that 'the policy of European unification is in reality a question of war and peace in the 21st century.'[83]

Born in 1930, Kohl shared the generational experience of coming of age during the Second World War with Delors and Mitterrand. As a result of the transnational collective memory rooted in the rupture of 1945 that he shared with the French president, Kohl also believed that 'nationalism means war.'[84] His deep personal commitment to the process of integration within community institutions was tied to his determination to lock the Federal Republic into European institutions before a younger generation of Germans, who had not personally experienced war and the atrocities of the Holocaust assumed the reins of leadership.[85] Despite its economic costs and the fact that it would necessitate German renunciation of its beloved Deutsche Mark, Kohl agreed to support the EMU as part of this process. For him, the project of monetary union was not primarily based 'on economic grounds, but as a means to forever preclude repetition of Europe's bloody and genocidal history.'[86] The resulting creation of a single currency thus 'represents the single greatest voluntary concession of sovereignty ever made to international institutions.'[87]

The close political partnership of Kohl and Mitterrand, supported by Delors at the Commission, was crucial to the achievement of EMU and the second phase of integration more generally. Although they were different in almost every way, the German Christian Democrat and French Socialist shared the tragic historical vision of their age. Despite their quarrels over policy, they were both determined to prevent another Verdun, another Auschwitz, another war. As generational contemporaries, they also saw themselves bound together through the institutions of a supranational Europe, which they both saw as a 'community of shared fate' (*Schicksalsgemeinschaft*). Their close relationship even allowed Kohl to forgive Mitterrand's attempt to block German unity by conspiring with Soviet president Mikhail Gorbachev and East German leader Egon Krenz in 1989.

Although it did not succeed in breaking apart the Franco-German partnership between Kohl and Mitterrand, the fall of communism in 1989 raised the stakes of integration, as the postwar German Problem once again reared its head. Kohl responded to these events by seeking to embed Germany irreversibly within European institutions, so that it would be unable to pursue purely nationalistic projects in the future. While the reunification of east and west fulfilled the long-standing aspirations of postwar Germany, Kohl tied this process firmly to the European dream. After the new *Bundesländer* of the former East

German Democratic Republic had joined the West German Federal Republic in 1990, Kohl argued that 'we had realized only half of our vision after the war. Before us lay – and still lies – the realization of the other half: the unification of Europe.'[88]

In addition to opening the door to the deepening of integration, the end of the forty-five-year division of the continent also created new opportunities for the broadening of Europe. Given the political liberalisation required by the EU's *acquis communautaire*, it was clear that the postcommunist states of East-Central Europe would need some time to adjust their legal and institutional regimes before being brought into the European fold. However, the rich, capitalist, and democratic states of the north, including Austria, Finland, and Sweden, who had been forced to maintain good relations with Moscow during the Cold War, were no longer constrained by the demands of neutrality. Additionally, with the deepening of integration signalled by the increased constitutionalisation of Europe and the expansion of the CM, these three 'neutrals' had a lot to gain through accession.[89]

While Sweden had managed to stay out of the Second World War, Austria and Finland had been involved in the war. In both cases the experience was decidedly ambivalent. After the 1938 *Anschluss*, Austria had officially been part of Nazi Germany. Similarly, while the Finns had fought the Lapland War against Germany and the Winter War against the USSR, they had also waged the so-called Continuous War against the USSR with the assistance of the Third Reich. Despite their existing ties to the west and the fact that a second northern expansion did not challenge the existing European narrative of integration, accession posed problems for the memorial cultures *within* all three of the new member-states.

This is particularly true in Austria. Although there was some denazification in the years immediately following the war, this was quickly abandoned in favour of a policy of silence and forgetting that did not address the fact that there was deep support for Nazism in the country. For example, reports of Jews returning to Vienna broadcast in cinemas after the war were greeted with cries of 'Gas 'em.'[90] For much of the postwar era Austria had been able to ignore the past by emphasising its status as 'Hitler's first victim.'[91] The opening of Austrian memory was driven by the fall of the Soviet Union and the revelation that President Kurt Waldheim had lied about his wartime service as an officer for German Army Group E in Greece.[92] In the aftermath of the Waldheim Affair, the EU played an important role in bringing Austria into the fold of European memory. Günter Bischof observes, 'Austria's more candid confrontation with her World War II past may also have been induced during its ... entry into the European Union.'[93]

While events were not as dramatic in Finland, its historical consciousness was also affected by accession to the EU. Although it fought against both Nazi Germany and Soviet Russia, it was the conflict Finland waged against the USSR that 'influences Finnish historical consciousness more than any other episode in the country's history.'[94] In the postwar period, the so-called Winter War continued in a different form. Although the Iron Curtain split the whole continent from north to south, Finland was the only democratic state in Western Europe that shared a border directly with the USSR. The imperative of maintaining good relations and the desire to keep from antagonising the Soviets had kept Finland from forging closer ties with the west in the first place.

The liminal geographic and geopolitical position between east and west was not just a feature Finland's foreign policy. On the contrary, 'It was a civic religion that guided domestic politics, economics, as well as individual Finns' contacts with and views of the world abroad.'[95] Given the centrality of the so-called Paasikivi-Kekkonen Line, the disintegration of the USSR represented a threat to Finnish national identity as it had been constructed in collective memory since 1945.[96] The decision to enter the EU after 1990 was a symbolic 'return' to Europe after nearly half a century of isolating 'Finlandization.'[97] Thirty-six-year-old Prime Minister Esko Aho saw Europe as a way to break with the past and move into the modern world. He made the 'historic decision' to place Finland on the path towards EU membership soon after being sworn into office in 1991.[98]

Discourses of collective remembrance played an increasingly important role in Sweden as well.[99] Much like Britain, the inability to draw on memories of defeat and occupation has made it much more difficult for the Swedes to justify the loss of national sovereignty involved in accession to the EU.[100] This has resulted in significant Euroscepticism. Unlike in Finland, where backing for EU membership was close to 2 to 1, only 52.3 per cent of Swedes voted in favour of accession. Even then, the vote was based on the understanding that, like Britain, Sweden would never join the common currency. Without the support of powerful collective memories of the Second World War to act as cognitive, motivational, and justificatory resources for the support of integration, Sweden's relationship to Europe has remained ambiguous.

The second northern expansion of 1995 was just a prelude of what was to come; the postcommunist states of East-Central Europe could clearly be seen on the EU's horizon. The expansion of Europe into an area that had been cut off from the rest of the continent for so long would have important consequences for narratives of memory in both east and west. With the entry of a large number of states who saw the defeat of communism in 1989 as just as important as the defeat of Nazism in 1945, Europe was facing not only a renegotiation of the past, but a clash of memories and memory cultures that would fundamentally challenge the central place of the Holocaust in established narrative of integration.

Conclusion

Since its start in the first period of integration in the 1950s, the European project has built on the desire to secure peace in Europe after the horrors of the Second World War and the divisions wrought by the Cold War. Despite the stagnation of the European Communities in the 1960s and 1970s, the Holocaust came to take a central place in Europe's narrative self-perception, as references to Auschwitz in documents coming out of European institutions multiplied. In particular, recognition of the Holocaust worked its way into the accumulated legislation, legal acts, and court decisions contained within the EC's *acquis communautaire*. As part of the second phase of integration, 'A forceful *Vergangenheitsbewältigung* ["struggle to come to terms with the past"] may well be part of the hidden agenda of the *acquis communautaire* and Europe's new value system.'[101]

Attempts to institutionalise the Holocaust and Auschwitz as the key image driving integration had a great effect on understandings of history within the member-states. Neil Fligstein points out that increasingly, 'One of the main issues in primary and secondary education has been how to educate students to be Europeans.'[102] As a result, history has come to be taught in a European framework centred on the Holocaust. Longitudinal studies of European textbooks show great and increasing acceptance of the narrative of Europe being born out of the Second World War within many member-states.[103] Although the Holocaust has taken on a global role, it still has special meaning for Europeans, who have come to treat it as an important starting point for a shared continental identity.[104]

This focus on the Holocaust continued throughout the second phase of integration, especially as Germany sought to assure its neighbours and the rest of the continent that a reunified Federal Republic should not be seen as a threat. The classic narrative thrived in the 1980s and 1990s as Europe was experiencing its greatest institutional 'deepening' since 1958. However, despite its increasing acceptance and influence, the classic narrative of integration focused on the Holocaust did not receive its paradigmatic statement until the beginning of the twenty-first century.

On 15 February 2003, Europe was the site of the largest mass demonstrations since the Second World War, as citizens across the continent gathered to protest the US invasion of Iraq. It was this event that prompted Jürgen Habermas to pen the definitive statement of the classic narrative of integration. In an article co-signed by his friend and colleague Jacques Derrida, he argued, 'It is memory of the moral abyss into which the excesses of nationalism led us that lends our current commitment [to a peaceful, postnational Europe] the status of an accomplishment.'[105] Although the European project had frequently been linked to the past from its very origins in the 1950s, it had never received such a full and succinct statement of how the rupture of 1945 was connected to the need to go beyond the boundaries of the nation-state. For Habermas and Derrida, 'Contemporary Europe has been shaped by the experience of the totalitarian regimes of the twentieth-century and through the Holocaust … Self-critical controversies about this past remind us of the moral basis of politics.'[106]

However, the argument Habermas and Derrida presented proved to be highly problematic. It was soon questioned on three fronts. Only a year later it was already being undermined by the accession of the new EU member-states from East-Central Europe. While 1945 was an important historical break in East-Central Europe, this symbolic date has a very different meaning on the eastern side of the Iron Curtain. Within the western narrative, 1945 stands the beginning of a new project of integration based on the lessons of a bloody history. By contrast, for postcommunist societies, '1945 means a transition from one occupation to another; from Nazi rule to Soviet rule. It is the beginning of two full generations of communist rule, which for most people was no experience of political progress.'[107] Although most of the massacres of the Holocaust had taken place in eastern Europe, their importance to the inhabitants of this region was overshadowed by the events that followed.

The onset of the Eurozone crisis in 2010 further eroded the classic narrative of integration. In addition to building on the past, the classical view of history 'has always appealed to some conception of peace (more broadly understood as "security") and some conception of prosperity (more broadly understood as "welfare").'[108] While the end of the Cold War undermined the former, the Eurozone crisis made many question the latter. Far from being the vehicle of prosperity Monnet envisioned, a tripartite crisis of finance, banking, and sovereign debt plunged Europe into a Great Recession that was exacerbated by the rules of the monetary union and the nationalistic, self-interested squabbling of the member-states. Far from being part of the solution, the EU appeared to be part of the problem, leading many to express a certain nostalgia for the image of the sovereign nation-state.[109]

The crisis of the Eurozone coincided with the onset of the European 'Age of Populism.'[110] On the one hand, this backlash against the mainstream postwar politics of free movement, open markets, and liberal cosmopolitan ideals is understandable in light of the economic hard times brought on by the Great Recession. However, on the other it is also very worrying as the rhetoric and symbolism of these movements recalls the rise of fascism in the 1930s in the aftermath of the Great Depression. Across the continent these movements have joined together in seeking to 'take back control' (Nigel Farage during the campaign for Britain to leave the European Union) by seeking to 'remove Jewry from power' (a mantra from the 'Independence March' in Poland) and preventing 'Europe being overrun' by migrants from the Middle East and Africa (President Viktor Orbán in Hungary).

Building on the framework of collective memory I have constructed, I argue that with the generational turnover we are witnessing at the beginning of the twenty-first century, '[i]gnorance about historical fascism and lack of personal experience and memories of the tragedies of World War II' play a key role in explaining these difficulties.[111] In the next chapter, I therefore examine how the eastward expansions of Europe since 2004 and the onset of the Eurozone crisis in 2010 both served to challenge and undermine the classical narrative of integration. These events have also coincided with a populist challenge of what William Connolly calls 'aspirational fascism,' which started on the periphery but has increasingly threatened to infest the centre of Europe as well.[112] Combined with the real threat of disintegration posed by the British decision to leave the EU – confirmed by referendum in June 2016 – seventy years after its creation the EU faces an unprecedented combined political, economic, institutional and social crisis that threatens its very existence. Chapter 4 therefore presents the pathology of Europe's present in its full form.

Notes

1   D. Sternberger, 'Die deutsche Frage,' *Der Monat*, 8/9 (1949); D. Sternberger, 'Versuch zu einem Fazit,' *Die Wandlung*, 4 (1949).

2   Herf, *Divided Memory*, 225.

3   N. Elias, *The Germans: Power Struggles and the Development of Habitus in the Nineteenth and Twentieth Centuries*, trans. E. Dunning and S. Mennell (New York: Polity, 1996), 261; C. Fogu and W. Kansteiner, 'The Politics of Memory and the Poetics of History' in Lebow *et al.*, *The Politics of Memory in Postwar Europe*, 293–298.

4   E. Pond, *The Rebirth of Europe* (Washington, DC: Brookings Institution Press, 2002), 158; N. Frei, *Vergangenheitspolitik: Die Anfänge der Bundesrepublik und die NS-Vergangenheit* (Munich: Beck, 1996); E. Wolfrum, *Geschichtspolitik in der Bundesrepublik Deutschland: Der Weg zur bundesrepublikanischen Erinnerung 1948–1990* (Darmstadt: Wissenschaftliche Buchgesellschaft, 1999).

5   L. van Middelaar, *The Passage to Europe* (New Haven: Yale University Press, 2013), 158, 164.

6   Thomas Hobbes, *Leviathan*, ed. Richard Tuck (Cambridge: Cambridge University Press, 1991), 90.

7   B. A. Misztal, *Theories of Social Remembering* (Philadelphia: Open University Press, 2003), 86; Y. F. Khong, *Analogies at War: Korea, Munich, Dien Bien Phu, and the Vietnam Decisions of 1965* (Princeton: Princeton University Press, 1992), 214.

8   E. J. Weber, *The Nationalist Revival in France, 1905–1914* (Berkeley: University of California Press, 1959).

9   De Gaulle, *Complete War Memoirs of Charles de Gaulle*, 3.

10 H. Arendt, *Essays in Understanding, 1930–1954* (New York: Harcourt, Brace & Co., 1994), 118.

11 Beloff, *The General Says No*, 19. This judgement was shared by the interwar French Ambassador to Germany and postwar High Commissioner, André François-Poncet, see Lenz, *Im Zentrum der Macht*, 682, 13 August 1953.

12 All quotes from de Gaulle above are found in C. de Gaulle, *France and Her Army* (London: Hutchinson, 1945), 7–23; S. Hoffmann and I. Hoffmann, 'The Will to Grandeur: De Gaulle as Political Artist,' *Daedalus*, 97:3 (1968), 829.

13 C. de Gaulle, *The Army of the Future* (Philadelphia: Lippincott, 1941), 31; Beloff, *The General Says No*, 20.

14 De Gaulle, *Complete War Memoirs of Charles de Gaulle*, 318.

15 De Gaulle quoted in A. Prost and J. Winter, *Penser la grande guerre: Un essai d'historiographie* (Paris: Editions du Seuil, 2004), 33; de Gaulle's address to the Oxford French Club at Oxford University on 25 November 1941 in C. de Gaulle, *The Call to Honor: Documents 1940–1942* (New York: Simon & Schuster, 1955), 318–319. My analysis is indebted to D. J. Mahoney, *De Gaulle: Statesmanship, Grandeur, and Modern Democracy* (Westport: Praeger, 1996), 103–105.

16 J. Lacouture, *De Gaulle: The Rebel 1890–1944*, trans. P. O'Brian (New York: W. W. Norton, 1990), 166; de Gaulle, *Complete War Memoirs of Charles de Gaulle*, 951; 'Speech delivered by General de Gaulle at the meeting of the "Français de Grand-Bretagne", at the Albert Hall, London, 18 June 1942,' in de Gaulle, *The Call to Honor*, 427.

17 A. Shennan, *De Gaulle* (New York: Longman, 1993), 18; P. Manent, 'De Gaulle as Hero,' *Perspectives on Political Science*, 21:4 (1992), 205.

18 FJM, AME 8/2/1, A. Salter and J. Monnet, 'Anglo-French unity,' (40.06.13), Annotations manuscrites.

19 FJM, AME 8/2/5, 'The declaration of liberty,' (40.06.15), Dactylogramme; 'Memorandum, de [J.M.] (40.12.02), Annotation de J.M. sur une photocopie, AME 14/4/4. FJM.

20 Mahoney, *De Gaulle*, 77; de Gaulle, *Complete War Memoirs of Charles de Gaulle*, 81–82, 951.

21 Cf. W. S. Churchill, *The Second World War, Volume II: Their Finest Hour* (Boston: Houghton Mifflin Company, 1986), 180–189.

22 Beloff, *The General Says No*, 43–45.

23 FJM, AME 56/1/1, '[Le but ultime est une organization du monde qui permette le développement maximum de ses ressources …],' Note, manuscrit., translation mine; also FJM, AME 31/1/2, '[Le développpment de la guerre est tel…],' manuscrit.

24 FJM, AME 33/1/8, 'Conversation du dimanche 17 octobre 1943,' Etaient présents: de Gaulle, J. M., A. Diethelm, R. Mayer, H. Alphand, translation mine. Reproduction available in Rieben, *Des guerres européennes à l'Union de l'Europe*, 286–291.

25 T. Ugland, *Jean Monnet and Canada: Early Travels and the Idea of European Unity* (Toronto: University of Toronto Press, 2011), 72.

26 Press conference at the Elysée Palace, 15 May 1962. In H. L. Wesseling, *Certain Ideas of France: Essays on French History and Civilization, Vol. 98* (Westport: Greenwood Press, 2002), 109.

27 Mahoney, *De Gaulle*, 136. See C. de Gaulle, *Major Addresses, Statements and Press Conferences of Charles de Gaulle: May 19, 1958–January 31, 1964* (New York: French Embassy, 1964), 92–93; H. Alphand, *L'Étonnement D'Être, Journal 1939–1973* (Paris: Fayard, 1977), 398. See also A. Malraux, *Felled Oaks: Conversation with de Gaulle* (New York: Holt, Rinehart and Winston, 1971), 123–124.

28 Shennan, *De Gaulle*, 48; F. Duchêne, *Jean Monnet: The First Statesman of Interdependence* (New York: Norton, 1994), 146; Blankenhorn, *Verständnis und Verständigung*, 333, 11 November 1958; 385, 8 September 1960.

29 Parsons, *A Certain Idea of Europe*, 119.

30 Shennan, *De Gaulle*, 88; J. Gaffney, *Political Leadership in France: From Charles de Gaulle to Nicholas Sarkozy* (Basingstoke: Palgrave Macmillan, 2010), 52; Mahoney, *De Gaulle*, 137.

31 G. Lundestad, *The United States and Western Europe since 1945: From 'Empire' by Invitation to Transatlantic Drift* (Oxford: Oxford University Press, 2003), 120–121.

32 J. Lacouture, *De Gaulle: The Ruler 1945–1970*, trans. P. O'Brian (New York: W. W. Norton, 1991), 345–350.

33 Adenauer and Heuss, *Unter vier Augen*, 278, 16 September 1958; Blankenhorn, *Verständnis und Verständigung*, 370, 14 June 1960; 383, 29 June 1960.

34 De Gaulle, *Major Addresses, Statements and Press Conferences of Charles de Gaulle*, 176.

35 In M. Schönwald, 'Walter Hallstein and the "Empty Chair" Crisis 1965/66,' in W. Loth (ed), *Crises and Compromises: The European Project 1963–1969* (Brussels: Bruylant, 2001), 157.

36 Van Middelaar, *The Passage to Europe*, 59. This account is based on H. Wallace and P. Winand, 'The Empty Chair Crisis and the Luxembourg Compromise Revisited,' in J.-M. Palayret, H. Wallace, and P. Winand (eds), *Visions, Votes and Vetoes: The Empty Chair Crisis and the Luxembourg Compromise Forty Years On* (Brussels: Peter Lang, 2006), 15–19.

37 F. Haynes-Renshaw and H. Wallace, 'Changing the Course of European Integration – or not?' in J.-M. Palayret *et al.*, *Visions, Votes and Vetoes*, 47.

38 Loth, *Crises and Compromises*, 157.

Origins and crisis diagnosis

39 Haynes-Renshaw and Wallace, 'Changing the Course of European Integration – or not?' 312–13; van Middelaar, *The Passage to Europe*, 63–70.

40 CIA special report, 'European Union: The Continuing search,' 18 November 1966, in in Wallace and Winand, 'The empty chair crisis and the Luxembourg compromise revisited,' 42.

41 Parts of the next two sections have previously been published as P. J. Verovšek, 'Expanding Europe through Memory: The Shifting Content of the Ever-Salient Past,' *Millennium – Journal of International Studies*, 43:2 (2015).

42 In J. Baylis, 'Britain, the Brussels Pact and the Continental Commitment,' *International Affairs*, 60:4 (1984), 615–617.

43 J. Charmley, *Splendid Isolation? Britain, the Balance of Power and the Origins of the First World War* (London: Hodder & Stoughton, 1999), 23.

44 S. Hoffmann, *The European Sisyphus: Essays on Europe, 1964–1994* (Boulder: Westview Press, 1995), 58; A. Siegfried, *L'Année politique 1950: Revue chronologique des principaux faits politiques économiques et sociaux de la France* (Paris: Editions du grand siècle, 1951), xiii.

45 W. S. Churchill, *The Sinews of Peace: Post-War Speeches* (Boston: Houghton Mifflin, 1949), 202; quoted in C. Lord, '"With but not of": Britain and the Schuman Plan, a Reinterpretation,' *Journal of European Integration History*, 4:2 (1998), 23.

46 H. Macmillan, *Tides of Fortune, 1945–1955* (New York: Harper & Row, 1969), 461.

47 E. B. Haas, *The Uniting of Europe: Political, Social, and Economic Forces, 1950–1957* (Notre Dame, IN: University of Notre Dame Press, 2004), xiii. J. Frankel, *British Foreign Policy 1945–1973* (London: Oxford University Press, 1975); F. S. Northedge, *Descent from Power: British Foreign Policy, 1945–1973* (London: G. Allen & Unwin, 1974).

48 A. Moravcsik, *The Choice for Europe: Social Purpose and State Power from Messina to Maastricht* (Ithaca, NY: Cornell University Press, 1998), 176.

49 In A. Horne, *Harold MacMillan: Volume II, 1957–1986* (London: Penguin, 1989), 446; in T. Judt, *Postwar: A History of Europe since 1945* (New York: Penguin Press, 2005), 308.

50 Judt, *Postwar*, 526; Beloff, *The General Says No*, 14–16.

51 Gaffney, *Political Leadership in France*, 105; A. Grosser, 'General de Gaulle and the Foreign Policy of the Fifth Republic,' *International Affairs*, 39:2 (1963), 208.

52 E. Jouve, *Le Général de Gaulle et la construction de l'Europe (1940–1966), Vol. 1* (Paris: Librairie generale de droit et de jurisprudence, R. Pichon et R. Durand-Auzias, 1967), 489.

53 Haynes-Renshaw and Wallace, 'Changing the Course of European Integration – or not?' 312.

54 Commission of the European Communities, 'General Considerations on the Problems of Enlargement. Communication sent by the Commission to the Council on 20 April 1978,' *Com*, Supplement 1 (1978), 6; also European Parliament, 'Débat d'actualité et d'urgence. Conseil Européen. 9 Juin.,' *Débats du Parlement Européen*, 1–300 (1983), 221.

55 M. Fennema, 'Stop Saying the EU is a Failure!' *De Volkskrant Amsterdam* (8 July 2013), www.presseurop.eu/en/content/article/3949421-stop-saying-eu-failure (accessed 8 July 2013).

56 'Greece's Gain,' *Time Magazine*, 112:21 (12 January 1981), 39.

57 F. Nicholson and R. East, *From the Six to the Twelve: The Enlargement of the European Communities* (Essex: Longman, 1987), 187, 192.

58 P. Preston, *The Triumph of Democracy in Spain* (London: Methuen, 1986), 8, 25.

59 P. Aguilar, 'Justice, Politics, and Memory in the Spanish Transition,' in A. Barahona de Brito, C. González Enríquez, and P. Aguilar Fernández (eds), *The Politics of Memory and Democratization* (Oxford: Oxford University Press, 2001), 97–99.

60 F. Agüero, *Soldiers, Civilians, and Democracy: Post-Franco Spain in Comparative Perspective* (Baltimore: Johns Hopkins University Press, 1995), 118; J. Díez Medrano, *Framing Europe: Attitudes to European Integration in Germany, Spain, and the United Kingdom* (Princeton: Princeton University Press, 2003).

61 A. Costa Pinto, 'Settling Accounts with the Past in a Troubled Transition to Democracy: The Portuguese Case,' in A. Barahona de Brito *et al.*, *The Politics of Memory and Democratization*, 65–67.

62 H. Janitschek, *Mário Soares: Portrait of a Hero* (London: Weidenfeld & Nicolson, 1985).

63 Soares on 12 June 1985, quoted in Nicholson and East, *From the Six to the Twelve*, 250.

64 C. Leggewie, 'Battlefield Europe: Transnational Memory and European Identity,' *Eurozine* (28 April 2009), www.eurozine.com/battlefield-europe/ (accessed 30 April 2009).

65 Van Middelaar, *The Passage to Europe*, 65.

66 One important exception to this statement is the European Court of Justice, which gradually asserted ever greater power to interpret European treaties and set out general principles of European law. J. H. H. Weiler, 'A Quiet Revolution: The European Court of Justice and its Interlocutors,' *Comparative Political Studies*, 26:4 (1994), 510–534.

67 Jabko, *Playing the Market*, 2.

68 *Ibid.*, 19.

69 Duchêne, *Jean Monnet*, 269. See also J. Gillingham, 'Jean Monnet and the Origins of European Monetary Union,' in D. J. Kotlowski (ed), *The European Union: From Jean Monnet to the Euro* (Athens, OH: Ohio University Press, 2000), 79–86.

70 European Commission, 'Commission Memorandum to the Council on the Co-ordination of Economic Policies and Monetary Co-operation within the Community,' 12 February 1969.

71 J. Delors, 'Report on Economic and Monetary Union in the European Community,' 17 April 1989, Committee for the Study of Economic and Monetary Union.

72 For economic interpretations, see T. H. Oatley, *Monetary Politics: Exchange Rate Cooperation in the European Union* (Ann Arbor: University of Michigan Press, 1997); K. H. F. Dyson, *Elusive Union: The Process of Economic and Monetary Union in Europe* (New York: Longman, 1994); Moravcsik, *The Choice for Europe*. For geopolitical interpretations, see G.-H. Soutou, *L'Alliance incertaine: Les rapports politico-stratégiques Franco-Allemands, 1954–1996* (Paris: Fayard, 1996); H. Simonian, *The Privileged Partnership: Franco-German Relations in the European Community, 1969–1984* (Oxford: Clarendon Press, 1985).

73 Parsons, *A Certain Idea of Europe*, 148.

74 Jabko, *Playing the Market*, 6.

75 J. Gillingham, *European Integration, 1950–2003: Superstate or New Market Economy?* (Cambridge: Cambridge University Press, 2003), 158.

76 A. Verdun, 'The Role of the Delors Committee in the Creation of EMU: An Epistemic Community?' *Journal of European Public Policy*, 6:2 (1999).

77 J. Delors, *L'Unité d'un homme* (Paris: Odile Jacob, 1994); J. Delors and J.-L. Arnaud, *Mémoires* (Paris: Plon, 2004), 171–228; C. Grant, *Delors: Inside the House that Jacques Built* (London: Nicholas Brealey, 1994), 66–67.

78 G. Ross, *Jacques Delors and European Integration* (New York: Oxford University Press, 1995), 107–135; Jabko, *Playing the Market*, 121–146.

79 K. Featherstone, *Socialist Parties and European Integration: A Comparative History* (New York: St. Martin's Press, 1988), 120.

80 Parsons, *A Certain Idea of Europe*, 203.

81 Quoted in R. Schneider, *Les dernières années* (Paris: Editions du Seuil, 1994), 88–89; also F. London, 'The Logic and Limits of *désimflation competitive*: French Economic Policy from 1983,' *Oxford Review of Economic Policy*, 14:1 (1998), 96–114.

82 Gillingham, *European Integration, 1950–2003*, 262.

83 H. Kohl, 'The Significance of European Integration,' speech, 2 February 1996, Louvain, Belgium, http://germanhistorydocs.ghi dc.org/sub_document. cfm?document_id=3740 (accessed 31 January 2013).

84 *Ibid.*

85 Lundestad, *The United States and Western Europe since 1945*, 282; Jabko, *Playing the Market*, 156; Pond, *The Rebirth of Europe*, 36.

86 E. Langenbacher, 'Changing Memory Regimes in Contemporary Germany?' *German Politics & Society*, 21:2 (2003), 46–47.

87 Kohl's tribute to Mitterrand in Le Monde after the French President's retirement from office in 1995, in *German Government Bulletin*, 41 (May 1995), 356ff.; Parsons, *A Certain Idea of Europe*, 202.

88 K. Diekmann and R. G. Reuth, *Kohl: Ich wollte Deutschlands Einheit* (Berlin: Propyläen, 1996), 483.

89 J. H. H. Weiler, 'The Reformation of European Constitutionalism,' *Journal of Common Market Studies*, 35:1 (1997); E. Oddvar Eriksen, J. E. Fossum, and A. J. Menéndez, *Developing a Constitution for Europe* (London: Routledge, 2004).

90 H. Uhl, 'From Victim Myth to Co-Responsibility Thesis: Nazi Rule, World War II, and the Holocaust in Austrian Memory,' in Lebow *et al.*, *The Politics of Memory in Postwar Europe*, 45.

91 T. U. Berger, *War, Guilt, and World Politics After World War II* (Cambridge: Cambridge University Press, 2012), 100.

92 Becker, 'Building Up a Memory,' 102–105.

93 G. Bischof, 'Victims? Perpetrators? "Punching Bags" of European Historical Memory? The Austrians and their World War II Legacies,' *German Studies Review*, 27:1 (2004), 23, emphasis in original; E. Langenbacher and Y. Shain, 'Introduction: Twenty-First-Century Memories,' in Langenbacher and Shain, *Power and the Past*, 5.

94 A. Paasi, 'Geographical Perspectives on Finnish National Identity,' *GeoJournal*, 43:1 (1997), 47.

95 J. Lavery, 'Finland at Eighty: A More Confident and Open Nation,' *Scandinavian Review*, 85:2 (1997), 13.

96 K. Armstrong, 'Ambiguity and Remembrance: Individual and Collective Memory in Finland,' *American Ethnologist*, 27:3 (2000), 591–608.

97 A. Paasi, *Territories, Boundaries, and Consciousness: The Changing Geographies of the Finnish-Russian Boundary* (Chichester: J. Wiley & Sons, 1996), 132–134.

98 R. J. Guttman, 'Finland's Prime Minister: Esko Aho,' *Europe* (1992), 28; 'Europe, Aho,' *Economist* (14 September 1991), 57; see section epigraph *supra*.

99 N. Ammert, 'To Bridge Time: Historical Consciousness in Swedish History Textbooks,' *Journal of Educational Media, Memory, and Society*, 2:1 (2010), 17–30.

100 P. Aronsson, 'Uses of the Past: Nordic Historical Cultures in a Comparative Perspective,' *Culture Unbound*, 2 (2010), 555–558.

101 Bischof, 'Victims?' 23, emphasis in original; Langenbacher and Shain, 'Introduction,' 5.

102   N. Fligstein, *Euro-Clash: The EU, European Identity, and the Future of Europe* (Oxford: Oxford University Press, 2008), 179.

103   B. Challand, 'European Identity and its External Others in History Textbooks (1950–2005),' *The Journal of Educational Media, Memory and Society*, 1:2 (2009), 60–96; C. Bottici, 'Europe, War and Remembrance,' in F. Cerutti and S. Lucarelli (eds), *The Search for a European Identity: Values, Policies and Legitimacy of the European Union* (London: Routledge, 2008), 45–58; H. Schissler and Y. Nuhoğlu Soysal, *The Nation, Europe, and the World: Textbooks and Curricula in Transition* (New York: Berghahn Books, 2005).

104   A. Assmann, 'Europe: A Community of Memory?' *GHI Bulletin*, 40 (2007), 12.

105   J. Habermas, *Time of Transitions*, trans. C. Cronin and M. Pensky (Cambridge: Polity, 2006), 105.

106   J. Habermas and J. Derrida, 'February 15, or what Binds Europeans Together: A Plea for a Common Foreign Policy, Beginning in the Core of Europe,' *Constellations*, 10:3 (2003), 297.

107   T. Snyder, 'Balancing the Books,' *Index on Censorship*, 34:2 (2005), 72.

108   G. Morgan, *The Idea of a European Superstate: Public Justification and European Integration* (Princeton: Princeton University Press, 2005), 19.

109   W. Streeck, 'Small-State Nostalgia? The Currency Union, Germany, and Europe: A Reply to Jürgen Habermas,' *Constellations*, 21:2 (2014), 213–221.

110   I. Krastev, 'The Age of Populism: Reflections on the Self-Enmity of Democracy,' *European View*, 10:1 (2011), 11–16.

111   A. Koronaiou, E. Lagos, A. Sakellariou, S. Kymionis, and I. Chiotaki-Poulou, 'Golden Dawn, Austerity and Young People: The Rise of Fascist Extremism among Young People in Contemporary Greek Society,' *The Sociological Review*, 63:2 (2015), 237; W. Streeck, 'The Crises of Democratic Capitalism,' *New Left Review*, 71 (2011).

112   W. E. Connolly, *Aspirational Fascism: The Struggle for Multifaceted Democracy Under Trumpism* (Minneapolis: University of Minnesota Press, 2017).

Chapter 4

The fragmentation and loss of European memory: the Eurozone crisis, Brexit, and possible disintegration

The revenge of memory has been slow ... If the problem in Western Europe has been a shortage of memory, in the continent's other half ... there is too much memory.

Tony Judt, 'The Past is Another Country' (1992)

Questioning the classic narrative

Transnationally shared collective memories of war and suffering – framed in terms of the rupture of 1945, which allowed for a re-evaluation of existing narratives and the creation of new ways of linking past and future to the present – have played an important role in 'imagining Europe' ever since it was first institutionalised as the ECSC in 1951. Acting as an important cognitive, motivational, and justificatory resource, remembrance of Europe's age of total war allowed leaders across the continent to imagine, impelement, and justify their decisions to push integration in a community direction. While such moves towards European unification outside the constitutional architecture of the sovereign state were opposed by various actors committed to more traditional approaches to European affairs, at key moments during the two phases of integration (1945–58 and 1985–2003) constellations of leaders with Europeanist ideas were able to push the project forward by implementing new institutional arrangements that built on their shared understandings of the past.

As I pointed out at the beginning of the previous chapter, the immediate postwar atmosphere was characterised by a silent acknowledgement of the crimes of the past and a desire to build on the experience of bloody nationalism using the postwar resources of collective memory. However, by the time of the first expansion of the European project in the 1970s the Holocaust had established itself as 'the European entry ticket.'[1] Using the memory-based foundation of war and suffering during the rupture of the first half of the twentieth century, Europe built the classic narrative of integration on its guarantee of peace and economic welfare within a community of liberal democracies.

The idea of the industrial slaughter of the Holocaust as the basis for European integration only makes sense in retrospect. Despite its constructed character, by and large the citizens within the member-states of Western Europe have bought into the narrative of integration as a response to 'bloody nationalism' and its many crimes, epitomised most powerfully by the ashes of the death chambers at Auschwitz.[2] This focus on the Holocaust and the desire to prevent further wars on the continent forms the temporal or horizontal axis of the classic narrative of integration as a project that advances over time. From the beginning of integration in the 1950s, the idea of increased eco-nomic prosperity has defined the vertical axis of the European project as one that gradually moves more deeply into areas previously considered the pur-view of sovereign nation-states. Working together, security and welfare have defined the narrative field of integration, presenting the EU as a vehicle of progress towards 'ever closer union.'[3]

In 2003 Jürgen Habermas and Jacques Derrida gave the definitive statement of the classical narrative of integration in the co-signed text they produced in order to commemorate what they saw as the birth of a European public sphere. While internal differences among the peoples of Europe remained, they argued that the continent had developed distinctive markers of 'how Europe at large presents itself to non-Europeans.' More specifically, they pointed out that the 'bellicose past [that] entangled all European nations in bloody conflicts' had led the continent to integrate based on a number of differences from other parts of the world – even from other parts of the developed west, such as the United States. These characteristics include the secular nature of European politics, the continental faith in government, a preference for the welfare state, a suspicion of under-supervised markets, an aversion to the use of force, and a desire for multilateral diplomacy conducted through the United Nations.[4]

However, instead of 'prompting the horizontal networking of national public spheres,' as Habermas and Derrida expected, in the first decades of the twenty-first century the classical narrative of integration has been undermined by a series of events.[5] First, the eastern enlargements of the EU into the postcommunist space, which started in May 2004, began to undermine the central place of the Holocaust in Europe's historic imaginary. As the Union expanded eastward in 2004, its new postcommunist member-states have made the 'legitimation of Europe though the creation of a common conception of history' more difficult by seeking to place communist crimes on par with Nazi atrocities. Whereas 1945 has entered collective memory throughout Western Europe as a rupture in the fabric of historic time, it is less of a turning point in Eastern and Central Europe. On this half of the continent 1989 competes with 1945 as the crucial societal rupture in collective remembrance. As such, it challenges the shared cognitive, motivational, and justificatory resources of the past that had driven integration up until 2003 by bifurcating Europe's previously shared (western) framework of collective memory.

By questioning the status of 1945 and the Holocaust as the focal points of European memory politics, the accession of postcommunist Europe has forced continental institutions and existing members of the EU to 'negotiate the past' in new and disruptive ways.[6] The post-Cold War 'revenge of memory' – as Tony Judt refers to this phenomenon in the epigraph to this chapter – also sparked memory-based conflicts between neighbours, further threatening the surprisingly thin veneer of the 'European spirit.' While the actual threat to European security posed by these conflicts is minor, the façade of the classic narrative of integration has already started to crack as a result. The differing cognitive, motivational, and justificatory resources that emerge from treating 1989 as a rupture instead of (or in addition to) 1945 has thus 'extended the EU's memory agenda and posed a number of new challenges to the Union.'[7]

The onset of the Eurozone crisis in 2010 caused these cracks to widen into broader fissures that threaten the structural integrity of the EU itself. The suffering brought about by the austerity that continental institutions deemed necessary to contain the concurrent financial, banking, and sovereign debt crises that roiled Europe exploded the welfare-based justifications of the classical narrative. These fiscal challenges also opened deep divisions between the rich, financially stable member-states of 'the north' and the less economically developed, crisis-ridden countries of 'the south.' As a result, nationalistic antagonisms and rioting spread across the continent, threatening both the internal security of the EU's member-states, as well as their relations with their European 'partners.'

For example, in Greece the anger directed towards Germany, the EU, and the domestic elite following the outbreak of the crisis led to the torching of over 800 buildings in cities around the country.[8] These divisions aggravated preexisting tensions over the past, which were further inflamed by the fact that the cohort of leaders in charge in Europe at the start of the twenty-first century can no longer draw on the resources of collective memory to bind them to the EU as a normative project. This chain of events triggered not only the fragmentation and loss of the shared European framework of collective remembrance emanating from the rupture of 1945; it also turned collective memory from a constructive into a destructive resource, as old grievances took the place of shared remembrance.

Unsurprisingly, this return or revenge of national memory has both spurred and reinforced the rise of populism in Europe, fuelling the increasing electoral success of far-right nationalist parties, including the Rassemblement national (previously Front national) in France, the United Kingdom Independence Party, the Greek Golden Dawn, Fidesz in Hungary, as well as Law and Justice in Poland. While the postcommunist states of East-Central Europe have sought to push the EU into a more 'illiberal' direction that opposes migration and the protection of minorities in favour of an emphasis on Christian values, the populist movements in its western 'core' have moved in a more Gaullist direction, calling for the scaling back of supranationalism towards a model of a *Europe des patries*. The rise of this 'axis of illiberalism' and its differing image of Europe – based on ethnic homogeneity, nationalism, and Christianity instead of diversity, multiculturalism, and toleration – has important implications, especially as the rupture of 1945 fades from active, personal recall into the historical imaginary of cultural remembrance.[9]

At a time when Europe is losing its 'generation of experience,' its leaders are increasingly sceptical of integration, favouring a return to the nation-state instead of deeper integration along the community model. As a result, these new leaders are reinvigorating older tropes of collective memory dating back to before Europe's age of total war. This is most visible in the United Kingdom in the aftermath of its vote to leave the EU on 23 June 2016. The neo-imperial dream of a 'global Britain' deployed by the Brexiteers, in which Britain can make up for the loss of its customs union with the EU by negotiating closer ties with erstwhile colonies, including the United States, India, and Australia, is a reflection of a return to a dark past that is remembered fondly by a certain segment of the predominately white population that is old enough to remember the heady days of the postwar economic miracle, but young enough to have no personal memories of the wars and suffering that preceded it. This phenomenon is not limited to the political right, as some older socialists have also sought to rebrand Brexit as 'Lexit,' presenting it as an opportunity for the left to pursue a project of 'socialism in one country.'[10]

Just as transnationally shared collective memories helped to drive the project of integration during the postwar period by serving as cognitive, motivational, and justificatory resources for the creation of the European Communities, today the fragmentation and loss of European memory jeopardises the entire project of the European Union. By detailing this threat, this chapter completes the 'origins and crisis diagnosis' phase of my project and sets the stage for the normative, prescriptive arguments on the future of European memory presented in Part II. The first section examines the damage done to the classical narrative by the eastern enlargements of the EU since 2004. An examination of the divisions opened by the Eurozone crisis follows. The third section then examines the possible destabilisations that face the EU in potential future rounds of expansion. A treatment of Brexit and the populist challenge to the EU and to European memory culture follows in the fourth section. The conclusion sums up the backward-looking *Zeitdiagnose* presented in Part I before transitioning to the forward-looking second phase of the argument.

Eastern enlargement (2004, 2007, 2013)[11]

The fall of the Berlin Wall was greeted enthusiastically throughout Europe. From its beginnings in the early Cold War atmosphere of the 1950s, the European project has seen itself as a bulwark against Soviet communism, with the ultimate goal of reuniting the continent under the banner of liberal democracy. In fact, the eastern half of the continent that remained behind the Iron Curtain was a central part of Jean Monnet's dream of a European federation stretching from the Atlantic to the Urals. Similarly, the states of Eastern and Central Europe, especially those that shared the Hapsburg imaginary of Catholic *Mitteleuropa*, interpreted their historical legacy as placing them firmly within western civilisation.[12]

From a purely economic perspective, the integration of the postcommunist states into the EU made little sense. Despite the obvious importance of economic prosperity and military security, the opening of new markets is not enough to explain the widening of integration. In particular, such 'hard' economic factors have trouble accounting for the enlargement to the east, which was very costly for existing member-states. The accession of Bulgaria and Romania in 2007, which proceeded as planned even though the costs far outweighed the benefits for states already in the EU, is the most difficult example for such approaches to explain.[13]

Constructivist scholars of international relations have sought to elucidate these difficult cases by arguing that expansion is the result of how applicant countries 'fit' within the ideas of Europe and European identity held by the leaders of existing member-states.[14] From this perspective, the potential losers of enlargement could not oppose the admission of Romania and Bulgaria because, in the words of a declaration from the EP, this would 'undermin[e] the European Community's credibility.'[15] In line with my broader thesis, I argue that the imperative to expand is not the result of an abstract moral argument, but of historical experiences of rupture interpreted through societal lenses and mediated by interactions with other European leaders. Collective memory thus functions as an important cognitive, motivational, and justificatory resource for expansion of the EU, even in cases where it does not necessarily further the material prosperity of the existing member-states.

From this perspective, 1989 presented an opportunity for Western Europe to free the 'captive nations' behind the Iron Curtain. Though the policy of Europe towards the USSR was often accomodationist in practice, its underlying goals were always dissolutionist and transformational. During the Cold War, differing understandings of the past in east and west were papered over, as the international politics was dominated by geopolitical struggles.[16] After the fall of the Iron Curtain, these unresolved issues rose up and became politically salient once more.[17]

In their response to the *Wende* ('turning point') of 1989, the EU and its officials sought to pre-empt these tensions by immediately making it clear that they were open to the accession of the new postcommunist states in the east. They spoke of the 'liberation' of East-Central Europe, which could now 'return' or come 'back to Europe.' The goal of European policy towards the east was to 'overcome division' and to fulfil 'the aspiration of the peoples of central and eastern Europe to "rejoin Europe."'[18] The EU's commissioner for enlargement, Günter Verheugen, routinely described eastern enlargement as 'a historic opportunity and an obligation for the European Union.'[19]

Ainius Lašas highlights the role of western feelings of collective guilt that stem 'from the historical mistakes that left [these states] behind the Iron Curtain for 50 years.' He focuses on what he calls the 'black trinity' of the Munich Agreement (1938), the Molotov-Ribbentrop Pact (1939) and the postwar agreements at Yalta and Potsdam (1945) as 'the historical mistakes that left the [East-Central Europe] behind the Iron Curtain for 50 years.' While not all the states of the western alliance participated in the events of the black trinity – and not all postcommunist states were equally affected by them – the feeling of collective responsibility and the desire to make up for these historical wrongs were incorporated into shared Euro-Atlantic identities vis-à-vis the east.[20]

For example, these dynamics were clearly visible during Margaret Thatcher's visit to Prague in 1990. While there the British prime minister acknowledged that the UK had 'failed you in 1938 when a disastrous policy of appeasement allowed Hitler to extinguish your independence.' She expressed her support for the widening of Europe by assuring her audience that the British 'still remember it with shame.' Similarly, although France was initially more reticent in their support for expansion eastward, the constructive resources of the past eventually helped to convince its leaders of their duties towards East-Central Europe as well. In 1997 French President Jacques Chirac expressed his support for the accession of the postcommunist east as well, noting that the events of the black trinity can be 'understood as a betrayal by Europe, or more probably as a betrayal by France.'

The historical legacy of the Second World War vis-à-vis East-Central Europe lay most heavily on Germany. The optics of the German position were particularly difficult. Given its historical legacy of collective guilt – and the fact that most of the atrocities of the Holocaust were actually carried out in territories occupied or annexed by the Nazis in Eastern and Central Europe – the Federal Republic could hardly deny the other postcommunist states entry into the EU while simultaneously integrating the former German Democratic Republic into its constitutional architecture.[21] As a result of these considerations successive German governments affirmed their support for the accession of the postcommunist states on historical grounds. In 1991, Christian Democratic Foreign Minister Hans-Dietrich Genscher noted that 'if they wish so, the German government would plead for their association with the [European Community].' Almost ten years later, Joschka Fischer, Genscher's successor from the Green Party, also spoke of German's 'historical responsibility' to support the eastern enlargement of Europe.

The leaders of the newly democratic postcommunist states sought to take advantage of these feelings of guilt and took every opportunity to remind the west of its historical responsibility for the partition of Europe, thereby activating the painful resources of collective memory that they felt they needed to ensure their accession to the EU. In Poland, 'British visitors usually receive a lecture from [former Solidarity leader] Mr. Walesa about Britain's role in the Yalta agreement that handed Poland to Stalin.' In a similar vein, Foreign

Minister Dariusz Rosati referred to 'eastern enlargement [as] an act of historic compensation.'[22] Although these statements were honest expressions of feelings in the region, it is also clear that the leaders of postcommunist Europe were well aware of the constitutive role the past had played in postwar Europe and had no compunctions about using the motivational and justificatory resources of the past to their advantage.

Despite the clear western feelings of guilt and responsibility, historical apologies did not flow uniformly from west to east. In the aftermath of the Second World War many communist regimes purged their societies of 'bourgeois' elements, often targeting ethnic Germans in revenge for the actions of the Nazi regime during the war. In addition to acknowledging the crimes of National Socialism, the German-speaking survivors of these '*erzwungene Wege*' ('forced journeys'), organised in *Vertriebenenverbände* (associations of exiles) to lobby their government for recognition of their suffering as well.[23] For example, bilateral German-Czech Declaration on Mutual Relations and their Future Development (1997), which enhanced the Czech candidacy for accession to the EU, is a good example of a mutual apology. While the Germans acknowledged responsibility for the crimes of the Nazis against the Czechs, the latter apologised for the expulsion of the Sudeten Germans after the Second World War: 'Both sides therefore declare that they will not burden their relations with political and legal issues which stem from the past.'[24]

The year 1989 was an important turning point in East-Central Europe because it put an end to the communist regimes that had been imposed upon the region's citizens after the Second World War. Much like the Mediterranean states transitioning from authoritarianism in the 1970s and 1980s, the postcommunist states saw entry into the EU as a pathway into the modern world. In this sense, '"Europe" was such an object of desire to aspirant members ... [because it represented] an escape route out of their past and an insurance policy for the future.' The existing member-states and European institutions were ready to take them in because they had considered East-Central Europe to be part of the region that Milan Kundera famously referred to as 'the kidnapped West.'[25]

Memory and guilt for the abandonment of the east played an important role as a cognitive, motivational, and justificatory factor in helping Western Europe to commit to eastern enlargement. However, the differences in historical experience and the diverent understandings of which transitions constitute a historical rupture in collective memory also caused more significant clashes of collective memory than were visible in any previous round of enlargement. While 1945 is an important historical break in East-Central Europe, it has a very different meaning in the postcommunist space.

Within the western narrative, the end of the Second World War stands for the beginning of a new project of integration based on the lessons of a bloody history. In contrast, for societies that experienced communist rule, '1945 means a transition from one occupation to another; from Nazi rule to Soviet rule. It is the beginning of two full generations of communist rule, which for most people was no experience of political progress.'[26] While they shared in the fascist memory of defeat and occupation, in East-Central Europe the 'entry ticket' focusing on the Holocaust had little resonance in light of the more recently experienced crimes of communism. Those who had suffered under the *ancien régime* saw the western focus on the events of 1939 through 1945 as an attempt to downplay or suppress their own experiences of suffering since the end of the war.[27]

Many westerners have found it difficult to give up the centrality of the Holocaust and to relate to the communist memories of the east. In part this is due to the presence of communist parties in Western Europe, which obscured the differences between socialism as a political ideal and communism as it actually existed behind the Iron Curtain.[28] Despite his attempts to understand the full import of what he calls Europe's 'ravaged century,' Robert Conquest admits that the only reason he can give for why he finds the Holocaust to be 'worse' than the Stalinist crimes is, 'I feel so.' Charles Maier has attempted to explain this 'feeling' – he too uses this word – concluding that 'Nazi violence and genocidal policies targeted terror in contrast with the stochastic terror of Stalinism.' Maier argues that this feature makes Nazi memory 'hot,' because the narrow targeting of a specific group is more shameful and makes bystanders feel more complicit than the 'cold' memories of the broad, societal crimes of communism.[29]

For many East-Central Europeans such attempts to explain away half a century of suffering on their part adds insult to injury. At the Leipzig Book Fair in March 2004, Latvian politician Sandra Kalniete argued that 'the two totalitarian regimes – Nazism and Communism – were equally criminal.' After her speech, western commentators accused her of making an 'illegal comparison,' of 'downgrading the Holocaust' and of 'anti-Semitism.'[30] Tatiana Zhurzhenko notes that 'communist memory is "hotting up" again in Eastern Europe. ... EU enlargement has become a catalyst for debates about the communist past and for memory politics in both the new EU member states and their neighbours.'[31]

Historical disagreements have also affected the bilateral relations of many states whose borders ran along the Iron Curtain, forcing them to negotiate the past as well. For example, a long-running dispute over restitution for Italians forced out of their homes in Yugoslavia during and after the Second World War has continued to sour relations between Italy and the successor states of the Socialist Federal Republic, especially Croatia and Slovenia. The claims of the *esuli* found a voice in Silvio Berlusconi's right-wing coalitions in the first decade of the twenty-first century. As prime minister, Berlusconi engaged in significant historical revisionism, at one point even claiming, 'Mussolini never killed anyone … Mussolini sent people on holiday to confine them.'[32] Additionally, the Foreign Minister in these governments was Gianfranco Fini of the post-fascist National Alliance, which received much of its support from the *esuli* resettled in northeastern Italy.

In the aftermath of this statement many in the west agreed with Slavoj Žižek, who argued Berlusconi's claim was part of a larger symbolic political and ideological project to destroy anti-fascist unity, which is the basis of modern European identity. Slovenian historian Jasna Fišer even reports being approached by diplomatic representatives from France and Germany in 2002 during her state's accession negotiations, because they were worried that Slovenia was distancing itself from its role in the coalition that defeated fascism in order to ensure that Italy did not veto the country's entrance into the EU. They warned her that Europe could not tolerate this kind of historical revisionism, since the project of integration is built on the victory over fascism.[33]

Debates over the meaning of the communist past vis-à-vis the legacy of National Socialism are not confined to bilateral relations. They also often play themselves out within the supranational institutions of the continent, particularly the EP. In 2005, Members of the European Parliament (MEPs) from East-Central Europe defeated a bill that would have extended the German ban on Nazi symbols like the swastika throughout the EU, arguing that the ban should also include communist symbols like the hammer and sickle. During the debate, Hungarian MEP Jozsef Szájer agreed with the desire to ban the swastika, but argued that if 'the Union wishes to propose a ban on the swastika, I suggest adding the symbols of the hated and bloody communist dictatorship as well … No more Nazism in Europe, no more communism in Europe!'[34]

This proposal produced a heated response, especially among representatives of social democratic parties.[35] After the uproar surrounding the debate on the banning of the swastika, the EP worked hard to create a consensus surrounding

European collective memory by recognising and emphasising the evils of communism alongside those of Nazism. A series of hearings and conferences organised by the European Commission and the Slovenian presidency of the EU in April 2008 'brought to light a strong feeling that the Member States in Western Europe should be more aware of the tragic past of the Member States in Eastern Europe.'[36]

These disputes led to the creation of a new European Day of Remembrance for the victims of Nazism and Stalinism, which commemorates the Molotov-Ribbentrop Pact signed between Nazi Germany and the USSR on 23 August 1939. While this has mollified MEPs from postcommunist Europe, this controversy remains in the background. Despite calls for the creation of a 'critical culture of remembrance' to secure an 'open-minded approach to conveying the past,' the declarations of European institutions continue to stress that 'the uniqueness of the Holocaust must nevertheless be acknowledged.'[37]

Debates about the relative place of Nazi versus communist memory do not always divide neatly between the states to the east and west of the defunct Iron Curtain. On the contrary, the legacy of communism is very controversial within many states of East-Central Europe, where former communists who have managed to maintain or regain power. Similarly, western member-states have sought to exploit the 'hotting up' of communist memory to make claims against the states of East-Central Europe for communist crimes while whitewashing their own histories of fascism.

In its declaration on 'European conscience and totalitarianism' (2009), the EP argued that 'Europe will not be united unless it is able to form a common view of its history, recognises Nazism, Stalinism and fascist and Communist regimes as a common legacy and brings about an honest and thorough debate on their crimes in the past century.'[38] Unfortunately, pulling the states of East-Central Europe into the EU has done little to ameliorate these tensions. Instead, these debates have led to a 'revenge of the past,' which has done little to further integration through a common historical narrative.[39] On the contrary, the accession of the postcommunist east posed a severe challenge to the classic narrative of integration and the Holocaust as 'Europe's entry ticket.' Given these difficulties it is no longer clear whether the EU can really be thought of as a common 'community' or a 'space' of memory.[40]

The clashes over the past brought on by the accessions of new member-states since 2004 opened an important east–west fault line within the EU. While both sides see the past as a constructive resource, they understand and apply these resources to make very different arguments. However, these difficulties represent only one aspect of the problems facing the EU at the start of the twenty-first century. In addition to the continental divisions over memory, the global financial crisis brought on by the fall of Lehman Brothers, one of the world's largest financial service providers, in September 2008 has opened new rifts in Europe.

In addition to the east–west fault lines created following the accessions of 2004, as a result of the Great Recession the EU and its common currency area, the Eurozone, now also face a widening gulf between north and south. These horizontal and vertical aspects of Europe's crisis at the start of the twenty-first century often intersect and reinforce each other. As a result, while shared collective memories and deeper integration used to reinforce each other by furthering both the security and prosperity of the European continent, since 2004 the fragmentation and loss of European memory have helped to deepen the economic downturn of 2008, thus threatening the future of the EU as a whole.

The crisis of the Eurozone[41]

Two decades after the fall of communism and the Berlin Wall allowed Eastern and Western Europe to reunite under the auspices of the EU, the continent faced renewed economic and political divisions. In August 2007 the world began to experience the longest and deepest economic downturn since the Great Depression. While the Cold War split nation-states ideologically, these financial 'hard times,' when 'some … experience misfortune while others achieve financial gain,' are turning 'equal nations into an unequal compulsory union of borrowers and creditors, one that threatens to divide the continent.'[42] Whereas the accession of the postcommunist space divided Europe horizontally between east and west, the financial crisis has divided it vertically between north and south.

The so-called Great Recession started as a subprime mortgage crunch, which eventually lead to the collapse of global 'financialised capitalism.'[43] Although it initially appeared that Europe had managed to avoid the contagion emanating from the other side of the Atlantic, by 2010 the crisis had shifted across two dimensions: what started in the United States in the business sphere had moved across the Atlantic and into the public sector. The result was a full-blown economic, banking, and sovereign crisis within the EU, centred on but not limited to the member-states that share its common currency, the euro.[44]

The Eurozone crisis has disproportionately affected the newer member-states of the EU's periphery, especially Portugal, Spain, Ireland, and Greece.

Economic and political responsibility is divided between the rich 'northern' core, whose investors financed irresponsible borrowing and whose leaders sought to protect their banking sectors from losses, as well as the elites of the 'southern' periphery, who took advantage of the low interest rates to bankroll unwise investments. While the crisis can be understood from the micro 'point of view of the individual decision-makers,' macro structural factors are also important, since 'the mechanisms for controlling speculation and unrestrained capital flows were insufficient.'[45]

The divisions between the 'rich north' and the 'lazy, crisis-ridden' south have built up gradually since the introduction of the euro. Although it allowed southern member-states used to selling sovereign bonds at higher interest rates to access capital on international financial markets at the same low rate as paragons of fiscal stability like Germany, 'The introduction of a common currency without a common authority and mechanisms of redistribution was intensifying regional imbalances, hurting workers in both core and periphery countries, yet benefiting the capital of the core European countries.'[46] In practice, the introduction of the euro represented a currency devaluation for the north, which enabled higher productivity and greater competitiveness in international trade, and an overvaluation in the south, leading to a decline in competitiveness in export markets. While the experience of a relatively weaker currency allowed the export-driven economies of the north to run large current accounts surpluses, the comparatively strong euro encouraged the southern member-states to import goods, causing them to run ever-larger deficits.

The crisis has shown that 'a monetary union which is based on loose rules on budget/tax/economic governance will remain incomplete and unsustainable.' The Maastricht model – named after the treaty that laid the legal foundations for the euro as a currency with a central bank but no treasury, with a common market but no common government – functioned during the economic boom of the early 2000s. However, its deficiencies were revealed during the financial downturn starting with the Great Recession of 2008.

The inability to devaluate government debt denominated in a currency no individual state controls, means that the member-states of the euro are faced with the risk of default. Crisis-ridden governments are forced to adopt austerity to regain their competitiveness while facing ever-higher rates. Successive taxpayer-financed rescues of the financial sector have sought to resolve the contradictory imperatives of lowering interest *premia* on southern bonds while protecting the investments of large northern banks. However, this merely served to convert private liabilities into public debt, further exacerbating the economic crisis.[47]

These difficulties have brought on what Claus Offe, a sociologist associated with the Frankfurt School, calls a 'crisis of crisis management.' Because policy repertoires and political interventions are continually 'recycled' without addressing structural causes, the citizens of Europe have lost faith in the ability of authorities at both the national and the European levels to address the economic contradictions of the euro.[48] Although EU communiqués and officials at the ECB often like to present their resolutions and decisions as the products of objective, technical analysis, 'The euro crisis has been … a "live-fire test", making more visible the politics within the Union that it aims to describe.'[49]

In most cases the political machinations revealed by the crisis have been decidedly divisive and distasteful, revealing little of the much-ballyhooed 'European spirit.' The fact that the divisions between north and south mirror the historically based divisions in European collective memory between east and west results in the intertwining of these two conflicts. Taken together, these developments mean that the member-states are increasingly running out of the cognitive, motivational, and justificatory resources of remembrance that they need to work together to resolve the crisis of the Eurozone precisely at the time they need them most.

As a result, instead of addressing shared problems, 'each country [has defended] its own interests while attempting to benefit from "free-rider" tactics.' While this position has a certain logic, much like the outcome of a prisoner's dilemma, over the course of the crisis the seemingly rational decision to free ride has left everyone worse off.[50] Given its strong fiscal tradition, large current accounts surplus, economic power, and political position, Germany has emerged as the key player in the crisis. Unfortunately, it has proved unwilling to understand the structural nature of the problems of the south or to sacrifice its own short-term economic interests for the long-term stability and prosperity of the Eurozone as a whole. Instead, 'all too often, lacking empathy to put themselves in the position of their neighbours, the Germans have a tendency to make moralizing judgments about what other euro members should or should not do.'[51]

The northern narrative has focused on the clientalist nature of politics in the south. For example, debates about the crisis in Greece are framed based on stereotypes of lazy Greeks lying on beaches as the government piles up debt to finance unfunded social mandates. Conversely, narratives in the south have deployed images of uncaring Germans in Nazi uniforms imposing their will on countries they occupied during the Second World War. The focus on nationalistic prejudices instead of on the structural imbalances within the institutional architecture of EMU has strengthened the 'intuitive, appealing' use of austerity as a response to a crisis that can be 'handily summed up in the phrase *you cannot cure debt with more debt.*' The moralisation of the Eurozone's difficulties has allowed leaders in the north to console themselves that the painful measures they are imposing are necessary.[52]

The perceived lack of concern exhibited by northern elites and the leaders of European institutions for the suffering of individuals in the southern member states resulted in protests and social upheavals throughout southern Europe, where more than half of those under thirty were unemployed at the height of the crisis. Comparable only to the dramatic events of May 1968 – a parallel drawn explicitly by French President Nicholas Sarkozy – these demonstrations coincided with rioting and the emergence of nationalistic extra-parliamentary movements. This has resulted not only 'in a general crisis of the state' throughout the crisis-ridden south, but in more 'struggle *against* the EU.'[53]

There is a certain irony to be found in the divisive effects the euro has had on the EU as a result of the Eurozone crisis. After all, the groundwork for the common currency was laid in the Eurosclerosis of the 1970s precisely in order to 'to generate a European consciousness' by making 'Europe more visible to residents' of the member-states. It has succeeded in doing just the opposite: 'Far from promoting convergence among member states, European Monetary Union has been a source of unrelenting pressure on workers that has produced systematic disparities between core and periphery resulting in vast accumulation of debt in the latter.'[54] These problems reveal the difficulties of sustaining the EU if it loses its basis in the moral demands of collective memory and becomes purely a project based on economic gain.

While the east–west divisions over the classic narrative of integration may have been overcome on their own, the addition of the economic crisis has merely served to further fracture the unity of the member-states and to weaken their ability to act together through the shared institutions of the EU. Whatever the substantive solutions, it is clear that the member-states will have to overcome these divisions before they will be able to implement anything. As Stanley Hoffmann points out, 'Politics is a matter of will … Either Europeans must develop more effectively the will to surmount their present divergences and build a common structure, or things will go on as they always have, with European states acting separately.'[55]

The destabilising potential of future expansion

In the end, the crisis of the Eurozone will most likely result in a significant 'deepening' of the EU behind the backs of its citizens. However, acute economic problems – and their effects on European politics and society – are not the only destabilising factor threatening the EU's future. Despite the 'expansion fatigue' that followed the accession of postcommunist Europe, it is also clear that Europe has not finished its widening either. In the course of its development since 1951 the transfer of competencies up beyond the nation-state to supranational institutions has also empowered subnational actors, especially regional assemblies within member-states. As a result of the EU's growing support for regions through the development of its cohesion policies, 'sub-national government has an increasing role to play in the formulation of EU policy, as well as in its implementation.'[56]

While these dynamics have affected the power of subnational actors within all the member-states, they have been especially pronounced in regions dominated by separatist substate minorities. In part, this is because non-state peoples like the Basques, Catalans, and Scots have sought to take advantage of their new possibilities for self-rule presented by the structures of continental unification. These active attempts to increase regional decision-making powers have also been supported by the EU's emphasis on minority rights and its regional development policy, which has given these areas direct access to European funds.[57]

The increased independence of these regions and the broader horizons of the CM have also made the potential loss of these provinces more palatable to their parent states than would have been the case in the past. However, the potential of this new regionalism to splinter Europe is explosive, since it could encourage the succession of other non-state peoples. The status of a newly independent region from an existing member-state is also unclear. While some legal experts argue that these potential new states would automatically be members, others contend that they would have to apply for membership and accede like any other state outside the union.[58] Despite the possible conflicts that would result, this form of expansion is unlikely to cause major disturbances to European memory culture.[59]

The same cannot be said for other potential member-states from this area, such as the successor states of post-conflict Yugoslavia, which face important internal problems. When it became clear that the fall of communism would destabilise the delicate ethnic balance in the southern Balkans, the leaders of the EU attempted to keep the country together by offering it fast track to membership to the EU if it remained unified. This attempt failed. In its aftermath, the EU committed itself to the eventual accession of all of the former Socialist Federal Republics.[60]

While it was clearly unsuited to undertake the military intervention necessary to stop the conflict, the EU's foundation on the reconciliation of France and Germany after 1945 seems to make it the ideal facilitator for the post-conflict memory politics of Yugoslavia. However, the triple legacy of the past – including occupation during the Second World War, the experience of communism through the postwar period, as well as war and ethnic cleansing in the 1990s – has made this process much harder. While Slovenia (2004) and Croatia (2013) have already joined the EU, it is unclear how long it will take for the other successor states of the former Yugoslavia to join the EU due to important domestic and European constraints.

Although all of these possible expansions pose interesting problems, the question of Turkish membership looms largest. As a large, powerful, developing, majority-Muslim state, Turkey presents many difficulties for the EU.[61] On one hand, Turkey's sense of belonging to the European *projet* is clearly diminished by the fact that it did not experience the events that form the historical background to the project of integration, particularly the Holocaust.[62] However, as demonstrated by the accession of Spain and Portugal, this cannot be considered an *a priori* criterion for membership. Despite its non-participation in the experience of Nazism, Turkey was an important outpost of the western alliance during the Cold War. It was frequently conceived as being part of Europe and this fact was used both to motivate and justify its acceptance as a candidate country. At the signing of the Agreement of Association between the European Communities and Turkey in September 1963, Commission President Walter Hallstein affirmed, 'Turkey is part of Europe.'[63]

Leaving aside all the other economic, social, and political problems posed by Turkey's application to join the EU, the place of the Armenian genocide in Turkish collective memory is a major issue. To date the demands for recognition of this historical event have remained largely implicit. In certain cases, it has actually become explicit as '[t]here was even talk in 2006 of making Turkish recognition of the genocide a precondition for entry into the European Union.'[64] These issues of collective remembrance are extremely explosive in Turkey. While the Turks recognise that many Armenians died in a regrettable 'massacre' (*katliam* or *kiyim*), they strongly deny that this constituted a planned, government orchestrated 'genocide.' When asked about these problems in

2008, Turkish Prime Minister Recep Tayyip Erdoğan answered diplomatic-ally: 'Our goal is full membership. We want to be treated in the same way as the other candidate countries.'[65]

Erdoğan's reaction to the statements of both French President Jacques Chirac and his successor Nicolas Sarkozy, insisting that if Turkey wants to join the EU it should accept the genocide, is understandable. Like many Central Europeans, Turks resent being told what to think of their past by the west. After the experience of postcommunist expansion, the leaders of Europe seem to be warier of the paternalism involved in teaching other nations their history. Despite this reticence, Turkey's refusal to come to terms with the past in a European fashion is highly problematic and goes against the basic values of the EU. In the words of the European Council's report on totalitarian crimes, the connection 'memory [of the horrors of the past] nourishes the commitment of the European Union to democracy and the respect of funda-mental rights, and to fight against modern manifestations of intolerance and extremism.'[66]

Insofar as a confrontation with the past has become 'an informal mem-bership criterion' and 'part of the hidden agenda of the *acquis communautaire*,' then Turkey is being 'treated in the same way as the other candidate coun-tries' in being pushed to confront the less appealing aspects of its history.[67] At this point, however, in the aftermath of the failed coup attempt against Erdoğan on 15 June 2016, hopes of further progress on Turkish member-ship appear slim at best. The Turkish president's response to the coup, which he blamed on secularist elements within the army, has resulted in an extreme judicial crackdown on political opposition and on the basic liber-ties the EU promotes through its *acquis communautaire*. While the prospect of Turkish membership may be revived in the future, it is unlikely in the short- to medium-term, or at least as long as Erdoğan and his AKP remain in power in Ankara.

Despite the EU's expansion fatigue and Turkey's deprioritisation of mem-bership as part of a broader move towards a more autocratic form of elect-oral dictatorship in the wake of Erdoğan's deconsolidation of democracy, the past continues to act as a 'pull' factor drawing states into Europe's orbit. This was most powerfully revealed in pro-Europe protests in Ukraine in 2013 and 2014, which were set off by President Viktor Yanukovych's last-minute deci-sion to sign an economic association agreement with the Russian Federation rather than the EU. As in all of the cases discussed above, 'hard' material con-siderations certainly played a role in the Ukrainian protesters' desire to join

Europe. However, collective memory was also a salient factor pulling parts of Ukraine towards the EU.

Ukraine has a deeply divided culture of remembrance. There have been attempts to create a national collective memory around the rupture of 1989 by stressing the nation's newfound freedom. However, the state continues to be bifurcated by 'the myth of the two Ukraines,' i.e. the western Ukraine of Galicia, whose people fought for independence against both Nazi and Soviet rule, and the eastern Ukraine of the Russian minority, which cannot accept the anti-Soviet version of historical memory propounded in the west. The fact that this divide mirrors the historical boundary between the 'western' Habsburg and the 'eastern' Russian empires, only serves to underline the historical complexity of these issues.[68]

Given the divisive effects the accession of the new postcommunist member-states has already had on the Union since 2004, it seems unreasonable to expect that the integration of states such as Serbia, Ukraine, and Turkey will go smoothly, especially considering their radically divergent memory cultures. In addition to these internal destabilisations, the further 'widening' of Europe also has important external geopolitical implications. The successor states of the former Yugoslavia and Ukraine are part of what Russia consideres its sphere of influence or 'near abroad,' while Turkey serves as a direct link between Europe and the Middle East. In addition to integrating these new memory cultures, the accession of these states would also require a renewed focus on strengthening and deepening the EU's commitment to a common foreign and security policy. This is likely to be a tall order, given that the EU is currently already internally divided on both its horizontal and vertical axes.

Populism, Brexit, and potential disintegration

Focusing on the crisis of the Eurozone and the problems involved in integrating the memory culture of the west with the differing sources of rupture in postcommunist Europe makes it seem like this is the source of all of the EU's problems at the start of the twenty-first century. Unfortunately, as is often the case with deep-seated pathologies, underlying problems tend to manifest at the periphery initially before becoming visible in the core. In this sense, these interlocking crises are 'not a temporary phenomenon' but build on the fact that 'democracies of trust' both in Europe and beyond have gradually come to be replaced by 'democracies of mistrust,' as Pierre Rosanvallon puts it.[69]

Fragmentation and loss of European memory

The difficulties the European political system has had in dealing with the interlocking crises at the beginning of the third millennium has driven much of this disillusionment. Given its pre-existing democratic deficits, much of this anger has been directed towards the EU in the form of anti-European far-right movements. Demographically, the supporters of these parties are drawn from older cohorts born during the period of unprecedented economic growth between 1945 and 1975. Using Eurobarometer data from the UK, Kieran Devine concludes that not all 'over-65s' favour Brexit, as the generations who experienced Europe's age of total war first-hand display 'significantly more positive views towards European integration than the immediate post-war generations.' In contrast to those born after 1945, this older cohort is 'more likely to associate the EU with peace, and thus have more positive attitudes towards integration.'[70]

By contrast, among the 'over-65s' born after the end of the Second World War, 'historical amnesia is favouring the rise of the populist right.'[71] In large part this seems to be due to the fact that these individuals associate the postwar era of prosperity, which also coincided with the creation of the welfare state, with the success of the sovereign nation-state. Given the fact that the EU only started to become more visible in continental economic policy and the everyday lives of Europeans towards the end of this period – that is in the 1980s and 1990s – they associate the subsequent decline in growth, living standards, and prosperity with European integration. These factors, combined with the rise in globalisation and multiculturalism that followed the end of the Cold War in 1989 as well as the austerity programme implemented by the Conservative Party in response to the Great Recession, have 'reinforced the sense that Europe only cares about liberalism, while the nation-state does democracy.'[72]

These cohort effects, which are driven by the passing away of the generations that had direct memories of Europe's age of total war as well as the concurrent loss of the cognitive, motivational, and justificatory resources that came with them, help to explain the nostalgic overtones of the rhetoric of the far-right in the aftermath of the economic downturn. Slogans like Nigel Farage's claim that leaving Europe would help the British to 'take back control,' which was devastatingly effective in the campaign for Brexit, encourage their audience to hearken back to a better, earlier time.[73] It projects an image of national sovereignty that is intimately bound up with what Timothy Snyder refers to as 'the fable of the wise nation.'

Like most myths, this image of the solitary sovereign state that is able to protect its citizens from unwanted external influence and provide for their needs internally builds on a historical fiction. Snyder notes that in order for this narrative to succeed 'nation-states must be imagined into periods when in fact they did not exist.' While the national state may appear to be the key player in postwar economic prosperity, this was not actually the case. Far from moving from empire to nation to integration, Snyder argues that the major states of Western Europe transitioned directly from colonialism to economic integration after the war. Although it was not particularly visible to European citizens at the time, the postwar prosperity was driven in large part by trade liberalisation through the action of the European Communities and the other institutions of the postwar world order (such as the Marshall Plan, the GATT, NATO, the WTO, etc.). As a result, Snyder concludes that in fact 'there was no era of the nation-state.' He argues that it is a mistake to think of integration as 'a national *choice* rather than as a national *necessity*' brought about the destruction wrought by the Second World War and the loss of empire that followed closely on its heels.[74]

In Western Europe, this false image of the powerful nation-state, which is better off going it alone, is most visible in the United Kingdom. The rhetoric of the Leave campaign was redolent with nostalgic references to the old policy of 'splendid isolationism' as well as Britain's 'past glories and "finest hour."'[75] The slogan calling on the people to 'take back control' implicitly referenced a better, more successful past, when Britain was a powerful player, both in economic terms and geopolitically. The cinematic successes of *Dunkirk* (2017) and *Churchill* (2017), two historical dramas that portrayed Britain's ability to survive even without its allies during both world wars, further reinforces the nostalgic overtones of the Brexit project.[76]

The UK's narrow vote to leave, with 51.89 per cent for Brexit and 48.11 per cent against on a relatively high turnout of 72.2 per cent, revealed a number of important divides within Britain. While England overwhelmingly voted to leave (joined narrowly by Wales), the Scots and the Northern Irish both voted Remain by large margins.[77] Regardless of these internal differences, multi-factor analyses of the vote revealed a powerful cohort effect, as age was strongly correlated with a desire to leave the EU. John Curtice notes that the splitting age was 45, as 'those aged less than 45 voted to Remain in the EU, while most of those aged 45 and over indicated that they wished to Leave.'[78]

This means that those born after 1970, who grew up on a continent of increasingly open borders and a more visible EU, voted to stay in the bloc, while those born during the economic boom, who could thus buy into the 'myth of the wise nation' as the source of postwar prosperity voted for Brexit. This is an extremely powerful cohort effect, which also highlights the absence of the pro-European 'missing generation' that has already passed away: those who could actually remember the war and the real reasons that underpin continental integration (i.e. the generations of the founders of Europe). Support for right-wing, nationalist parties is thus driven by a cohort of individuals who 'are young enough not to have experienced world war, but ... are old enough to idealise the pre-1989 era and a simpler, pre-globalization world.'[79]

In addition to these national and generational dynamics, policy attitudes also played an important role in the vote. Most notably, those who voted Leave noted that their primary concerns were high levels of immigration – driven by the EU's guarantee of the freedom of movement – and the loss of national identity (particularly English national identity). These nostalgic preferences were correlated with more 'authoritarian' attitudes confirming the findings of the Frankfurt School and Adorno's classic study of the authoritarian personality.[80]

In particular, recent research demonstrates that voting Leave in the Brexit referendum correlates strongly with favouring the death penalty and approval of strict parenting techniques that require obedience from children. By contrast, Remain voters tend to care more about economic performance and hold more cosmopolitan views on issues of identity.[81] These results are also in line with my arguments about the important generational effects resulting from the rupture of 1945. As Robert Inglehart and Pippa Norris point out, 'Authoritarian populist support is concentrated among the older generation, the less-educated, men, the religious, and the ethnic majority – groups that hold traditional cultural values.'[82]

These British dynamics mirror the anti-European populist movements on the continent. Although Geert Wilders's Partij voor de Vrijheid (Party for Freedom, PVV) and Marine Le Pen's National Rally have not succeeded in winning an election or scheduling a referendum for 'Nexit' or 'Frexit,' it is no accident that these movements are most powerful in large, traditional nation-states like the Netherlands and France, both of which can fall back on nostalgic colonial histories of empire (much like Britain). These facts confirm Seymour Martin Lipset's argument that support for fascism in the 1920s and 1930s drew from the economically and politically threatened members of the majority, especially the elderly.[83] Within Europe's increasingly multicultural societies the white majority has come to blame its economic problems on recent arrivals, who they perceive as a threat to their prosperity as well as their national and religious traditions. This has produced an authoritarian or xenophobic reaction, where individuals revert back to traditional values, close ranks behind strong leaders, and seek solidarity with their in-group.[84]

Despite their differing memory cultures and experiences of the postwar era that ended in 1989, the new member-states of East-Central Europe have also been caught up in the wave of reactionary populism that has swept the continent in the aftermath of the Great Recession. Although Western Europe has largely succeeded in neutralising this threat – with the notable exception of Brexit and the unstable populist coalition that took power in Italy in the spring of 2018 – the same cannot be said of postcommunist Europe. For example, in both Hungary and Poland far-right parties have taken hold of the reins of state. While Orbán's Fidesz and Kaczyński's Prawo i Sprawiedliwość (Law and Justice) parties have worked hard to avoid 'evok[ing] the images familiar from twentieth century dictatorships' by eschewing overt violence and maintaining the outward trappings of democracy, they have secured single-party rule by more modern means. These include gerrymandering, the writing of electoral laws that guarantee constitutional majorities, the neutering of the judiciary, and the takeover of the media by friendly tycoons.[85]

Although they took hold of power in different ways, these two regimes have sought to spread their values by reinvigorating the Visegrád Group. Initially formed by communist dissidents committed to liberalism, these 'aspirational fascists' have sought to reinvigorate this constellation. As Jacques Rupnik points out, 'Today, particularly on the migrant issue, Visegrád asserts itself in opposition to Brussels and Berlin, with Orbán and Poland's Jarosław Kaczyński calling for a counter-revolution in Europe.'[86]

Interestingly – compared to the movements led by Farage, Wilders, and Le Pen in the west – these parties within the new member-states are not anti-European per se: they just have a different understanding of what it means (or should mean) to be European. In contrast to the multiculturalism and cosmopolitanism of supporters of the EU in Western Europe, the postcommunist narrative sees itself as the 'rampart of Christianity' (*antemurale christianitatis*), fighting to save a European civilisation based on 'nations of culture' (on the model of the German nineteenth century ideal of the *Kulturnation*) from a cultural, economic, and social threat emanating from the Middle East, Africa, and Russia.[87]

I have already noted some of the important differences in memory culture that result from postcommunist focus on 1989 in comparison to the western emphasis on 1945 and the Holocaust as the key rupture that defines the cognitive, motivational, and justificatory resources of the past. My argument is that in Western Europe the revival of fascist symbols and rhetoric has been driven by generational turnover – both among voters and their leaders – who no longer carry personal memories of the destruction fascism unleashed in the 1930s and 1940s. Given that passage of time, these same effects are also present in Central Europe. However, among the new member-states this turnover is further augmented by the memory narratives encouraged and enforced by the communist regimes before 1989. Although these governments did not erase the Holocaust from national history, they portrayed it as an exclusively German crime connected with capitalism. In so doing they also papered over the complicity of the 'ordinary men' throughout the territories the Nazis occupied and/or annexed during the war.[88]

This externalisation or distancing of the Holocaust has a number of effects in the postcommunist member-states. To start with, it further diminishes whatever power the rupture of 1945 might have had as a moral imperative of collective memory. Additionally, it helps to explain the rise of the incredibly restrictive memory laws that are becoming ever more common in Central Europe. For example, in 2018 the Polish parliament passed a law that criminalised references to 'Polish Death Camps' as well as any other insinuation that the Polish nation may have been complicit in what occurred in the camps located on its territory.[89] As a result of this distancing from the legacy of fascism and any complicity with it, it is even harder for younger generations in East-Central Europe to recognise its dangers than those in the west, who were raised with an awareness of the Holocaust, even if that awareness is receding with the passage of time.

The damage done to the classical narrative by the eastern enlargements of the Union in 2004, the onset of the Eurozone crisis in 2010, Brexit, and the other populist challenges to mainstream politics all build on each other, posing what could well turn into an existential threat to the EU. Although these difficulties are driven by important economic factors, demographic turnover and the impact this has on collective memory across the continent also plays an important role. As the generation that remembers Europe's age of total war dies out, there is a real danger that the 'moral demands of memory' that the rupture of 1945 brought about will die with them.[90] These interlocking crises are potentially existential because it is unclear if Europe can survive without the cognitive, motivational, and justificatory resources of the past.

Conclusion

Europe's classical narrative of integration has invariably appealed to peace (or security) and prosperity (or welfare) in seeking to justify the creation of shared institutions based on the community model. Both of these arguments have been called into question by events since 2004. For most West Europeans the goal of putting 'an end to the bloody history of warfare between European nations … has already been achieved.'[91] As a result of this fact, and of the fragmentation and loss of European memory that I detailed in this chapter, Europeans and their leaders are increasingly unwilling to endure more growing pains in order to integrate states further to the east. Additionally, the Great Recession of 2008 and the Eurozone crisis that followed have made arguments about prosperity increasingly hard for the citizens of the EU to believe. This doubt, in turn, has led to Brexit and the rise of new populist movements that seek to return to the nation-state in a nostalgic effort to recreate the halcyon days of the postwar era.

Despite these problems, the current perspective, shaped as it is both by the weak financial position of the Eurozone and by its peaceful western location, may be too myopic. The Ukrainian 'Euro-Maidan' protests, named after the square the supporters of EU membership occupied in Kiev, have pointed to the continuing relevance of Europe's traditional narrative of peace and prosperity, at least in the east. While observers in Western Europe have concluded that 'Europe can no longer play the war card,' this argument is still salient in the Ukraine.[92] Snyder observes that 'it is the simple desire for peace, and the achievement of peace, that makes the European Union attractive in Kiev and elsewhere' outside of the EU's West European core.

Notwithstanding the massive recession and ongoing economic crisis of banking, finance, and sovereign debt, even the prosperity argument still has legs. Snyder observes that for many young, middle-class Ukrainians, the EU association agreement 'seemed to hold out … a symbolic assurance that a future of normal, civilized, European life awaited.'[93] The example of Ukraine shows that in addition to the European narrative of peace and prosperity, collective memories of the past will also continue to push potential applications to pursue membership in the EU for the foreseeable future. This argument will only become more powerful if the EU – and especially the Eurozone – manages to overcome its economic paralysis.

Whereas chapters 2 and 3 argued that the leaders of postwar Europe successfully built the EU the memory of the European rupture of 1945, the pathologies of the present show how both the integration of the postcommunist member-states of the east and the Eurozone crisis have undermined the achievements of integration. This chapter wraps up Part I, the 'explanatory-diagnostic' phase of this volume. As the generation of memory has died off and left public life – taking the cognitive, motivational, and justificatory resources of the past with them – the EU has had difficulty maintaining itself and continuing its development as a political project with important normative goals. Building on this critical diagnosis of the present (*kritische Zeitdiagnose*), I now turn to the future. Following the two-stage methodology of the Frankfurt School of critical theory, in Part II I build on the past to chart 'anticipatory-utopian' paths for the future of European collective memory.

Notes

1   Judt, *Postwar*, 803.
2   The paradigmatic statement of this narrative of integration can be found in Habermas and Derrida, 'February 15,' 291–297. References to the Second World War have played an important role in justifying integration in public debates over the EU as well. Bottici, 'Europe, War and Remembrance,' 45–58.
3   G. Morgan, 'European Political Integration and the Need for Justification,' *Constellations*, 14:3 (2007).
4   J. Habermas, 'February 15, or: What Binds Europeans,' in *Old Europe, New Europe, Core Europe: Transatlantic Relations After the Iraq War*, trans. M. Pensky (London: Verso, 2005), 8–12. Also P. J. Verovšek, 'Meeting Principles and Lifeworlds Halfway: Jürgen Habermas on the Future of Europe,' *Political Studies*, 60:2 (2012), 371–373.
5   C. Cronin, 'Editor's Preface,' in J. Habermas, *The Divided West* (London: Verso, 2006), xx.
6   K. H. Jarausch, 'Zeitgeschichte zwischen Nation und Europa. Eine transnationale Herausforderung,' *Aus Politik und Zeitgeschichte*, 54:B39 (2004), 3; A. Eriksen and J. Viðar Sigurðsson (eds), *Negotiating Pasts in the Nordic Countries: Interdisciplinary Studies in History and Memory* (Lund: Nordic Academic Press, 2009).
7   A. Sierp, 'Drawing Lessons from the Past: Mapping Change in Central and South-Eastern Europe,' *East European Politics and Societies*, 30:1 (2016), 5.
8   P. Bratsis, 'Legitimation Crisis and the Greek Explosion,' *International Journal of Urban and Regional Research*, 34:1 (2010), 190.
9   B. Vezjak, 'Axis of Illiberalism,' *Eurozine* (9 July 2018), www.eurozine.com/axis-of-illiberalism/ (accessed 10 July 2019); Verovšek, 'Memory and Forgetting in Central Europe.'
10 P. J. Verovšek, 'Lexit Undermines the Left: It will be no Prize for Labour,' *LSE Brexit Blog* (16 October 2018), https://blogs.lse.ac.uk/brexit/2018/10/16/lexit-undermines-the-left-it-will-be-no-prize-for-labour/ (accessed 17 October 2018).
11 Parts of this section were previously published as Verovšek, 'Expanding Europe through Memory.'
12 J. O'Brennan, *The Eastern Enlargement of the European Union* (New York: Routledge, 2006), 1. Also Gillingham, *European Integration, 1950–2003*, 410. For more on the

relationship between Christendom and the idea of Europe, see P. Anderson, *The New Old World* (London: Verso, 2009), 475–476. For more on the rediscovered concept of *Mitteleuropa*, see Judt, *Postwar*, 720.

13 C. J. Schneider, *Conflict, Negotiation and European Union Enlargement* (New York: Cambridge University Press, 2009), 3, 33; H. Sjursen, 'Why Expand? The Question of Legitimacy and Justification in the EU's Enlargement Policy,' *Journal of Common Market Studies*, 40:3 (2002), 497 and citations therein. Defenders of this approach have argued that barring relatively poor candidates from entry would destabilise the EU politically, threatening the existing benefits member-states already enjoy. See L. Friis and A. Murphy, 'The European Union and Central and Eastern Europe: Governance and Boundaries,' *Journal of Common Market Studies*, 37:2 (1999). This explanation is both ad hoc and unconvincing, given that the EU has blocked states such as Turkey from membership for decades without seriously undermining its political stability.

14 F. Schimmelfennig, *The EU, NATO and the Integration of Europe: Rules and Rhetoric* (Cambridge: Cambridge University Press, 2003); K. M. Fierke and A. Wiener, 'Constructing Institutional Interests: EU and NATO Enlargement,' *Journal of European Public Policy*, 6:5 (1999); U. Sedelmeier, 'Sectoral Dynamics of EU Enlargement: Advocacy, Access and Alliances in a Composite Policy,' *Journal of European Public Policy*, 9:4 (August 2002); H. Sjursen, *Questioning EU Enlargement: Europe in Search of Identity* (London: Routledge, 2007).

15 *Europe* 6094 (27 October 1993), 10.

16 R. N. Lebow, 'The Memory of Politics in Postwar Europe,' in Lebow *et al.*, *The Politics of Memory in Postwar Europe*, 25.

17 Paradigmatic works of nationalism generally all maintain that a shared past is a necessary precondition for any form of nationality. See C. J. Huntley Hayes, *Essays on Nationalism* (New York: The Macmillan Company, 1926); H. Kohn, *Prophets and Peoples: Studies in Nineteenth Century Nationalism* (New York: The Macmillan Company, 1946); K. W. Deutsch, *Nationalism and Social Communication: An Inquiry into the Foundations of Nationality* (Cambridge: Cambridge University Press, 1953). For a more recent treatment of these same issues, see Smith, *Stories of Peoplehood*.

18 F. Andriessen, *Prosperity and Stability in a Wider Europe*, Speech at the Atlantic CEO Institute (Dobris, Czechoslovakia: Europa Press Release, 10 June 1991), http://europa.eu/rapid/pressReleasesAction.do?reference=SPEECH/91/71&format=HTML&aged=1&language=EN&guiLanguage=en (accessed 27 February 2012). See also B. Kovrig, *The Myth of Liberation; East-Central Europe in U.S. Diplomacy and Politics since 1941* (Baltimore: Johns Hopkins University Press, 1973); J. I. Torreblanca, *The Reuniting of Europe: Promises, Negotiations and Compromises* (Aldershot: Ashgate, 2001); K. Henderson, *Back to Europe: Central and Eastern Europe and the European Union* (London: UCL Press, 1999).

19 O'Brennan, *The Eastern Enlargement of the European Union*, 5; European Commission, Directorate General for Enlargement, Information and Interinstitutional Relations Unit, *European Union Enlargement: A Historic Opportunity* (Brussels: European Commission, 2000), 4.

20 A. Lašas, 'Restituting Victims: EU and NATO Enlargements through the Lenses of Collective Guilt,' *Journal of European Public Policy*, 15:1 (January, 2008); A. Lašas, *European Union and NATO Expansion* (New York: Palgrave Macmillan, 2010), 101–104, 721–742.

21 K. Jaspers, *The Question of German Guilt*, trans. E. B. Ashton, ed. Joseph W. Koterski SJ (New York: Fordham University Press, 2001); T. Snyder, *Bloodlands* (New York: Basic Books, 2010).

22 All quotations in Lašas, 'Restituting Victims,' 106–107.

23 P. Ther, 'Die Last der Geschichte und die Falle der Erinnerung,' *Transit – Europäisches Revue*, 30 (2006). For more on the *Vertriebenenverbände*, see P. Ahonen, 'Domestic Constraints on West German Ostpolitik: The Role of the Expellee Organizations in the Adenauer Era,' *Central European History*, 31:1/2 (1998); P. Ahonen, *After the Expulsion: West Germany and Eastern Europe, 1945–1990* (Oxford: Oxford University Press, 2003).

24 H. Kohl and V. Klaus, 'German-Czech Declaration on Mutual Relations and their Future Development' (Government Declaration, Prague, 1997), http://eudocs.lib.byu.edu/index.php?title=Czech-German_Declaration&oldid=5101 (accessed 28 February 2012), art. IV; see also E. Barkan and A. Karn, 'Group Apology as Ethical Imperative,' in E. Barkan and A. Karn (eds), *Taking Wrongs Seriously: Apologies and Reconciliation* (Stanford: Stanford University Press, 2006), 9.

25 Judt, *Postwar*, 734; M. Kundera, 'The Tragedy of Central Europe,' *The New York Review of Books*, 31:7 (26 April 1984).

26 Snyder, 'Balancing the Books,' 72.

27 T. Snyder, 'Holocaust: The Ignored Reality,' *The New York Review of Books* (16 July 2009).

28 This debate over the idea of communism is still active today. See C. Douzinas and S. Žižek, *The Idea of Communism* (New York: Verso, 2013); A. Badiou, *The Communist Hypothesis* (New York: Verso, 2010). My thanks to one of the reviewers from this journal for making this point.

29 R. Conquest, *Reflections on a Ravaged Century* (New York: W. W. Norton, 2000), xii; C. S. Maier, 'Hot Memory ... Cold Memory: On the Political Half-Life of Fascist and Communist Memory,' *Transit – Europäisches Revue*, 22 (2002).

30 Quoted in S. Troebst, 'Halecki Revisited: Europe's Conflicting Cultures of Remembrance,' in M. Pakier and B. Stråth (eds), *A European Memory? Contested Histories and Politics of Remembrance* (New York: Berghahn Books, 2010), 60.

31 T. Zhurzhenko, 'The Geopolitics of Memory,' *Eurozine* (10 May 2007), www.eurozine.com/the-geopolitics-of-memory (accessed 12 May 2007).

32 J. Hooper, 'Mussolini Wasn't That Bad, Says Berlusconi,' *Guardian* (12 September 2002). For more on the *esuli*, see P. Ballinger, *History in Exile: Memory and Identity at the Borders of the Balkans* (Princeton: Princeton University Press, 2003).

33 Reported in J. Golob, P. Vodopivec, T. Hribar, J. Prunk, and M. Basta, 'Razprava' in J. Golob, P. Vodopivec, T. Hribar, J. Prunk, and M. Basta (eds) *Zbornik: Žrtve vojne in revolucije* (Ljubljana: Državni svet Republike Slovenije, 2005), 185; S. Žižek, 'Kazen mora biti stroga, a pravična,' *Delo, Sobotna priloga* (12 February 2005), 9; B. Repe, 'Uvodni poudarki,' in Z. Čepič and T. Velagič (eds), *Odpor 1941: Zbornik s posveta ob 60. obletnici Osvobodilne fronte slovenskega naroda* (Ljubljana: Društvo za preučevanje zgodovine, literature in antropologije in Glavni odbor Zveze združenj borcev in udeležencev narodnoosvobodilnega boja Slovenije, 2001), 9.

34 European Parliament, 'Report of Proceedings,' P6_CRE(2005)01–27, 27 January 2005, www.europarl.europa.eu/RegData/seance_pleniere/compte_rendu/traduit/2005/01–27/P6_CRE(2005)01–27_DEF_EN.pdf (accessed 29 February 2012).

35 BBC, 'Call for Europe-Wide Swastika Ban,' *BBC News* (17 January 2005), http://news.bbc.co.uk/2/hi/uk_news/4178643.stm (accessed 15 September 2006); BBC,

'EU Ban Urged on Communist Symbols,' *BBC News* (3 February 2005), http://news. bbc.co.uk/2/hi/europe/4234335.stm (accessed 15 September 2006); O. Lungescu, 'EU Rejects Communist Symbol Ban,' *BBC News* (8 February 2005), http://news.bbc. co.uk/2/hi/europe/4248425.stm (accessed 15 September 2006).

36 European Commission, 'The Memory of the Crimes Committed by Totalitarian Regimes in Europe: Report from the Commission to the European Parliament and to the Council,' (Brussels, COM(2010) 783 final, 22 December 2010, www.europarl. europa.eu/RegData/docs_autres_institutions/commission_europeenne/com/2010/ 0783/COM_COM(2010)0783_EN.pdf (accessed 29 February 2012), 6;

37 M. J. Prutsch, *European Historical Memory: Policy Challenges and Perspectives* (Brussels: Directorate-General for Internal Policies: Culture and Education, 2013), 30; European Parliament, 'European Parliament Resolution of 2 April 2009 on European Conscience and Totalitarianism,' P6_TA(2009)0213, 2 April 2009, www.europarl. europa.eu/RegData/seance_pleniere/textes_adoptes/definitif/2009/04–02/0213/ P6_TA(2009)0213_EN.pdf (accessed 29 February 2012), §H, G.

38 European Parliament, 'European Parliament Resolution of 2 April 2009 on European Conscience and Totalitarianism,' §K; K. Hammerstein, 'Europa und seine bedrückende Erbschaft. Europäische Perspektiven auf die Aufarbeitung von Diktaturen,' in W. R. Assmann and A. Graf von Kainein (eds), *Erinnerung und Gesellschaft. Formen der Aufarbeitung von Diktaturen in Europa* (Berlin: Metropol Verlag, 2011), 11.

39 R. G. Suny, *The Revenge of the Past: Nationalism, Revolution, and the Collapse of the Soviet Union* (Stanford: Stanford University Press, 1993).

40 Assmann, 'Europe,' 11–25. See also J.-W. Müller, 'Europäische Erinnerungspolitik revisited,' *Transit – Europäisches Revue*, 33 (2007).

41 Parts of this section were previously published as P. J. Verovšek, 'The Immanent Potential of Economic Integration: A Critical Reading of the Eurozone Crisis,' *Perspectives on Politics*, 15:2 (2017).

42 M. J. Shapiro, 'The Moralized Economy in Hard Times,' *Theory & Event*, 14:4 (2011); G. Soros and G. P. Schmitz, *The Tragedy of the European Union: Disintegration or Revival?* (New York: Public Affairs, 2014), xxix.

43 M. Aglietta, 'The European Vortex,' *New Left Review*, 75 (2012), 15.

44 This chronology follows the analysis of the former head of the European Central Bank (ECB), Jean-Claude Trichet, 'The State of the Euro,' paper presented at the Center for European Studies, Harvard University, Cambridge, MA, USA, 16 October 2013. For a summary, see C. Lapavitsas, 'Financialised Capitalism: Crisis and Financial Expropriation,' *Historical Materialism*, 17:2 (2009), 114–148.

45 H.-W. Sinn, *Casino Capitalism: How the Financial Crisis Came About and What Needs to be Done Now* (Oxford: Oxford University Press, 2010), 20; D. Lizoane and M. Ecke, 'European Youth Need a Change from a New German Government,' *Social Europe Journal* (14 November 2013), 2.

46 S. Sakellaropoulos and P. Sotiris, 'Postcards from the Future: The Greek Debt Crisis, the Struggle against the EU-IMF Austerity Package and the Open Questions for Left Strategy,' *Constellations*, 21:2 (2014), 263.

47 J.-C. Piris, *The Future of Europe: Towards a Two-Speed EU?* (Cambridge: Cambridge University Press, 2012), 42; D. Marsh, *The Euro: The Battle for the New Global Currency* (New Haven: Yale University Press, 2011); Sinn, *Casino Capitalism*, 228.

48 C. Offe, *Contradictions of the Welfare State* (Cambridge, MA: MIT Press, 1984); C. Hay, *Re-Stating Social and Political Change* (Philadelphia: Open University Press, 1996).

49 Van Middelaar, *The Passage to Europe*, xiv.

50 R. Tuck, *Free Riding* (Cambridge, MA: Harvard University Press, 2008).

51 Aglietta, 'The European Vortex,' 24; D. Marsh, *Europe's Deadlock: How the Euro Crisis could be Solved, and Why it Won't Happen* (New Haven: Yale University Press, 2013), 23.

52 M. Blyth, *Austerity: The History of a Dangerous Idea* (Oxford: Oxford University Press, 2013), 7; C. Joerges, 'Law and Politics in Europe's Crisis: On the History of the Impact of an Unfortunate Configuration,' *Constellations*, 21:2 (2014), 250.

53 Bratsis, 'Legitimation Crisis and the Greek Explosion,' 194; Sakellaropoulos and Sotiris, 'Postcards from the Future,' 270.

54 Dutch MEP Ieke van den Burg quoted in van Middelaar, *The Passage to Europe*, 265; C. Lapavitsas *et al.*, *Crisis in the Eurozone* (London: Verso, 2012), 90–91.

55 In A. Burr Overstreet, 'The Nature and Prospects of European Institutions: A Report on the Second Carnegie Endowment Conference on International Organization,' *Journal of Common Market Studies*, 3:2 (1964), 131–132.

56 R. Bellamy and A. Warleigh, 'From an Ethics of Integration to an Ethics of Participation: Citizenship and the Future of the European Union,' *Millennium*, 27:3 (September, 1998), 449.

57 C. K. Ansell, C. Parsons, and K. A. Darden, 'Dual Networks in European Regional Development Policy,' *Journal of Common Market Studies*, 25:3 (1997), 347–375.

58 S. Castle, 'After Scots' Referendum, into the Unknown,' *International Herald Tribune* (11 February 2012).

59 For more, see A. Sierp and J. Wüstenberg, 'Linking the Local and the Transnational: Rethinking Memory Politics in Europe,' *Journal of Contemporary European Studies*, 23:3 (2015).

60 J. Glaurdić, *The Hour of Europe: Western Powers and the Breakup of Yugoslavia* (New Haven: Yale University Press, 2011).

61 O. Anastasakis, K. Nicolaïdis, and K. Öktem, *In the Long Shadow of Europe: Greeks and Turks in the Era of Postnationalism* (Boston: Martinus Nijhoff, 2009), Part I.

62 S. Benhabib and T. Isiksel, 'Ancient Battles, New Prejudices, and Future Perspectives: Turkey and the EU,' *Constellations*, 13:2 (2006), 221.

63 W. Hallstein, *Europäische Reden*, ed T. Oppermann and J. Kohler (Stuttgart: Deutsche Verlags-Anstalt, 1979), 439.

64 Langenbacher, 'Collective Memory as a Factor in Political Culture and International Relations,' 21.

65 *Frankfurter Allgemeine Zeitung* (13 March 2008), translation mine.

66 European Commission, 'The Memory of the Crimes Committed by Totalitarian Regimes in Europe,' 10.

67 Bischof, 'Victims?' 23.

68 T. Zhurzhenko, 'Land of Confusion: Ukraine, the EU and the Tymoshenko Case,' *Eurozine* (14 December 2011), www.eurozine.com/land-of-confusion/ (accessed 17 December 2011); T. Zhurzhenko, 'The Myth of Two Ukraines,' *Transit – Europäisches Revue*, 23 (2002); K. A. Darden, *Resisting Occupation: Mass Literacy and the Creation of Durable National Loyalties* (Cambridge: Cambridge University Press, 2012).

69 Krastev, 'The Age of Populism,' 12; P. Rosanvallon, *Counter-Democracy: Politics in an Age of Distrust*, trans. A. Goldhammer (Cambridge: Cambridge University Press, 2008).

70 K. Devine, 'Not All "Over-65s" are in Favour of Brexit: Britain's Wartime Generation are Almost as Pro-EU as Millennials,' *LSE Brexit Blog* (21 March 2019), https://blogs.lse.ac.uk/europpblog/2019/03/21/not-all-the-over-65s-are...rexit-britains-wartime-generation-are-almost-as-pro-eu-as-millennials/ (accessed 23 March 2019).

71 R. Wilson, *Meeting the Challenge of Cultural Diversity in Europe: Moving Beyond the Crisis* (Cheltenham: Edward Elgar, 2018), 90.

72 J.-W. Müller, *What is Populism?* (Philadelphia: Pennsylvania University Press, 2016), 59. For more on the period of postwar prosperity, see T. Piketty, *Capital in the Twenty-First Century*, trans. A. Goldhammer (Cambridge, MA: The Belknap Press of Harvard University Press, 2014).

73 For an academic statement of this desire, see Streeck, 'Small-State Nostalgia.'

74 T. Snyder, *The Road to Unfreedom: Russia, Europe, America* (London: Bodley Head, 2018), 119, 76, 79 (emphasis added). For more on the economic side of this narrative, see D. Rodrik, *The Globalization Paradox: Democracy and the Future of the World Economy* (New York: W. W. Norton & Company, 2011), 67–88. See also P. J. Verovšek, 'History and the Inevitability of Eternity,' *Eurozine* (24 July 2018), www.eurozine.com/mapping-road-unfreedom/ (accessed 25 July 2018).

75 Charmley, *Splendid Isolation?*, 23; Hoffmann, *The European Sisyphus*, 58.

76 S. Rose, 'The Dunkirk Spirit: How Cinema is Shaping Britain's Identity in the Brexit Era,' *Guardian* (20 July 2017).

77 These differences may reflect important differences in the collective remembrance of the constituent nations within the United Kingdom. Unfortunately, I cannot go into these variations here.

78 J. Curtice, 'Brexit: Behind the Referendum,' *Political Insight*, 7:2 (2016), 7.

79 J. Bittner, 'Europe's Angry Old Men,' *New York Times* (25 June 2016), A21; S. B. Hobolt, 'The Brexit Vote: A Divided Nation, a Divided Continent,' *Journal of European Public Policy*, 23:9 (2016).

80 See T. W. Adorno, E. Frenkel-Brunswik, D. J. Levinson, and R. Nevitt Sanford, *The Authoritarian Personality*, introduction by P. Gordon (London: Verso, 2019).

81 E. Kaufmann, 'Brexit Voters: NOT the Left Behind,' *Fabian Review* (24 June 2016), 5.

82 R. Inglehart and P. Norris, 'Trump and the Populist Authoritarian Parties: The Silent Revolution in Reverse,' *Perspectives on Politics*, 15:2 (2017), 446.

83 Seymour Martin Lipset, *Political Man: The Social Bases of Politics* (Garden City: Doubleday, 1960), ch. 5.

84 R. Inglehart, *The Silent Revolution: Changing Values and Political Styles among Western Publics* (Princeton: Princeton University Press, 1977); Inglehart and Norris, 'Trump and the Populist Authoritarian Parties,' 444.

85 J.-W. Müller, 'Homo Orbánicus,' *New York Review of Books* (5 April 2018).

86 J. Rupnik, 'Evolving or Revolving? Central Europe since 1989,' *Eurozine* (15 December 2017), www.eurozine.com/evolving-or-revolving-central-europe-since-1989/ (accessed 30 December 2017).

87 J. Rupnik, 'Surging Illiberalism in the East,' *Journal of Democracy*, 27:4 (2016), 83–84.

88 C. R. Browning, *Ordinary Men: Reserve Police Battalion 101 and the Final Solution in Poland* (New York: Penguin, 2001); J. T. Gross, *Neighbors: The Destruction of the Jewish Community in Jedwabne, Poland* (Princeton: Princeton University Press, 2001); Lebow *et al.*, *The Politics of Memory in Postwar Europe*; J. Mark, *The Unfinished Revolution: Making Sense of the Communist Past in Central-Eastern Europe* (New Haven: Yale University Press, 2010).

89 K. Gebert, 'Projecting Poland and its Past,' *Eurozone* (27 April 2018); D. E. Lipstadt, *Denying the Holocaust: The Growing Assault on Truth and Memory* (New York: The Free Press, 2012).

90 J. Blustein, *The Moral Demands of Memory* (Cambridge: Cambridge University Press, 2008).

91 J. Habermas, 'Why Europe Needs a Constitution' in Oddvar Eriksen *et al.*, *Developing a Constitution for Europe*, 18.

92 P. Scheffer, 'EU Can No Longer Play the War Card,' *De Morgen* (19 January 2012), www.presseurop.eu/en/content/article/1416561-eu-can-no-longer-play-war-card (accessed 20 January 2012).

93 T. Snyder, 'A Way Out for Ukraine,' *New York Review of Books Blog* (5 December 2013), www.nybooks.com/blogs/nyrblog/2013/dec/05/ukraine-protests-way-out (accessed 5 December 2013).

Part II

Memory and the future of Europe

Chapter 5

Changing generations, negative memory, and non-economic resources

'The pardon and the promise': This magnificent formula by the philosopher Hannah Arendt illustrates the approach of the founding fathers of Europe. To pardon the enemies of yesterday is not to forget. To promise is to ensure future generations ... have their full place in the international community.
    Former President of the European Communities, Jacques Delors (2007)

The economically necessary and the politically possible

Following critical theory's two-stage approach to social research, my explanatory-diagnostic reconstruction of the history of European integration in the first two chapters of Part I showed how the leaders of Europe built on the cognitive, motivational, and justificatory resources of collective memory to create a European political community over the course of the second half of the twentieth century. In the previous chapter I traced how the project has started to sputter with the passing of the generations that had experienced the rupture of 1945 first-hand. Since the turn of the millennium these new leaders have found it difficult to resolve the interlocking economic and political problems plaguing Europe without the resources of collective remembrance that had previously served as the engine for integration through community-based institutions at the continental level.

In addition to providing a diagnostic analysis of the crisis of the present, the approach of the Frankfurt School also calls on the social critic to identify pathways for emancipation 'from those forms of social life and of the juridical, political, and cultural orders which have become a straitjacket.' Unlike empirical or positivistic approaches, critical theory does not merely identify phenomena in a dispassionate manner. Instead, it is also invested in resolving the social pathologies it identifies. In his programmatic text outlining the differences between 'Traditional and Critical Theory' (1937), Max Horkheimer notes that the Frankfurt School's 'presentation of societal contradictions is not merely an expression of the concrete historical situation but also a force within it to stimulate change.'[1]

I take up this agenda in Part II. My reflections on memory and the future of European integration in this second, 'anticipatory-utopian' section of this book are situated within the shadow of the crisis of the Eurozone and the spread of far-right populism across the continent. The economic problems of the EMU and the return of nationalism feed off each other as part of a broader attack on the postwar European project. In fact, the latter is increasingly preventing the resolution of the former, as the rise of populism is preventing the cross-border cooperation necessary to repair the 'flaws in the construction of the single currency.'[2] These disputes have a decidedly tragic quality, as there is broad agreement that no lasting solution to Europe's current malaise is possible without 'significantly increasing the degree of political union.' Christine Lagarde, who has served as the head of both the International Monetary Fund and the ECB, has encouraged the political leaders of the EU to 'get on with the union. Make sure you have a banking union, down the road fiscal union, and that you keep that currency zone together and solid.'[3]

Unfortunately, the nationalistic desire to protect individual state interests has stood in the way of the cooperation necessary to resolve the European crisis. Jürgen Habermas therefore argues that the EU is 'trapped in the dilemma between, on the one side, the economic policies required to preserve the Euro and, on the other, the political steps to closer integration.' His colleague Claus Offe makes a similar point, noting that 'the mismatch between what is economically necessary and what is politically feasible can be seen on both sides of Europe's north–south divide.' The crisis of the Eurozone thus presents the peoples of the continent with a choice: either dismantle the euro by repatriating monetary policy to the member-states, or complete the EMU through 'greater centralisation and political unification.'[4]

Building on my crisis diagnosis, I argue for the latter course of action. In an increasingly globalised, multicultural, and interdependent global order, stepping back and decreasing cooperation is not realistic, nor is it desirable, as the difficulties delivering Brexit in Great Britain and Northern Ireland make clear. To paraphrase Jean Monnet, it is impossible to unscramble the eggs once they have been scrambled. Resolving the issues facing the EU at the start of the twenty-first century will require Europeans to expand their conception of the politically possible once more, just as their leaders were able to do at the beginning of the postwar era by drawing on the cognitive, motivational, and justificatory resources of the rupture of 1945. However, whereas in earlier periods such moves were supported by a 'permissive consensus' among the citizens of Europe, the recent development of a 'constraining dissensus' has increased the danger that this will occur as an elite-driven project.[5]

This chapter begins my reflections on collective memory and the future of Europe by arguing that the EU's problems are driven by the fragmentation and subsequent loss of the cognitive, motivational, and justificatory resources of the European rupture. As 1945 has ceased to be the central pivot around which European narratives of collective memory are organised, 'negative' conflictual narratives of memory have replaced the 'positive' constructive frameworks that defined the first sixty years of integration. I argue that the return of divisive narratives of economic suffering – especially those based on the collective memory of the hyperinflation of the 1930s instead of the cooperative lessons of the European rupture – help to explain the rise of protectionism and the re-emergence of right-wing nationalism on the continent at the start of the twenty-first century.

This insight leads me to address the problems that the change in political generations poses for the EU in the second section. I argue that the economic focus of integration, which worked as long as it was backed by normative resources of collective remembrance, endangers the entire project at a time when leaders with no personal memories of total war increasingly calculate their European interests in terms of short-term cost–benefit analysis. The following section focuses on political education and the development of a supranational understanding history as the foundation for a truly postnational European identity. Similar to the current generation of leaders, the cohort born after 1980 also does not have personal memories of Europe's age of total war. However, this younger generation is equipped with new, pro-European resources as a result of growing up on a continent of open borders. Since waiting for this cohort to revitalise the European project of community integration is a long-term solution at best, I argue that it is only possible to maintain hope for the future if Europe can survive the crisis it faces at the start of the twenty-first century.

The final section addresses the need for the citizens of Europe to take control of their own destinies by becoming more assertive in the processes of opinion- and will-formation at the supranational level. Habermas and other critical theorists have focused on the issue of leadership precisely because the member-states have the power to shift the contours of the politically think-able, just as 'the Six' did in forming the first supranational institutions of the ECSC. However, unlike their predecessors in the 1950s, it is unfeasible to do so solely 'from above.' Leaders must rally public support so that they can actualise these goals 'by adopting [them] as a conscious aim.'[6] The goal of a hopeful, forward-looking, emancipatory critical theory of European inte-gration must be to convince those on the continent most affected by these problems that they can change the conditions around them through active citizenship, instead of simply accepting them as passive consumers.

The dangers of negative memory[7]

Immediately following the onset of the crisis of the Eurozone in 2010, the logic of instrumental rationality led the member-states of northern Europe to take a principled stand against cross-border fiscal transfers. Citing the treaties and the inflation-fighting mandate of the ECB, Germany and the Netherlands defended their national-interest and the letter of European law to rebuff calls for greater solidarity and financial assistance from Portugal, Ireland, Spain, and Greece. The northern narrative against bailouts held that the south needed to suffer the pain of austerity in order to learn the lessons of past profligacy.

Over the course of the crisis this seemingly principled narrative has become less instrumentally attractive. Although Germany profited from the early stages of the crisis as a result of greater investment and low interest rates on its sover-eign bonds, the economic downturn in other member-states eventually started to impact growth in the Federal Republic, demonstrating the dependence of its export-driven model on the rest of the EU.[8] This conclusion is supported by evidence that a Greek exit from the Eurozone could cost Germany more than €64 billion in lost credit and €73 billion in economic growth. Such a 'Grexit' could also 'trigger a wave of further Eurozone exits in Europe's south' with 'devastating' implications for Germany and the rest of Europe.[9]

In earlier periods of integration, constructive narratives of collective memory based on the rupture of 1945 gave political leaders new perspectives on the present, motivating them to make difficult political choices, and helping them explain these decisions to the public. Despite the reversal in the instru-mental logical of economic support among political elites as a result of the length and depth of the economic crisis, they are faced with the need to (re)-convince their populations to buy into a non-nationalistic, European narrative.

Unfortunately, the taglines of 'lazy Greeks' and 'profligate southerners' that northern European elites implanted in the early stages of the crisis are still broadly accepted. Similarly, the southern narrative of northern Europeans as 'pitiless' and 'uncaring' taskmasters has also proven difficult to dislodge. Political leaders are thus constrained by their overly successful initial framing of Europe's problems through a nationalistic lens.

This has led to a return to the kinds of conflictual frameworks of remembrance that dominate the literature within collective memory studies. In the early stages of the crisis (roughly 2010–12), pre-rupture memories were deployed to justify nationalistic stances based on short-term economic interests within each individual member-state. In the south, images of war and occupation have been transplanted into economic debates over the common currency and fiscal reform. As a result, *Der Spiegel* notes, 'Hardly a day goes by without Chancellor Angela Merkel being depicted in a Nazi uniform somewhere. Swastikas are a common sight as well.' This is especially true in Greece, where European officials are portrayed as the National Socialists who occupied the country during the Second World War. As the crisis has spread to other countries, so has this Nazi imagery. For example, in Italy *Il Giornale* portrayed Merkel waving in a Hitleresque salute while declaring the 'Fourth Reich' under the headline, 'Germany has won; Italy, Europe and the euro have lost.'[10]

Collective memory has increasingly played a negative role in northern Europe as well. Most notably, the German fear of inflation is rhetorically tied to remembrance of the economic crisis of 1923, which was caused by the government's use of the printing press to finance public expenditure. The so-called 'Great Inflation' had far-reaching consequences, destroying the German middle class, the credibility of the Weimar Republic, and German faith in democracy in the aftermath of the First World War. The lessons of German collective memory contained within these experiences were institutionalised within the conservative, inflation-fighting mandate of the ECB. However, despite its historical grounding, the deployment of this narrative has been highly strategic. Like most uses of negative memory, it takes historical events out of context and deploys the lessons of the past in a divisive way to pin the blame on out-groups (Greece and the rest of the European south), while shielding in-groups from responsibility for its actions (German and northern financial elites).

Although the narrative of the Great Inflation sounds plausible, it is actually a recent construction of German political elites used to justify an economically driven, nationalistic stance vis-à-vis Greece and the other crisis-ridden southern states. Upon closer examination, linking the German fear of inflation to the experience of the 1920s is not backed up by historical evidence. From 1960 to 1999, average annual inflation in Germany under the leadership of the German Central Bank – the *Bundesbank* or *Buba* – was 3.2 per cent. Since the introduction of the common currency in 2000, inflation has been 1.5 per cent.

Despite this fact, the collective memory of German hyperinflation has been deployed to support strident criticism of the ECB's profligacy. This framing has proved to be highly successful, as polling data shows that the German fear of inflation has only risen since the end of the Cold War. The increased salience of this narrative since 1990 is difficult to explain if the fear of inflation were actually the result of memories of 1923 and not merely of their strategic deployment as a way of asserting German economic preferences within the ECB, as well as a loss of the lessons of the rupture of 1945 resulting from generational turnover.[11]

The use of these 'negative' frameworks of collective memory to further short-term German interests is not new. They were also deployed early in the creation of the EMU by German Chancellor Helmut Kohl in order to justify his insistence that the ECB be modelled on the single, inflation-fighting mandate of the *Buba*, not on the dual mandate of the American Federal Reserve, which seeks to manage both inflation and unemployment. This allowed Germany to build its ordoliberal preferences for price stability into the institutional DNA of the Eurozone.[12] The insistence on enshrining teutonic approaches based on German collective memories of the interwar crisis reflects what Habermas has referred to as the Federal Republic's 'Deutschmark nationalism' (*DM-Nationalismus*). This turn of phrase describes how 'German pride in West Germany's economic accomplishments … has not lacked an edge of condescension toward those of Germany's postwar allies who are its economic competitors and have not done so well.'[13]

The basic problem is that the German *economic* narrative of hyperinflation forgets and silences the *political* lessons of the interwar years.[14] The Great Inflation was just one episode in the collapse of the economic and political order in the aftermath of the First World War. By constructing a narrative of the dangers of inflation to justify imposing austerity on Greece, the German political elite seems to have forgotten that it was actually the austerity and unemployment brought on by the Great Depression of 1929 – building on the previous suffering associated with hyperinflation – that set the stage for Hitler's rise to power.

Drawing on this broader perspective could help the leaders of Europe (and of the Federal Republic) to reinvigorate the older, postwar narrative of the past that ties into Europe's origins as a reaction against the crimes of totalitarianism. Although the comparison may seem facile at first glance, there are striking similarities in the conditions that led to the rise of Nazism in Germany and the deteriorating situation in Greece in the wake of the Great Recession.[15] By focusing excessively on its own memories of rapid inflation, Germany is overlooking the fact that its policy prescriptions are creating the preconditions for a renewal of fascism in Europe. The danger is that long-term economic stagnation may result in growing support for fascism and the extremist views of groups like the Greek Golden Dawn party, whose electoral flag features a swastika-like emblem, just as they did in Germany during the Great Depression. To a certain extent, this may already be visible in the rise of illiberal democracy in Poland and Hungary and the success of far-right popu-list parties such as the Rassemblement national in France, the Lega in Italy, and the Alternative für Deutschland in Germany.[16]

Totalitarianism – in both its fascist and its communist flavours – remains surprisingly salient in European narratives of collective memory. Deteriorating economic conditions on top of the hopelessness created by seemingly never-ending austerity not only threatens the EU as an institution; it also directly endangers the anti-fascist foundations of the postwar European project. The spectre of a resurgent fascism might help Europeans to remember the whole narrative of the European rupture in its proper perspective. Despite its recent negative usages, the leaders of the current generation may be able to reinvig-orate collective memory as a positive, constructive resource for European cooperation by abandoning their reliance on economic thinking and their div-isive use of the past to fan the flames of nationalism.

Whereas the political project of integration built on the constructive resources of collective remembrance, the economic crisis has signalled a return of memory in its negative form, as opposed to the positive or 'constructive' postrupture valence I outlined in chapter 1. This is dangerous both for the institutions of the EU and for the stability of Europe as a whole. Such strategic uses of the past for nationalistic, self-interested economic gain also threaten the immanent potential for transcendence through deeper integration that exists within the EMU. However, this does not mean that all hope is lost.

Generational change and new justifications for Europe

The founders of the European Communities consistently credited their trans-nationally shared collective memory of the past for helping them to imagine, motivate, and justify the creation of Europe as a community-based project.

Memory and the future of Europe

For early postwar leaders such as Jean Monnet, Robert Schuman, and Konrad Adenauer, the European Communities were born out of the rupture of 1945 and the confrontation with totalitarianism in both its fascist and communist forms. Ever since the Schuman Declaration of 9 May 1950, the narrative of supranational Europe as a product of the experience of war and suffering has dominated the continent's political discourse.[17]

Despite its importance in the early history of integration, it is unclear what role collective memories of the rupture of 1945 can continue to play on the continent in the future. At the beginning of the third millennium, the generations that experienced and could remember the war directly are no longer active in public life. As a result, it is becoming increasingly clear that 'Europe can no longer play the war card.' The crumbling of the moral imperative of the past has robbed the EU of its normative foundations, making it more vulnerable to the problems raised by both the accession of the postcommunist states of East-Central Europe and the Eurozone crisis.

It is well established within memory studies that the collective remembrance of key experiences loses its salience with the passage of time. As Paul Scheffer points out, 'Nightmare images of a possible return to previous violent conflicts serve only as a distraction ... Beyond "never again," there is a need for a renewed justification for European integration.' Neil Fligstein reinforces this point by showing that older cohorts who can still remember the war express more support for integration and generally have more European identities.[18]

The need to find new arguments for integration highlights the importance of generational dynamics in political life. As the individuals that can still remember the war have started to pass away, the cognitive, motivational, and justificatory resources that had driven the push towards community-based integration have also dried up. For the previous generations of West Europeans, economics was the gateway to European political unity. During the postwar era, collective memory provided a corrective balance to the narrow, nationalistic cost–benefit calculations of economics. At the start of the twenty-first century this is no longer the case. The loss of the normative resources of collective memory helps explain the inability of the current generation of leaders to articulate a vision that goes beyond the instrumental reasoning of economics.

The so-called *Erfahrungsgeneration* ('generation of experience') defined the early history of integration. Having come of age before the Great War, they lived through the rupture of 1914 through 1945 as adults. It was the break in historical time created by these experiences that transformed their 'historical knowledge ... into expectations' that allowed them to conceive of a new future in the present.[19] As the world they had grown up in was torn asunder, this constellation of leaders, including Monnet, Schuman, and Adenauer, was forced to build on the resources provided by their lived experience of the past to redefine the place of nation-states and nationalism within Europe. The result was the foundation of the European Communities in the 1950s. In this early period, the European movement received vocal philosophical support from individuals like Max Horkheimer in Germany and Jean-Paul Sartre in France. Both of these philosophers and public intellectuals believed that the European experience of wartime resistance should play a role in the revival of democratic values on the continent.[20]

By the late 1960s this temporal grouping was replaced by the *Flakhelfer-Generation* ('anti-aircraft helper generation'), which draws its name from the fact that many of its members – at least in Germany – were called up from reserve units and the Hitler Youth to help defend the German fatherland as teenagers in the last days of the war. Unlike the previous cohort, these so-called 'forty-fivers' experienced the break in tradition caused by the Second World War as young adults. This phase of life – roughly between fifteen and thirty – is a key period for the development of generational memories.[21] From a philosophical perspective this generation was defined by the work of Jürgen Habermas.

The political achievements of the *Flakhelfer* resulted in the second major phase of European integration in the late 1980s and early 1990s. By 'playing the market,' Jacques Delors, François Mitterrand, and Helmut Kohl pushed through the Single European Act (1986) to complete the common market, opened intra-European borders with the Schengen Agreement, and laid the foundation for the euro in the Treaty on European Union (1992) signed at Maastricht.[22] These steps to 'deepen' the institutional roots of integration set the stage for the 'widening' of Europe to the postcommunist states of East-Central Europe starting in 2004.

At the start of the twenty-first century the leadership positions in Europe have passed to a cohort of leaders with no shared collective memory of the Second World War. While this generation still pays homage to the ideal of Europe, their commitment is not as deep. Although more than sixty years of integration and the development of European law have given them the cognitive tools for thinking about integration, they have neither the motivational commitment nor the justificatory arguments to convince populations that increasingly do not remember the war either.

This change is perhaps most obvious in the handover of the German Chancellorship from Helmut Kohl to Gerhard Schröder in 1998. Born in 1930, Kohl used his position as chancellor to deepen integration by laying the foundations for the EMU. By contrast, while Schröder accepted the EMU as a given, he admitted that it was not a high priority. Born in 1944, two decades after the forty-fivers, Schröder rejected the seemingly ingrained Europeanist instinct of postwar German foreign policy. He argued that it was time for Berlin to pursue its national interest without shame for its Nazi past. Schröder noted that for his generation of Germans, being European was a matter of choice, not obligation.[23] This perspective is shared by his successor, Angela Merkel, as well as many other leaders at the start of the twenty-first century.

Habermas has observed these changes with angst, noting the 'remarkable contrast between the expectations and demands of those who pushed for European unification immediately after World War II, and those who contemplate the continuation of this project today.'[24] It is obvious that with the passing of time, 'The original scorched memory of Hitler and Stalin and the craving for obverse reconciliation [can] no longer drive the process of European integration as they once did.'[25] Whereas the European movement originally used economics as a means to achieve political ends, economic welfare has increasingly become its sole *raison d'être*.

The Great Recession of 2008 exacerbated these pre-existing problems. Commenting on Europe's downward spiral, Habermas has described the current generation of leaders as 'normatively disarmed' (*normativ abgerüstet*), since they lack the cognitive, motivational, and justificatory resources to think beyond narrow economic self-interest. He notes that 'since Gerhard Schröder took office a normatively unambitious generation has been in power which has become preoccupied with a short-winded approach to the day-to-day problems … Conscious of the diminishing room for political manoeuvre, these people shy away from farsighted goals and constructive projects, let alone an undertaking like European unification.'[26]

What is most interesting – and most frightening as well – is the extent to which the Eurozone crisis seems to be the product of the same impulses that drove the Great Depression in the late 1920s and early 1930s. During the early years of the Institute for Social Research, the first generation of the Frankfurt School identified the inability of instrumental reason to think about ends as one of the underlying pathologies of European development. As production becomes an end in itself, reason develops into a slave of profit, thus losing the ability to set goals beyond the assurance of greater economic welfare. In the words of Herbert Marcuse, the triumph of instrumental reason results in a 'comfortable, smooth, reasonable, democratic unfreedom [that] prevails in advanced industrial civilization.' This leads to the creation of '*one-dimensional thought and behaviour*' among individuals in society, who no longer conceive of themselves as active citizens, but merely as passive consumers. Despite their differences, the members of the Frankfurt School saw the expansion of instrumental rationality as one of the driving forces in the rise of fascism and of what they called the 'authoritarian personality.'[27]

The most alarming aspect of this development is that from the perspective of the individual the descent into the trap of instrumental reason is completely logical. In 'Some Implications of Modern Technology' (1941), Marcuse illustrates this development through the quintessentially modern example of driving an automobile on a highway. Unlike earlier modes of transportation, which adapted to the land, the highway treats topographical features as obstacles in its path, restructuring the experience of the countryside for the driver through the use of tunnels and raised viaducts.

This change is not only physical, but is communicated to individuals directly: 'Numerous signs and posters tell the traveller what to do and think; they even request his attention to the beauties of nature or the hallmarks of history.' Disobeying the directions will not only disrupt the functional equilibrium of the highway as a feat of human engineering; it is also inherently illogical. As Marcuse points out, from the perspective of the driver, the highway 'is a rational apparatus, combining utmost expediency with utmost convenience, saving time and energy, removing waste, adapting all means to the end, anticipating consequences, sustaining culpability and security.'[28]

The reflections of the early Frankfurt School on the pathologies of instrumental reason can readily be applied to the EU. Monnet's economistic vision of an '*état metallurgique*' incorporated many of the dystopian elements that the first generation of critical theorists associated with modernity and industrialisation. Given its basis in economic policy, the institutional policies of Europe have tended to promote an economic model of citizenship. This strategy of treating citizens as what Horkheimer and Adorno refer to as 'eternal consumers' worked as long as it was backed up by a broader, normative vision of solidarity based on the common experience of war and suffering. However, it has perverse consequences when cut from this mooring. As Alexandra Beasley points out, 'EU institutions are stifling the imagination of citizens, promoting a passive citizenship, in which dialogue and invention are not encouraged.'[29]

In her 'critical political theory of the post-totalitarian moment,' Hannah Arendt interprets the project of European unification as a possible solution to the 'European crisis which made possible the German conquest of the continent.'[30] However, much like the thinkers of the early Frankfurt School, she also worries about the increasing consumerisation of political life. In particular, Arendt deplored the increasing encroachment of economics into politics, a phenomenon she refers to as 'the rise of the social.' In ancient times, politics had been a forum for individuals to assert their uniqueness before their peers. Appearing in the political life of the *polis* allowed individuals to go beyond labour and work by expressing their unique human ability to act.[31]

By contrast, in the modern world politics is ruled by the laws of mass production and consumption, where unique individuals are reduced to interchangeable entities, acting not with respect to each other, but merely responding to their external, material environment. The 'substitution of behaviour for action' – which Marcuse refers to as the 'mechanics of conformity' – that comes with the replacement of citizens by consumers explains the rise of economics as the modern field of public policy *par excellence*.[32] After all, as Arendt points out, 'Economics ... could achieve a scientific character only when men had become social beings and unanimously followed certain patterns of behaviour, so that those who did not keep the rules could be considered to be asocial or abnormal.'[33]

Arendt locates the rise of the social in the thought of Karl Marx and the modern nation-state. Ironically, while the EU was founded as part of the Atlantic alliance against the Soviet Union and communism more generally, these dangers are even more prevalent within the EU, given its organisation around a common market with the goal of increasing productivity across national borders. The increasing embrace of neoliberal economic rights and freedoms by European institutions through its drive to what is usually referred to as 'negative integration' has only reinforced these tendencies. The economisation of life is reflected in schooling as well, as the goal educating individuals to be enlightened civic participants is replaced by the training of productive workers.

Marcuse observes that this approach transforms individual differences in 'insight and knowledge ... into different quanta of skill and training, to be coordinated at any time within the common framework of standardised performances.' The largest problem is that the pathologies of instrumental reason and the economisation of politics reinforce each other: 'Reason has found its resting place in the system of standardized control, production and consumption … [as a result of which] society has become indifferent and insusceptible to the impact of critical thought.'[34]

The true costs of focusing almost exclusively on economics are clearly visible in the Eurozone crisis. In the face of a crisis that requires common solutions with a shared vision, parochialism dominates. It is unfair to blame the situation solely on current political leaders, since many of their constituents share the same perspective. While the decision of the *pères de l'Europe* to use economics to achieve their political goals is understandable, this approach has clashed with the goal of 'ever closer union' among the peoples of Europe. On the contrary, the development of an 'economic and selfish model of citizen-ship … does not promote participation and solidarity among people, and does not focus on the possibility of a common future.'[35]

Noneconomic resources for the present

While the mismatch between the stated goals of the European monetary order and its actual effects may allow for the Eurozone to integrate further in order to transcend its economic troubles, a critical theory of the EU cannot be content to simply wait for these issues to work themselves out on their own. It has been a long-standing tenet of the Frankfurt School that 'phenomena assuming economic form are rarely purely economic'; on the contrary, eco-nomic problems are linked to deeper pathologies in politics and society.[36] New resources are needed precisely because the old ones rooted in the experi-ence of Europe's 'age of total war' no longer provide the necessary cognitive, motivational, and justificatory power.

This loss of normative force is due to the fact that most Europeans believe that the goal of putting 'an end to the bloody history of warfare between European nations … has already been achieved.' Additionally, welfare-based arguments in support of European integration have also increasingly been called into question. The expansions of the EU east into the postcommunist space, which were economically costly for existing member-states, and the Euro-crisis have both eroded the prosperity argument.[37] Offe notes, 'The European public needs a normatively convincing defense of the integration project, and that need grows more pressing as the project moves forward.'[38]

Although the goal of ensuring peace in Europe has largely been attained, this does not mean that the totalitarian past – in both its fascist and com-munist variations – can simply be forgotten. On the contrary, doing so would endanger this very achievement. Current imagery depicting German chancellor Angela Merkel as an invading Nazi soldier shows the continuing salience of memory in Europe. Thomas McCarthy observes, 'We cannot have a future qualitatively different from [the past] as long as we refuse to deal with it.' Unfortunately, the process Theodor Adorno referred to as 'working through the past' (*Aufarbeitung der Vergangenheit*) has no determinate endpoint.[39]

What has clearly been exhausted is the narrative of 'never again' (*nie wieder Krieg, plus jamais la guerre*). It is no longer possible to think of, motivate, and argue for Europe by raising the spectre of another world war. However, collective memories of warfare are still the foundation for the European ascriptive self-understanding. This narrative has the potential to connect past and present Europeans, even those who have no personal memories of Europe's age of total war, by 'giving them a place in a larger intergenerational story.'[40] Despite the increasing inadequacy of 'never again,' the collective memory of the rupture of 1945 brought about by the experiences bookended by the two world wars is part of what Paul Ricœur calls the European 'social imaginary.' Much like Benedict Anderson's famous image of the nation-state as an 'imagined community,' this concept brings together the collective stories and histories that inform a community's understanding of its historical roots. By giving a plot to events and our experience of time, narratives drawing on the past give order 'to what might otherwise be construed as haphazard and disconnected.'[41]

While the past must not be forgotten, the European experience of 1914 through 1945 must make the transition from the lived memory of individuals into a tradition capable of grounding a European social imaginary. The citizens of Europe must actively appropriate this new tradition. As Jeremy Waldron points out, 'Only the deliberate enterprise of recollection can sustain the moral and cultural reality of self and community.'[42] What this means can perhaps best be demonstrated by examining the role the traditions drawn from the founding of the United States, which is often seen as a large, multi-ethnic model for the EU (I present a deeper analysis of this comparison in the next chapter). The United States has long passed the point where anyone can remember its creation in 1776. However, as the origin of the American social imaginary these events continue to provide an important touchstone for the values and identity of the United States. The plot lines drawn outward in time from these events towards the present act help Americans define the markers of their particular identity and help them agree on the basic values of the American republic.[43]

Changing generations and negative memory

In order to make the transition from collective memory to tradition, from experience to a European social imaginary, Europe's foundational moments must fulfil this same two-fold purpose. As an identity marker, Scheffer argues that the 'never again' doctrine 'directs its focus inward, while the essential imperative for integration lies outside the continent.'[44] Umberto Eco echoes this sentiment. He points out that while it may be difficult to observe from the continent itself, 'a European identity reveals itself as soon as we come into contact with a non-European culture, including American culture.' While internal differences and identities will remain – just as they do between Texans and Californians in the United States – a common, European identity structures how Europeans see themselves and how others see them in external contexts. As Habermas points out, beyond the continent 'others often recognise us as Europeans, rather than as Germans or French.'[45]

In addition to being a marker of identity, the origins of a community also identify its fundamental values. Defining such European characteristics is very difficult in the abstract. Based on his sociological research, Fligstein notes that 'if Europe stands for anything, it is the completion of the Enlightenment project of democracy, rule of law, respect for the difference of others, and principles of rational discourse and science.'[46] However, there is a danger in claiming these values for Europe. On one hand, it smacks of a kind of neo-colonial attempt to impose supposedly European values on everyone. This sentiment is expressed in Tony Blair's (in)famous observation that 'Ours are not Western values. They are the universal values.' On the other hand, it also risks claiming ownership of these values too narrowly, putting them outside the domain of other parts of the world.[47]

Tying essential European values to the continent's transnationally shared experience of war and suffering between 1914 and 1945 avoids many of these problems.[48] While it does not repudiate the core values of the Enlightenment, it places them in a specific historical context, upon which Europeans can draw exclusively without claiming ownership or denying access to others. This approach allows the citizens of the member-states to identify what Bassam Tibi, one of Adorno's students, calls a 'European guiding culture' [*europäische Leitkultur*] within a historically grounded 'consensus of values and identity.'[49]

Most directly, this consensus involves a commitment to working through the many differing collective memories of totalitarianism, which are shared in some form by all member-states whether they focus on the rupture of 1945, 1989, or both.[50] Based on this experience, Europe can build on a sensitivity to human suffering, especially state-sponsored genocide, and a commitment to multilateral approaches to international affairs that favour normative, civilian power over violent intervention.[51] This historical approach to continental values specifically reflects 'Europe's memory of continental war.' It defines the European experience without excluding anyone from committing to the same basic values as a result of similar but distinct historical experiences.[52] Unlike the 'never again' doctrine, this is a perspective on collective memory that makes it 'essential that we remember the previous war, but never again use it as a pretext.'[53]

The necessity of getting Europeans to appropriate this social imaginary raises the issue of political and civic education. The importance of schooling in the education of active citizens has long been recognised within critical theory. As Seyla Benhabib points out, 'Schools are major public institutions … in that they are settings through which the future generations of a polity are formed. Schools are not "services"; they are crucibles of identity formation.'[54] Approaching education in this way assumes that it is about more than merely training the next generation of workers in the skills they will need to function as part of a productive labour force. On the contrary, schooling is the civic education of individuals so that they can become active citizens in a free and open society. Historical education can thus come to 'play the inoculating role of the direct experience of the post-war generation who had lived through the Holocaust.'[55]

Former US President Thomas Jefferson argued that civic education ought to be 'chiefly historical.' Jefferson's reasoning was that 'by apprising them of the past, [it] will enable them to judge of the future; it will avail them of the experience of other times and other nations; it will qualify them as judges of the actions and designs of men.'[56] This is the approach that I argue Europe should adopt. Understanding European postnational history in this way does not require abandoning ethnic elements or national narratives. Instead, it involves a commitment to the process of writing and debating history together in a European context.[57]

To a certain extent, this movement is already underway. Fligstein notes, 'One of the core groups involved in creating European society is the education establishment.' Since the start of the twenty-first century Ministers of Education across Europe have started to reform European schooling through the standardisation of curricula across borders and by encouraging the teaching of second or even third languages in primary schools. These reforms have had the greatest impact on the discipline of history. Instead of focusing on the emergence of their respective nation-state, teachers and students across the continent are encouraged to see national traditions within a broader

European context that 'seeks to place the good things that have occurred in a country's history as attributable to the unfolding of a European set of values.' It does not abandon the national narrative, but instead situates it in a broader continental context.[58]

In addition to creating a common historical imaginary, these changes also encourage students to study in other European states. The most successful and widespread example is the Erasmus programme, which funds university students to spend up to a year studying in another member-state. Since its inception in 1987, millions of students have taken advantage of this opportunity to study abroad.[59] This programme has also had a great sociological impact on the lives of many European students. In the words of Umberto Eco, 'Erasmus has created the first generation of young Europeans. I call it a sexual revolution: a young Catalan man meets a Flemish girl – they fall in love, they get married and they become European, as do their children.'[60]

This observation is backed by estimates that twenty-five years after the programme's inception over one million babies have been born to parents who met while they were on an Erasmus exchange. These couples and their children are predisposed to tolerant, cosmopolitan attitudes as a result of their early and intimate experience of identity within the family as culturally 'multiple and overlapping.'[61] More importantly, given the educational level of their parents, their comfort with multiple languages and different surroundings, these Erasmus children are positioned to become leading figures in politics and economics in the future.

Unfortunately, while schooling may be an important source of hope for the future, resolving the existing crisis cannot be left to a background developmental pressure that allows the people to remain in 'a state of unthinking inertia.'[62] This kind of systemic pressure leaves individuals alienated and disillusioned from their concrete forms of life (*Lebenswelten*). In order to overcome this condition, 'the agents themselves must appropriate the interpretations, explanations and criticisms proposed by the theorist.' Only through self-conscious realisation and acceptance can the peoples and leaders of Europe truly come to identify with the new forms of communal, political life that are immanent in the existing institutions of the Eurozone.[63]

Leadership, democracy, and the European public

The emancipatory vision of the future provided by both the economic and the noneconomic dimensions of my argument is plagued by two potential pitfalls.

The first is the possibility that the generation born after 1980, which grew up on a continent of open borders, might lose its pro-European predispositions as a result of the hardships inflected on this cohort by the economic austerity adopted in response to the crisis of the Eurozone. Given that nearly half of Europeans under the age of thirty-five were unemployed in parts of southern Europe at the height of the crisis of the Eurozone, at the turn of the millennium the EU risks alienating what ought to be the most pro-European generation to date. While balancing budgets on the backs of the youth may make sense in terms of a short-term national electoral calculus, it could well doom Europe's future. Second, although Europe's leaders have managed to muddle through the Eurozone crisis, they have not fully resolved the underlying pathologies that brought it about.[64] Looking to the Europeanism of the coming generations provides some hope for the future, but does little to solve the EU's current problems.

Given the deficiencies of leadership in the first generation without any collective memory of the experience of total war, it is clear that the citizens of Europe must take a stronger role in European affairs. This leads me to repose what Arendt called 'the most crucial political issue ... the question of Who rules Whom?' Historically there have been many different responses to this query. However, 'in most cases in complex societies the answer will be the naming of an office, position, or institution.' Things are not so simple in the EU. Given the complex, quasi-federal supranational community model of the EU, there are many different actors who can all claim to answer Lenin's basic political question of 'who, whom?' (кто кого?).[65] The candidates include (but are not necessarily limited to) the leaders of the member-states, the European Council, the President of the European Commission, the President of the European Council, and the President of the EP.

While this question is difficult in the abstract, 'thanks to its economic might, Germany has been catapulted by the financial crisis and the crisis of the Euro into the position of the undisputed great power.'[66] Any changes to structure of the Eurozone must have the support of Europe's economic, financial, and monetary hegemon. Instead of making decisions regarding the steps necessary to resolve the crisis jointly through the European Council or the EP, Germany's national parliament has emerged as the primary check on the democratic will-formation in Eurozone as a whole. This development has largely been driven by the Federal Republic's Constitutional Court, which has used its powers of constitutional review to ensure that all crisis measures negotiated between European leaders have to be voted on by the German Parliament. As a result, it has been acting as the *de facto* legal arbiter for all of Europe. Much like the Bundestag, the Bundesverfassungsgericht has exercised its power over all of the member-states, despite only representing the interests of one.

Although previous imperatives towards deeper integration have been met by calls for European leadership – represented by constellations of men such as Robert Schuman, Konrad Adenauer, and Jean Monnet, who spurred the creation of the first European Communities, as well as François Mitterrand, Helmut Kohl, and Jacques Delors, who undertook Europe's transition from Community to Union – leadership on its own will not resolve the problems of the EMU. In fact, the cohort of politicians in office during the crisis has shown little desire to push for the further integration that is necessary to deal with the crisis of the Eurozone. Far from leading the way, 'Politics seems to be holding its breath and dodging the key issues at the threshold leading from the economic to the political unification of Europe.' Since the EU has failed to deliver on its promises of prosperity, Europeans have 'let themselves be bothered only by problems that emerge in day-to-day affairs' with an increasingly nationalist focus.[67]

While the gradual pressure of events has pulled the EU towards greater integration, the increasingly economistic and nationally focused perspectives of many European leaders, who increasingly view integration as a zero-sum game, where each member has to hold onto as much of what they have as possible instead of expressing solidarity with others, does not inspire much hope for the future. Given its dominant position within the EU, the answer to the question of 'who rules whom?' is increasingly that Germany rules the Eurozone.[68] This response is unsatisfactory to everyone – including the Germans – who have expressed little desire to play a hegemonic role on the continent.

Despite the Federal Republic's commanding position on the continent, it is clear that given the democratic nature of all of the member-states, the answer to the question of rule *should* be the citizens of Europe. This normative realisation is reinforced by the fact that the crisis has caused the EU to impinge on the welfare and fiscal policies of member-states, i.e. to issues that are of great interest to the citizens of the EU. Although the vast majority of the effects of the crisis have been profoundly negative, the transnational economic difficulties brought on by the crisis have furthered the creation of a continental public sphere, pushing European citizens to discuss issues relating to monetary and political union across national borders in new processes of transnational opinion-formation.[69]

Memory and the future of Europe

Before 2010 the EU was often seen as a technocratic organisation that had little effect on daily life. The crisis has shattered both of these myths. It is now clear that the EU is immensely political and has huge effects on the daily lives of Europeans. As a result, the citizens of the EU are increasingly debating and 'address[ing] the same critically filtered issues and contributions at the same time.'[70] While national media still dominate, in this nascent transnational public sphere 'European issues are debated as questions of common concern using similar frames of reference.' These developments reflect a 'return of politics' to the EU in the aftermath of the interlocking monetary, financial, and fiscal crisis.[71]

It is still unclear whether the rise of these common debates will engender the kind of social solidarity necessary to promote fiscal policy across borders or whether the European public sphere can succeed in shifting the continental political centre of gravity from national leaders to the directly elected EP with an EU-wide mandate.[72] Both these tasks are daunting. However, it is important not to fatalistically bow to these difficulties, but to reassert the hope that the agitation of active European citizens unsatisfied with the status quo – as all in both the north and south seem to be – can make a difference. Despite the difficulties they face, the citizens of Europe must maintain the belief that they can embrace their necessary role as the actors who should be exercising sovereignty over the EU.[73] The experience of Europe's age of total war clearly demonstrates the perils of allowing Europe to be dominated by any one nation. If nothing else, the collective memories of the European rupture must be preserved in order to keep this lesson alive. From this perspective it is indeed true that 'memory is essential for democracy.'[74]

Conclusion

Given the EU's democratic deficit, which is caused by the high level of bureaucratisation within European institutions and the perceived distance between the Brussels-based 'Eurocrats' and the populations of the member-states, whether a more active citizenry could even affect policy on the European level without significant institutional reform is an open question. However, given recent moves towards greater democratisation, I contend that basic problem is not institutional; instead, it is rooted in the fragmentation and loss of the collective memory of the rupture of 1945. As a result, both the leaders and the peoples of Europe increasingly think about politics in terms of short-term economic gains. Whereas leaders now lack the normative resources to see integration as part of a broader moral project and have become complacent about the true stakes of politics, which can lead to death and destruction on a massive scale, most voters also display a consumerist attitude that is apathetic to political developments unless they directly affect their pocketbooks.[75]

I argue that a more active, civically engaged, less instrumentally rational population could take advantage of the bureaucratic nature of the EU to fight against the neoliberal economic interests that seem to dominate Europe at the start of the twenty-first century. Marcuse points out that if 'the will of the people can assert itself, the public bureaucracy can be a lever of democratisation,' by acting as 'the weapon that protects the people from the encroachment of special interests upon the general welfare.'[76] The activity of the EU in promoting environmental regulations against the interests of energy companies and consumer rights to privacy vis-à-vis technology giants like Apple and Google demonstrate the potential of the continent's bureaucracy to look out for the interests of its citizens, a point to which I return below.

A politically active European citizenry that uses its popular sovereignty to assert its will through the supranational institutions of the EU is crucial for the future of Europe. Despite the successes of Italy and Greece in fighting off neo- and ordo-liberal policy prescriptions from financial markets and their backers in northern Europe, the popular sovereignty of the people will have to go 'beyond the nation-state' to resist the power of international financial markets and multinational corporations in the long term: 'it is only through such new transnational steering capabilities that the *social* forces of nature that have been unleashed at the transnational level – i.e. the systemic constraints that operate without hindrance across national borders, today especially those of the global banking sector – can also be tamed.'[77]

This sceptical note should not be seen as fatalistic. On the contrary, a thicker European society that builds on a more integrated continental public sphere may well succeed in turning the existing centrifugal forces into centripetal pressure that might succeed in 'promoting a European identity across social class groups.'[78] However, this will require the citizens of the northern member-states, who have managed to ride out the crisis, to express greater solidarity for the economic and social suffering recent events have caused individuals in the south. It is only in this way that the more long-range hopes for a brighter, European future based on a common historical imaginary and the renewed pro-integration leadership of a younger generation that grew up on a continent of open borders can come to fruition.

Notes

1 M. Horkheimer, 'Traditional and Critical Theory,' in *Critical Theory: Selected Essays*, trans. M. J. O'Connell (New York: Continuum Publishing Company, 1972), 230, 215.

2 A. Giddens, *Turbulent and Mighty Continent: What Future for Europe?* (Cambridge: Polity, 2013), 25. U. Beck, *Das deutsche Europa: Neue Machtlandschaften im zeichen der Krise* (Berlin: Suhrkamp, 2012); W. Streeck, 'Interview with Wolfgang Streeck,' *The Current Moment* (3 January 2012), http://thecurrentmoment.wordpress.com/2012/01/03/interview-with-wolfgang-streeck/ (accessed 5 January 2012).

3 P. De Grauwe, 'The Governance of a Fragile Eurozone,' *Centre for European Policy Studies (CEPS)*, Brussels (4 May 2011); Lagarde quoted in Jeanna Smialek, 'IMF Chief Lagarde Calls Merkel "Unchallenged Leader" in Germany,' *Bloomberg* (10 April 2013).

4 J. Habermas, 'Democracy, Solidarity and the European Crisis,' *Social Europe Journal* (2013), www.social-europe.eu/2013/05/democracy-solidarity-and-the-eu (accessed 9 May 2014); Claus Offe, 'Europe Entrapped,' *Eurozine* (6 February 2013), www.eurozine.com/europe-entrapped/ (accessed 9 February 2013); Michael Spence, 'Five Steps to Fix the World,' *Newsweek* (31 January 2011).

5 L. Hooghe and G. Marks, 'A Postfunctionalist Theory of European Integration: From Permissive Consensus to Constraining Dissensus,' *British Journal of Political Science*, 39:1 (2008).

6 S. Benhabib, *Critique, Norm, and Utopia: A Study of the Foundations of Critical Theory* (New York: Columbia University Press, 1986), 7.

7 Parts of the following sections have previously appeared in P. J. Verovšek, 'Memory and the Euro-Crisis of Leadership: The Effects of Generational Change in Germany and the EU,' *Constellations* 21:2 (2014), 239–248.

8 P. Kaczmarczyk, 'Germany Sticks to its Mercantilist Model,' *Social Europe Journal* (6 December 2018), www.socialeurope.eu/germany-sticks-to-its-mercantilist-model (accessed 7 December 2018).

9 T. Petersen and M. Böhmer, 'Economic Impact of Southern European Member States Exiting the Eurozone,' *Bertelsmann Stiftung Policy Brief*, 6 (2012); U. Guérot, 'The Euro Debate in Germany: Towards Political Union?' *European Council on Foreign Relations: Reinvention of Europe Project* (September, 2012).

10 J. Fleischhauer, 'We have Become the New Villain,' *Der Spiegel* (27 February 2012); F. Norris, 'Why Not Give Greeks their Say?' *New York Times* (3 November 2011); A. Sallusti, 'Quarto Reich: I no della Merkel e della Germania rimettono in ginocchio noi e l'Europa,' *Il Giornale* (3 August 2012), translation mine.

11 S. Dullien, 'Euro View: The German Fear of Inflation,' *European Council on Foreign Relations Blog* (30 November 2011), www.ecfr.eu/blog/entry/view_the_german_fear_of_inflation (accessed 1 December 2011).

12 M. Aglietta, 'The European Vortex,' *New Left Review* 75 (2012), 19; S. Dullien and U. Guérot, 'The Long Shadow of Ordoliberalism: Germany's Approach to the Euro Crisis,' *ECFR Policy Brief*, 49 (2012), 1–15.

13 J. Habermas, *Die nachholende Revolution* (Frankfurt am Main: Suhrkamp Verlag, 1990), 205; W. Pfaff, 'The Absence of Empire,' *The New Yorker* (10 August 1992), 59, 62.

14 V. Vinitzky-Seroussi and C. Teeger, 'Unpacking the Unspoken: Silence in Collective Memory and Forgetting,' *Social Forces*, 88:3 (2010).

15 M. Mazower, 'Weimar 2013?' *Project Syndicate* (31 December 2013).

16   J. Rupnik, 'La démocratie illibéral en Europe centrale,' *Espirit*, 6 (2017); R. S. Foa and Y. Mounk, 'The Dangers of Deconsolidation: The Democratic Disconnect,' *Journal of Democracy*, 27:3 (2016); R. Inglehart and P. Norris, 'Trump and the Populist Authoritarian Parties: The Silent Revolution in Reverse,' *Perspectives on Politics*, 15:2 (2017).

17   D. Dinan, 'The Historiography of European Integration,' in D. Dinan (ed), *Origins and Evolution of the European Union* (Oxford: Oxford University Press, 2006), 297.

18   P. Scheffer, 'EU Can No Longer Play the War Card'; N. Fligstein, *Euro-Clash: The EU, European Identity, and the Future of Europe* (Oxford: Oxford University Press, 2008), 141.

19   R. Koselleck, *The Practice of Conceptual History: Timing History, Spacing Concepts*, trans. T. S. Presner (Stanford: Stanford University Press, 2002), 127.

20   J. Herf, *Divided Memory: The Nazi Past in the Two Germanys* (Cambridge, MA: Harvard University Press, 1997), 327. As an early supporter of integration, Horkheimer was an outlier among critical theorists in the 1950s.

21   B. A. Misztal, *Theories of Social Remembering* (Philadelphia: Open University Press, 2003), 86; Y. F. Khong, *Analogies at War: Korea, Munich, Dien Bien Phu, and the Vietnam Decisions of 1965* (Princeton: Princeton University Press, 1992), 214.

22   N. Jabko, *Playing the Market: A Political Strategy for Uniting Europe, 1985–2005* (Ithaca, NY: Cornell University Press, 2006).

23   P. Norman and R. Atkins, 'Schröder Proposes Alliance to Cut German Joblessness,' and 'Germany's Modernizer,' *Financial Times* (11 May 1998). See also H. Kohl, *Aus Sorge um Europa: Ein Appell* (Munich: Verlag Droemer Knaur, 2014).

24   J. Habermas, 'Why Europe Needs a Constitution,' in E. O. Eriksen, J. E. Fossum, and A. J. Menéndez (eds), *Developing a Constitution for Europe* (London: Routledge, 2004), 17.

25   E. Pond, *The Rebirth of Europe* (Washington, DC: Brookings Institution Press, 2002), 227.

26   J. Habermas, 'Wir brauchen Europa!' *Die Zeit* (20 May 2010), translation mine; J. Habermas, *The Crisis of the European Union: A Response*, trans. C. Cronin (Cambridge: Polity Press, 2012), 124. For more on Habermas's views on Europe and their relationship to his broader social and political theory, see P. J. Verovšek, 'Meeting Principles and Lifeworlds Halfway: Jürgen Habermas on the Future of Europe,' *Political Studies*, 60:2 (2012), 376–377.

27   H. Marcuse, *One-Dimensional Man: Studies in the Ideology of Advanced Industrial Society* (New York: Routledge Classics, 1964), 3, 14, emphasis in original. Also Adorno *et al.*, *The Authoritarian Personality*.

28   H. Marcuse, 'Some Social Implications of Modern Technology,' in A. Arato and E. Gerhardt (eds), *The Essential Frankfurt School Reader* (New York: Urizen Books, 1977), 143.

29   M. Horkheimer and T. W. Adorno, *Dialectic of Enlightenment: Philosophical Fragments*, trans. Gunzelin Schmid Noerr (Stanford: Stanford University Press, 2002), 113; A. Beasley, 'Public Discourse and Cosmopolitan Political Identity: Imagining the European Union Citizen,' *Futures*, 38 (2006), 139. By stifling imagination and the ability to fantasise [*Phantasie*], which is crucial to creating new structures that go beyond the nation-state, the EU is dooming its own project.

30   S. Benhabib, *The Reluctant Modernism of Hannah Arendt* (Lanham: Rowman & Littlefield, 2003), xliv; H. Arendt, 'Approaching the German Question,' in Jerome Kohn (ed), *Essays in Understanding, 1930–1954* (New York: Harcourt, Brace & Co., 1994), 108.

31   H. Arendt, *The Human Condition* (Chicago: University of Chicago Press, 1998), 179.

32   *Ibid.*, 45; Marcuse, 'Some Social Implications of Modern Technology,' 145.

33 Arendt, *The Human Condition*, 42.

34 Marcuse, 'Some Social Implications of Modern Technology,' 142, 146, 8.

35 Beasley, 'Public Discourse and Cosmopolitan Political Identity,' 136.

36 D. Schecter, *Critical Theory in the Twenty-First Century* (New York: Bloomsbury Academic, 2013), 178; P. M. R. Stirk, *Critical Theory, Politics and Society: An Introduction* (New York: Continuum, 2000), 142.

37 Habermas, 'Why Europe Needs a Constitution,' 18; C. J. Schneider, *Conflict, Negotiation and European Union Enlargement* (New York: Cambridge University Press, 2009), 3, 33; H. Sjursen, 'Why Expand? The Question of Legitimacy and Justification in the EU's Enlargement Policy,' *Journal of Common Market Studies*, 40:3 (2002), 497.

38 Claus Offe, 'The Democratic Welfare State in an Integrating Europe,' in M. Greven and L.W. Pauly (eds), *Democracy Beyond the State? The European Dilemma and the Emerging Global Order* (Lanham: Rowman & Littlefield, 2000), 83–84.

39 T. A. McCarthy, *Race, Empire, and the Idea of Human Development* (New York: Cambridge University Press, 2009), 233; T. W. Adorno, 'What does Coming to Terms with the Past Mean?,' in G. H. Hartman (ed), *Bitburg in Moral and Political Perspective*, trans. T. Bahti (Bloomington: Indiana University Press, 1986).

40 Smith, *Stories of Peoplehood*; J. Blustein, *The Moral Demands of Memory* (Cambridge: Cambridge University Press, 2008), 162; P. Connerton, *How Societies Remember* (New York: Cambridge University Press, 1989), 6.

41 S. Kattago, 'Agreeing to Disagree on the Legacies of Recent History,' *European Journal of Social Theory*, 12:3 (2009), 377–378; P. Ricœur, 'The Human Experience of Time and Narrative,' in M. J. Valdés (ed), *A Ricoeur Reader: Reflection and Imagination* (Toronto: Toronto University Press, 1991), 99–116.

42 J. Waldron, 'Superseding Historic Injustice,' *Ethics*, 103:1 (1992), 6; Habermas, 'February 15, or: What Binds Europeans,' 10. For more on the importance of tradition within new institutions, see M. Halbwachs, *On Collective Memory*, trans. L. A. Coser (Chicago: University of Chicago Press, 1992), 125–126.

43 B. A. Ackerman, *We the People* (Cambridge, MA: Belknap Press of Harvard University Press, 1991), and the remaining volumes.

44 Scheffer, 'EU Can No Longer Play the War Card.'

45 U. Eco, 'An Uncertain Europe between Rebirth and Decline,' in D. Levy, M. Pensky, and J. C. Torpey (eds), *Old Europe, New Europe, Core Europe: Transatlantic Relations After the Iraq War* (London: Verso, 2005), 15, 9.

46 Fligstein, *Euro-Clash*, 178.

47 S. Jeffrey, 'Key Quotes: Tony Blair's Speech to US Congress,' *Guardian* (18 July 2003); I. M. Young, 'De-Centering the Project of Global Democracy,' in D. Levy, M. Pensky, and J. C. Torpey (eds), *Old Europe, New Europe, Core Europe: Transatlantic Relations After the Iraq War* (London: Verso, 2005), 153–159.

48 P. J. Verovšek, 'Historical Criticism without Progress: Memory as an Emancipatory Resource for Critical Theory,' *Constellations*, 26:1 (2019).

49 B. Tibi, *Europa ohne Identität? Die Krise der multikulturellen Gesellschaft* (Munich: C. Bertelsmann, 1998), xiv.

50 European Commission, 'The Memory of the Crimes Committed by Totalitarian Regimes in Europe: Report from the Commission to the European Parliament and to the Council' (Brussels, COM(2010) 783 final, 22 December 2010), esp. 8–10.

51 H. Bull, 'Civilian Power Europe: A Contradiction in Terms?' *Journal of Common Market Studies*, 21:2 (1982), 149–164; Ian Manners, 'Normative Power Europe:

A Contradiction in Terms?' *Journal of Common Market Studies*, 40:2 (2002), 235–258; T. Diez, 'Constructing the Self and Changing Others: Reconsidering "Normative Power Europe,"' *Millennium – Journal of International Studies*, 33:3 (2005), 613–636.

52 As Robert Kagan points out, this European approach to international affairs 'is a perspective on power that Americans do not and cannot share, inasmuch as the formative historical experience on their side of the Atlantic have not been the same.' R. Kagan, *Of Paradise and Power: America and Europe in the New World Order* (New York: Vintage Books, 2004), 29, 55.

53 Scheffer, 'EU Can No Longer Play the War Card.'

54 Benhabib, *The Reluctant Modernism of Hannah Arendt*, 151.

55 Wilson, *Meeting the Challenge of Cultural Diversity in Europe*, 90.

56 Quoted in R. Conquest, *Reflections on a Ravaged Century* (New York: W. W. Norton, 2000), 217.

57 A. Chalmers, 'Refiguring the European Union's Historical Dimension,' *European Journal of Political Theory*, 5:4 (2006), 451.

58 Fligstein, *Euro-Clash*, 25, 179–180.

59 For more information on the programme, see European Commission, *Erasmus – Facts, Figures and Trends: The European Union Support for Student and Staff Exchanges and University Cooperation in 2010–11* (Brussels: European Commission, 2012).

60 Eco, quoted in G. Riotta, 'Umberto Eco: "It's Culture, Not War, that Cements European Identity,"' *Guardian* (26 January 2012).

61 A. Appiah, *Cosmopolitanism: Ethics in a World of Strangers* (New York: W. W. Norton & Company, 2007), xviii; 'Erasmus Impact Study Reveals: 1 Million Babies Born to Erasmus Couples since 1987,' *ViEUws: The EU Policy Broadcaster* (22 September 2014).

62 P. Strydom, *Contemporary Critical Theory and Methodology* (London: Routledge, 2013), 122; G. W. F. Hegel, *Phenomenology of Spirit*, ed. J. N. Findlay, trans. A. V. Miller (Oxford: Clarendon Press, 1977), 17.

63 R. Celikates, 'Recognition, System Justification and Reconstructive Critique,' in C. Lazzeri and S. Nour (eds), *Reconnaissance. Identité et intégration sociale* (Paris: Presses Universitaires de Paris Ouest, 2009), 97. Also Geuss, *The Idea of a Critical Theory*, 62; A. Linklater, *The Transformation of Political Community: Ethical Foundations of the Post-Westphalian Era* (Columbia: University of South Carolina Press, 1998), 5.

64 U. Guérot, 'He Who Comes Late is Punished by Life,' *European Council on Foreign Relations Blog* (accessed 11 July 2012), www.ecfr.eu/blog/entry/he_who_comes_too_late_is_punished_by_life (15 July 2012).

65 H. Arendt, 'Reflections on Violence,' *Journal of International Affairs*, 23:1 (1969), 15; R. Geuss, *Philosophy and Real Politics* (Princeton: Princeton University Press, 2008), 25.

66 U. Beck, *German Europe* (New York: Polity, 2013), 3.

67 Habermas, *The Crisis of the European Union*, 7; J. Habermas 'Wir brauchen Europa!' *Die Zeit* (20 May 2010), translation mine; also Habermas, 'Leadership and Leitkultur,' *New York Times* (28 October 2010).

68 Beck, *German Europe*.

69 J. Habermas, 'Zur Prinzipienkonkurrenz von Bürgergleichheit und Staatengleichheit im supranationalen Gemeinwesen. Eine Notiz aus Anlass der Frage nach der Legitimität der ungleichen Repräsentation der Bürger im Europäischen Parlament,' *Der Staat*, 53:2 (2014), 184–185.

70 J. Habermas, *Europe: The Faltering Project*, trans. C. Cronin (Cambridge: Polity Press, 2009), 53; H.-J. Trenz and K. Eder, 'The Democratizing Dynamics of a European

Public Sphere: Towards a Theory of Democratic Functionalism,' *European Journal of Social Theory*, 7:1 (2004), 5–25.

71   T. Risse, *A Community of Europeans? Transnational Identities and Public Spheres* (Ithaca, NY: Cornell University Press, 2010), 5; G. Delanty and C. Rumford, *Rethinking Europe: Social Theory and the Implications of Europeanization* (London: Routledge, 2005), 79; L. van Middelaar, 'The Return of Politics: The European Union After the Crises in the Eurozone and Ukraine,' *Journal of Common Market Studies*, 54:3 (2016), 495–507.

72   J. Habermas, '"In Favor of a Strong Europe": What does this Mean?' *Juncture* (2 February 2014); U. Beck *et al.*, 'Vote for Europe!,' *Allianz Kulturstiftung*, 2014.

73   W. Streeck, 'Vom DM-Nationalismus zum Euro-Patriotismus? Eine Replik auf Jürgen Habermas,' *Blätter für deutsche und internationale Politik*, 58:9 (2013), 91; T. Biebricher and F. Vogelmann, 'Die Zukunft Europas zwischen Demokratie und Kapitalismus,' *Politische Vierteljahresschrift*, 55:1 (2014), 8.

74   P. J. Verovšek, 'La memoria è essenziale per la democrazia,' *VoxEurop* (8 March 2019), https://voxeurop.eu/it/2019/gli-europei-e-la-storia-5122733 (accessed 9 March 2019).

75   Morgan, *The Idea of a European Superstate*, 17. Also Moravcsik, 'In Defense of the "Democratic Deficit",' 603–624; P. J. Verovšek, 'Review: Rosanvallon, Democratic Legitimacy: Impartiality, Reflexivity, Proximity; Eriksen, the Unfinished Democratization of Europe,' *Political Studies Review*, 10:3 (2012), 457–458.

76   Marcuse, 'Some Social Implications of Modern Technology,' 155.

77   Habermas, *The Crisis of the European Union*, 10, emphasis in original.

78   Fligstein, *Euro-Clash*, 18.

Chapter 6

The future of Europe from a comparative perspective

We … found ourselves the legal inheritors of [certain institutions]. We toiled not in the acquirement or establishment of them; they are a legacy bequeathed us by a once hardy, brave, and patriotic, but now lamented and departed, race of ancestors … '[T]is our [task] only to transmit these … to the latest generation that fate shall permit the world to know. This task of gratitude to our fathers, justice to ourselves, [and] duty to posterity … all imperatively require us faithfully to perform.

Abraham Lincoln, Lyceum Address, Springfield, Illinois (1838)

The end of the European dream?

The project of European unification is one of the most important and theoretically interesting political developments since 1945.[1] Despite its humble origins in the ECSC in 1952, at the beginning of the twenty-first century the influence of the EU can be felt in the everyday lives of Europeans in a myriad of ways, including the creation of the CM, the euro, and the Schengen border free zone. Even though the EU is officially still composed of independent, sovereign nation-states who act as the proverbial 'Masters of the Treaties' (*Herren der Verträge*) that bind them together, in pooling significant portions of their decision-making capacity to create a 'functional constitution' at the supranational level, its member-states have created a new, pluralistic paradigm of transnational politics that questions the foundations of the state system dating back to the Treaty of Westphalia (1648).[2]

Within this new architecture of governance 'political practices of mediation and reconciliation have a primary role, to which legal means and institutions [have been] subordinated.'[3] The development of a postnational political community on a continent haunted by violence, bloodshed, and unprecedented atrocity is unexpected, to say the least.[4] Instead of standing in the way of international cooperation by increasing historical grievances, the experience of the rupture of 1945 provided Europeans with the impetus to pursue peace through integration. From the beginning, collective remembrance of the atrocities of war and fascism served as important cognitive, motivational, and justificatory resources for integration, culminating in what I call the 'classic narrative of integration.'

The period of optimism following the end of the Cold War only increased interest in the Euro-polity. A united, more muscular and financially integrated continent that deployed power in a civil, 'normative' manner instead of focusing on its hard, military aspects, made '[t]he European Dream [into] a beacon of light in a troubled world.'[5] With the accession of the first postcommunist states to the EU in 2004, its formula of community-based integration seemed to be 'destined eventually to serve as a model for the nations of the world.' Indeed, for a time the EU appeared to be 'a paragon of international virtues: a community of values held up by Europeans and non-Europeans alike.'[6] While the European project experienced some difficulties along the way, chapters 2 and 3 of this volume detail how community-based integration succeeded during the postwar period by building on the shared, collective memories of the rupture of 1945.

In the aftermath of the combined crises of the Eurozone and the increased flow of refugees from Africa and the Middle East during the second decade of the twenty-first century, this previous narrative seems hopelessly optimistic, if not Panglossian. In chapter 4 I diagnosed how these events have undermined what I call the 'classic narrative of integration.' It is certainly ironic that precisely the changes that defined so much of the post-Cold War 'EU-phoria' have actually destabilised Europe internally and harmed its international standing. As a result of the fragmentation and loss of European memory, the continent is increasingly divided between a western/northern core and an eastern/southern periphery. Far from acting as 'a model of post-Westphalian political organisation which is [to be] emulated by regions elsewhere,' the crisis of the EU at the beginning of the third millennium has put its very future into doubt.[7]

Although I outlined some reasons for hope in the previous chapter, this existential crisis has been reinforced by the loss of the generation of individuals, who pushed integration forward by fusing their deep-seated desire to put an end to the cycles of hatred by unifying the continent through joint, community-based institutions. For political leaders like Monnet, Schuman, and Adenauer, as well as Delors, Mitterrand, and Kohl, the economic aspects of the project – which had costs as well as benefits when looked at from a purely nationalistic, economistic point of view – were not only balanced by, but actually overshadowed, the broader normative project of integration. Building on the theoretical framework I presented in chapter 1, I argue that it is no accident that all of these leaders had direct, personal memories of Europe's age of total war. As a result of the cognitive, motivational, and justificatory resources they drew from their lived experience of the past, they were able to keep the project going through hard times by prioritising its political-normative goals over short-term economic considerations.

The loss of the founding generation of a political community is always a difficult time, as the comparison to the United States makes clear. On the eve of the American Civil War (1861–65) future President Abraham Lincoln reflected on the effects of the passing of 'a once hardy, brave, and patriotic, but now lamented and departed, race of ancestors.' The dangers posed to political institutions following the passing of the individuals that toiled in their establishment reveals the important generational dynamics involved in the (re)-founding of political communities. As time passes and circumstances change, future generations begin to think about the political forms of life they have inherited from the dead in new ways. To a certain extent, this is part of a natural process. However, it can also have negative effects as new leaders forget the lessons of the past and no longer recognise the benefits of the institutions that have been bequeathed to them.

This is the position of Europe at the beginning of the twenty-first century. Much like the United States of Lincoln's time, the EU is confronting the loss of the generation of the founding in the midst of a broader economic, social, and political crisis. As a result of the Great Recession, a new cohort of leaders with no memory of the European rupture of 1945 is increasingly calculating its interest in the EU in narrow, nationalistic terms.[8] This reaction can be understood in terms of what economists call 'motivation crowding'. As economic considerations have taken on a more central role vis-à-vis the normative imperatives of integration, this transformation has made the leaders and peoples of Europe – particularly in the northern/western core – less willing to express transnational solidarity with their southern/eastern counterparts. Such a focus on thinking in terms of price incentives can actually 'undermine … [the] sense of civic duty,' leading to the breakdown of intrinsic, community-oriented behaviour.[9]

In this chapter I explore the theoretical affinities between my project on the role of collective memory in the creation of the emerging European polity and importance of the past in the many refoundations of the American republic.

Although Jacques Delors was right to describe the EU as a 'UPO' or 'a sort of unidentified political object,' I argue that as two examples of new political communities that span entire continents, the development of the American republic in the nineteenth century may hold lessons for European unification at the beginning of the twenty-first.[10] At both these times the United States and the EU were the respective sites of important political innovations. Whereas the American republic sought to create a democratic people who could legitimately constitute their own government by 'seiz[ing] the mantle of authorization ... even as they explicitly [broke] from the established procedures or rules for representing popular voice,' postwar Europe has tried to move beyond the traditional logic of the nation-state by separating the *ethnos* of national belonging from the *demos* of political membership.[11]

To this end, the next section examines the role of memory as a source of stability and political innovation within the founding of the United States and at key moments of constitutional crisis. It connects these insights to my work on the origins of Europe by pointing to important differences in the origins of the American and European constitutional projects. In the third part, I examine the generational dynamics of collective memory and the crises that come about when the founding generations of a political community pass away. By looking at how the United States dealt with the problems posed by the loss of the generation of the founders, I maintain a sense of optimism for the future of the EU 'by relat[ing] the comprehensive picture of the social process offered by critical theory to currently existing and emerging forms of opposition, no matter how fragmented, distorted, or hopeless they may seem at the moment.'[12] I conclude by opposing fatalistic interpretations of the EU's disintegration, arguing instead that with the support of proper leadership and the activism of the European peoples, the continent can build on its legacy of political innovation in the twentieth century to find collective solutions to collective problems it faces at the start of the twenty-first.

Remembering the founding

In the theoretical section at the beginning of this project I argued that although collective memory acts as a conservative force during periods of normal politics, it can also provide political leaders and communities with important cognitive, motivational, and justificatory resources for political change in the aftermath of traumatic events that tear the fabric of historical time asunder. My thesis was based on a reading of early twentieth-century continental social and political theory, focusing especially on the critical theorists of the Frankfurt School. Their experience of the rupture of 1945 activated the constructive potential of collective memory as a spur to the imagination (*Phantasie* in Herbert Marcuse's terms), as they sought new solutions to the old problems of war and peace on the continent.

In comparing the political innovation of twentieth-century Europe to the foundation of the United States, it is interesting to note that similar arguments were made about the role of collective remembrance in eighteenth-century America. For the American founding fathers, the faculty of imagination was not only important in helping individuals to create coherent conceptions of themselves as persons; it was also crucial in 'establishing the sympathetic relationships that formed the basis of society and economic and political orders … Imagination was construed as the very basis of individual and collective identity.' Much like the thinkers of the Frankfurt School, who sought to balance the imperative for new thinking in the aftermath of two world wars with the importance of collective memories as a source of tradition, the philosophers working in the wake of the American and the French Revolutions, such as David Hume, also had to 'navigate the imagination's internal ambivalence,' since it is 'at once the faculty of transformative malleability and of securing an enabling, sedimented stability.'[13]

Just as the leaders of Europe in the second half of the twentieth century built on their transnationally shared collective memories, the founding fathers of the United States also recognised the importance of ensuring that the people of a new polity see themselves as 'united in the imagination.'[14] This was particularly true of the authors of *The Federalist Papers* (Alexander Hamilton, James Madison, and John Jay). Writing under the pseudonym Publius, these early American leaders understood the dangers posed by the imagination in the postrevolutionary United States. In particular, they highlighted its 'tendency to inflame the passions, betray the intellect, and subvert political authority.' However, they also saw its potential. As Jason Frank points out, 'At key points in his argument Publius invoked the imagination to secure the authority of the proposed constitutional regime; he converted imagination from a subversive or destabilizing force—the enthusiastic imagination—to a support of power.'[15] This was particularly important in helping the American founders to establish the respect necessary to create and sustain a new form of political authority and to shift citizen loyalty to the federal government.

Publius supported 'a remembrance of the endearing scenes which are past' to orient political action in the present.[16] This would not only bind individuals to the project inaugurated by the founding; it would also play a positive role in limiting the boundaries of the politically possible after the revolutionary moment had passed and a new form of normal politics had been established. However, this is not to say that the innovative potential of the founding to enact political change had been completely exhausted. On the contrary, much of the scholarship on American constitutionalism has stressed how the United States has repeatedly returned to its historical memories (i.e. not personal or individual) of its founding in moments of political crisis.

The clearest and most influential example of this comes from Bruce Ackerman's two-volume opus, *We the People* (1991, 1998). In this work, Ackerman develops a theory of 'constitutional moments,' which he defines as moments of dramatic constitutional revision and higher lawmaking after the close of the creative moment of the founding itself. As opposed to the drudgery of normal politics, in these moments 'the people' is able to recapture their role as a deliberative body of law writ large, harnessing the creative potential of their sovereign *constituent power* to endow their institutions of government with new *constituted powers*.[17]

In his reconstruction of the constitutional history of the American republic, Ackerman argues that the Reconstruction (1865–77) following the Civil War, the era of the New Deal (1933–36) following the Great Depression of the interwar years, and the postwar civil rights movement (1955–68) each constitute moments of higher lawmaking when 'the people' were able to break through the tedium of quotidian governance to transform the nature of the polity. These 'constitutional moments' are ruptures, marking 'a radical break' or a 'drastic change' from the past that results in an Arendtian new beginning. Like the European rupture of 1945, each allow follows a traumatic experience that serves as a narrative break in tradition. Ackerman's work is therefore part of 'a revival of the doctrine of constituent power in the United States.' Although they were developed in a different geographic and temporal context, Ackerman's ideas bear a strong resemblance to my understanding of rupture, even though he draws on radically divergent sources to formulate his argument.[18]

Another of the key thinkers in this same revival is J. G. A. Pocock, who also stresses the importance of returning the narratives of political founding in times of crisis. His concept of the 'Machiavellian moment' relates both to the creation of the political community and to later periods of corruption and crisis, when the republic returns to the principles it was founded upon. Pocock's ideas demonstrate how the shared collective memory of the founding can help to create a retrospective relationship between a historical consciousness of the past and political action in the present. For Pocock, Machiavellian moments are periods of rupture 'in which the republic was seen as confronting its own temporal finitude, as attempting to remain morally and politically stable in a stream of irrational events conceived as essentially destructive of all systems of secular stability.'[19] In light of the theoretical framework I have developed, Pocock's Machiavellian moments also highlight the important role that the founding plays in later 'narratives of justification.' These stories – much like the 'classic narrative of integration' I describe in postwar Europe – are 'more than literary superstructure.' In the words of Melissa Mathes, they 'are integral to the construction of the republic's political identity.'[20]

Both Hannah Arendt and Jürgen Habermas pick up this emphasis on narratives of founding. Arendt's experience of the rupture of 1945 leads her to develop a new form of historiography based on storytelling, which allows political actors 'to understand without preconceived categories and to judge without the set of customary rules which is morality.'[21] After immigrating to the United States in 1941, Arendt seeks to understand the dynamics of postrevolutionary politics based on her reading of the early history of the American republic. While founding a new political community creates opportunities to address fundamental problems and injustices, sweeping away the collective memories contained within existing laws and institutions, it also has the potential to backfire, as it removes barriers that traditionally restrain political leaders.

Arendt argues that the key move that allowed the American founding fathers to resist the temptations created by the 'lost continuity of the past' – to which the *Jacobin* had succumbed during the Terror that followed the onset of the French Revolution – was their commitment to obeying the new laws they had created.[22] She approved of the attempts to ensure that the founding itself, guaranteed by the constitution, would be shrouded in 'an atmosphere of reverent awe ... shield[ing] both event and document against the onslaught of time and changed circumstances.' However, Arendt also wanted to ensure that this veneration would not prevent future generations from engaging in higher lawmaking through Ackermanian constitutional moments.

It is at this point that collective remembrance once again comes into play.[23] Arendt sees collective memory and narratives of the founding as crucial to enabling the future use of constituent power to modify existing institutions of government. She argues that 'the authority of the republic will be safe and intact as long as the act itself, the beginning as such, is remembered whenever constitutional questions in the narrower sense of the word come into play.'[24]

Arendt refrains from tying future generations completely to the decisions of the founders by allowing them to make fundamental changes to the institutions of political governance within constitutional moments, i.e. through what Seyla Benhabib calls 'democratic iterations.' Future generations can therefore legitimately recapture the deliberative force of constituent power, only as long as they remember and seek to act within the spirit of the founding fathers.[25]

In his work Habermas also provides an account of the founding that serves to legitimise the use of constituent power to create laws that are not themselves legally constituted. In a response to the question 'How can people ever make the laws?' Habermas argues that the paradox of the illegal origins of law in constituent power 'resolves itself in the dimension of historical time, provided one conceives of the constitution as a project that makes the founding act into an ongoing process of constitution-making that proceeds across generations.' Future generations retroactively legitimate the founding by 'actualizing the still untapped normative substance of the system of rights laid down in the original document of the constitution.'[26]

This interpretation of 'constitutional history as a learning process (*Lernprozess*)' only works if we accept what Habermas admits is 'the nontrivial assumption that later generations will start with the same standards as did the founders.' Remembrance plays a key role in this process. Habermas argues that historical narratives can establish a continuous relationship between the past and the present, which enables future generations to see the founding as part of the tradition within which they locate themselves: 'The descendants can learn from past mistakes only if they are "in the same boat" as their forebears.' Habermas reiterates, 'All participants must be able to recognise the project as the same through history and judge it from the same perspective.'[27]

Although the EU is never far from Habermas's thought, most thinkers interested in what Bonnie Honig has called 'the paradoxes of the founding' – including Pockock and Arendt – base their reflections on the example of the American republic.[28] However, I argue that these theories can be insightfully transported to the case of twentieth-century Europe. In some cases, this comparison is explicit. For example, in thinking about how his theory of constitutional moments applies to the European context, Ackerman observes that although the 'American experience differs from the European in countless respects … the movement toward European Union has succeeded remarkably well.'[29] Similarly, although Arendt did not live to see the second major phase of European constitutionalisation, it is clear that she supported the attempt to apply the lessons of the American republic beyond the nation-state in Europe.

After all, her experience of the rupture of 1945 had convinced Arendt that the nation was 'the cheapest and the most dangerous disguise … in the political realm.'[30]

In other cases, such a comparison is explicitly subversive. For instance, Pocock was a trenchant critic of the EU, which he saw as a surrender of both of the conditions necessary for democracy: state sovereignty and national identity. He was particularly wary of Europe developing into what he called 'an "empire" of the market in which residual political authority was unequally distributed between the political entities subject to its supra-political authority.'[31] However, despite Pocock's Euroscepticism and his hostility to the EU, this does not mean that his reflections on the role of founding narratives are less useful to understanding integration than those of the more Europhilic Ackerman.

The broader literature in legal and political theory on the role of imagination and narrative in the founding of new political communities relates to European integration by bringing to light an important conceptual difference between the American and the European constitutional projects. Ackerman notes, 'If the first half-century of American Union was built on the foundations of hope and pride, European developments have been driven by fear and humiliation. The prelude for the Treaty of Rome was the disastrous destruction of World War II, not some triumphant collective act of liberation from imperial rule.' The exact implications of this are unclear, but he concludes, 'It seems that fear and humiliation can do as good a job as hope and pride in fuelling the engine of political construction.'[32]

I would take this argument even further. Basing political innovation on the cognitive resources of 'fear and humiliation' as opposed to 'hope and pride' does make a difference in the ability of political actors to enchant the imaginations of regular citizens. In reflecting on the role of the imagination in the early American republic, Frank argues that one of its key achievements was in helping to 'shift citizen loyalty from the state and local level to the newly energized federal government.' Publius makes the same point in *The Federalist Papers*.[33] Within the American republic, the recourse to a political imagination of the founding based on hope and pride was crucial in the creation of a new, central, postrevolutionary authority that would not only be respected and obeyed, but also venerated by its citizens.

It is obvious that despite the strong discourse of states' rights, America has succeeded in transferring the loyalties of its citizens to the federal government in Washington to a much greater extent than the Europeans have been able to do. Although Europe, less than a century after its foundation, may simply need more time to establish the loyalty of its peoples to a strong central authority in Brussels, it is also possible that this failure is driven by the fact that, 'The rising generations are no longer eye-witnesses to the destruction of Berlin or London and they cannot share their predecessors' grim determination to avoid a repetition.' As Ackerman argues, the EU would be better served by 'appeal[ing] to the next generation's hope and pride in their emerging role as citizens of a new Union.'[34] There are obviously also other factors at play in this change of political generations, a point to which I turn in the next section.

Reflecting on the differences between the founding of the American republic in the eighteenth century and the creation of the EU in the twentieth century reveals another important difference. In establishing the United States, its constituent colonies explicitly engaged in a revolutionary act by breaking the established laws and constitutional traditions of the British parliament by claiming the rights of an as yet non-existent people: 'There is ... a dynamic tension between what the rebelling colonists explicitly claimed and what they did, between the constitutionally defensive people they invoked to justify their resistance and the self-authorizing people whom this resistance enacted.'[35] The colonists resolved this dilemma by calling upon their constituent power to authorise their actions based on the authority of the people as a new democratic subject.

The founding of the American republic on the basis of constituent power has affected the subsequent development of the United States in various ways. On one hand, the dilemmas of constituency caused by the creation of a self-authorising subject meant that after independence various institutions could make competing claims to speak in the name of the people; once it is unleashed, the revolutionary spirit of the people as constituent power is hard to contain. However, on the other hand, this clean break by the people in the event of the revolution itself also served as an important form of popular legitimation that the founding fathers could draw upon as a concrete event of political enactment.[36]

This point is made most powerfully and eloquently by future US President Abraham Lincoln in his 1848 'Address before the Young Men's Lyceum of Springfield, Illinois.' On this occasion, Lincoln reminds his audience of the imaginative power of peoplehood that lay within the individual and collective memories of the American Revolution against the British. He observes,

> At the close of that struggle, nearly every adult male had been a participator in some of [the Revolution's] scenes. The consequence was that of those scenes,

in the form of a husband, a father, a son, or a brother, a living history was to be found in every family — a history bearing the indubitable testimonies of its own authenticity, in the limbs mangled, in the scars of wounds received, in the midst of the very scenes related — a history, too, that could be read and understood alike by all, the wise and the ignorant, the learned and the unlearned.[37]

Although the use of constituent power in the break of the United States away from British rule posted many potential problems for the reestablishment of normal politics in its aftermath, the revolutionary foundation of the United States also provided a strong basis for a common, American 'story of peoplehood.'[38]

By contrast, the founding of the European Communities through international treaties, signed by the representatives of already established *constituted* powers within existing nation-states, bypassed the democratic dilemmas of *constituent* power. Creating a supranational Europe was a revolutionary act in the sense that it involved the delegation of certain sovereign competencies to community institutions outside of the constitutional infrastructure of the Westphalian state. However, it did not need to draw on constituent power since there was never any doubt about the constitutional legality of government ministers like Robert Schuman and heads of state like Konrad Adenauer to sign legally binding treaties giving up their decision-making authority to external institutions outside the institutional architecture of the sovereign state.

Although it was revolutionary in substance, the *pères de l'Europe* drew on the established constitutional rules of constituted power to found the European Communities in the 1950s. From a certain perspective, this is clearly beneficial; the EU, as the product of treaties between existing nation-states, sidesteps the problems of the democratic paradox that confronted the early American republic. However, in avoiding the problems of constituent power, Europe also loses the popular legitimation that comes with the democratic paradox and constitutive authenticity of an experience of 'the people as event.'[39]

The origins of the United States and the EU in constituent and constituted power respectively may help to explain the greater success of the American republic in establishing a self-conscious, unified population as compared to the EU, where feelings of Europeanness have been largely confined to the elite that undertook and benefits most from integration.[40] Although drawing on constituent power poses greater problems in the short term, I contend that once these initial *aporias* are overcome, the creation of a self-authorising people in the event of the revolution creates a stronger foundation for political community, by providing the nascent polity with a deeper reserve of collective memory to draw on in creating their own stories of peoplehood. While collective remembrance of the experience of the rupture of 1945 helped Europeans to overcome some of the pathologies of nationalism by creating a supranational European community, it is unclear whether these memories will be enough to support Europe in the future.

The future of a young polity

The comparison of the United States and the EU raises further questions as well. Despite the achievements of European constitutionalism, it is important to remember that the institutions of the EU and the European constitutional project are still relatively young; at the beginning of the twenty-first century the European polity is only beginning to experience the passing away of its founding generation.[41] Despite the success of the American founding fathers in exciting the people's imaginary enough to 'inspire [within them] ... an active sentiment of attachment' to the institutions of the central government, this did not happen overnight. On the contrary, despite America's ability to build on what Lincoln called the living 'history bearing the indubitable testimonies of its own authenticity, in the limbs mangled, in the scars of wounds received, in the midst of the very scenes related' to the founding, the United States was a deeply divided, fragile project during its first generation of existence.[42]

Although the founding fathers succeeded in creating a people unified through a weak form of American patriotism, this fellow feeling was restrained by strong localism and state sovereignty during the first half of the nineteenth century. By the early 1860s, these tensions threatened to break the United States in two over the issue of slavery. It was only after the fighting of the bloody, fratricidal Civil War that the United States truly became a unified nation, whose imagined community stretched beyond local attachments. This change is symbolically visible in important changes in linguistic identification. Whereas before the Civil War Americans would usually say, 'The United States *are* a republic,' after this conflict they instinctively declared, 'The United States *is* a republic.'[43]

My emphasis on the importance of collective memory and the generational dynamics that shape it allow me to argue that the timing of the Civil War, seventy years after the colonies ratified the constitution in 1790, is hardly accidental. On the contrary, it corresponds to the passing away of the founding generation of the American republic. The importance of this fact was not lost on Americans leading up to the outbreak of the war. Reflecting on the loss of the revolutionary generation, Lincoln foresaw the coming war in a speech he delivered in 1838. He observed,

> [The living] histories [of the Revolution] are gone. They can be read no more for-ever ... They [the revolutionaries] were pillars of the temple of liberty; and now that they have crumbled away that temple must fall unless we, their descendants, supply their places with other pillars ... furnish[ing] all the materials for our future support and defense.[44]

The United States had to experience a brutal civil war to resolve the consti-tutional crisis brought about, at least in part, by the passing away of the gen-eration of the American founders. Despite this bloodshed, the descendants of the founding generation of the American republic succeeded in passing on the institutions they inherited to posterity – which Lincoln calls a 'task of gratitude to our fathers.'

Sixty years after its foundation in 1950, Europe began to experience a similar crisis of collective memory, as the veterans of the wars that bookended the rupture of 1914 through 1945, the soldiers who literally bore 'the scars of wounds received' started to pass away. Despite the divisions that have emerged between east and west over historical differences, as well as between lenders and debtors, north and south, rich states and poor states as a result of the Euro-crisis, no one on the continent expects that these disagreements will lead to open warfare. War in Europe is a thing of the past, as the Norwegian Nobel Committee recognised in awarding the 2012 Nobel Peace Prize to the EU in light of 'the EU's most important result: the successful struggle for peace and reconciliation, and for democracy and human rights.'[45]

However, this is not to say that the EU can rest on its laurels. As a result of this existential crisis, Europe needs to recapture the normative, political resources of collective memory in order to balance the narrow, nationalistic, economic self-interests that are dividing the continent. The leaders of the current generation need to remember and embrace the normative vision of the *pères de l'Europe*, which in the words of Nobel Committee, 'helped trans-form Europe from a continent at war to a continent at peace.' As Habermas observes, 'The Nobel Peace Prize makes it clear to the governments that are presently steering the Eurozone countries that they must step out from their own shadow and so move the European project forward.'[46] Just like the United States after the Civil War, the leaders of the EU today must hark back to the normative resources of collective memory provided by the founders of the Union and reappropriate them for the present to ensure that these shared, community institutions are transmitted to the next generation. If they do not, the increasingly fractured project of unification could indeed tear itself apart.

The failure of the EU has political implications far beyond the continent. At the start of the twenty-first century, the western model of combining politics, society, and economics based on the principles of democracy, liberalism, and capitalism is increasingly under threat. New models of governance that accept free markets but reject both liberalism and democracy have started to challenge western assumptions about modernisation and development, most notably in Central Europe through the development of the Visegrád Group, which I addressed in chapter 4. Instead of admiring the EU's innovative postnational forms of governance, these populists – and their intellectual supporters – look back fondly on the heyday of the welfare state during the postwar *trente glorieuses*, a time when it appeared that democracy had managed to tame capitalism by establishing the priority of people over markets.

The most powerful and nuanced statement of this position comes from Wolfgang Streeck. He starts by noting that integration in general – and monetary union in particular – was supposed protect the European peoples against the growing power of globalised financial markets by combining them into a supranational unit large enough and powerful enough to tame twenty-first-century financialised capitalism, just as the welfare state had been able to do during the postwar *Wirtschaftswunder*. However, in an argument he first elaborated in his Adorno Lectures at the Institute for Social Research in Frankfurt in 2012, Streeck observes that integration has done just the opposite by promoting the neoliberal interests of financial markets *against* the welfare of the people. Instead of acting as a shield protecting the peoples of Europe against the dangers posed by the globalisation and financialisation of capitalism, the monetary union has turned into a Trojan horse. By taking away their ability to devaluate their currency, the presence of the euro has forced the peoples of the Eurozone to accept neoliberal labour market liberalisation, putting them at the mercy of international lenders as they seek to service their debts during a global economic downturn.[47]

Streeck's analysis leads him to argue that Europeans must fall back on the only structures that have proved capable of taming capitalism in the name of the people: the institutions of the nation-state.[48] This argument has generated a surprisingly rancorous dispute between Streeck and Habermas, despite their shared relationship to the legacy of critical theory. The latter has characterised the former's 'nostalgic option' as unrealistic, given the weakening of the steering capacities of the nation-state in the face of financial globalisation since the 1970s. Streeck has responded to Habermas by noting that the whole debate about the size of states (*Klein- v. Großstaaterei*) is irrelevant, since there is little evidence that large states are any better at standing up to international markets than smaller ones. To substantiate this point, Streeck notes that 'if one wants to see how even a large state can appeal to market constraints to dispossess democratically and economically the ordinary-people majority of its population, one need look no further than the United States.'[49]

Size is certainly no guarantee against the legal and regulatory capture of political elites by international financial interests.[50] However, while the leaders of the United States may be just as beholden to globalised capitalism as those of many small states, this does not mean that they do not have a greater *ability* to do so. On the contrary, size does matter in terms of steering capacity vis-à-vis markets, even if it is not exercised. Streeck's arguments, despite their force, fail to provide any real alternatives to the dominance of markets over peoples in the present. By merely looking back to the golden age of the nation-state and forward to the end of the capitalist system, Streeck falls into a fatalistic pessimism that passively waits for capitalism to fall apart while providing no guidance for action in the present.[51]

In order to deal with the crisis of the Eurozone and the other challenges the twenty-first century will inevitably bring, Europeans will have to build on their legacy of innovation by continuing to reinvent the institutions and practices of their post-Westphalian union. Reflecting on the tradition of critical theory, David Held points out that the history of emancipation 'is also the history of crisis. There is no guarantee that these crises will be resolved – there is no guarantee of progress.'[52] Instead of succumbing to a passive fatalism, the citizens of Europe must find new ways to mediate between politics and economics so that they can emancipate themselves from external domination by continuing to exercise their autonomy through decision-making as a self-conscious, democratic community.

Conclusion

In this chapter I have engaged in a comparison of the United States and the EU in order to see what lessons the former can teach about the problems political communities face when confronted with the loss of the generations that literally 'bear the scars of the founding.' Where the EU goes from here is unclear. Much like the United States in the middle of the nineteenth century, in order to survive the current crisis Europe must either 'cooperate or fail.'[53] The United States fought a civil war before deciding to pursue the former. This is not the most appealing or inspiring prospect for Europe.

Although I highlighted some reasons for hope in chapter 5, it is difficult to be overly optimistic about the future of the project of integration. Europe's problems, most obviously expressed in the devastation wreaked by the Great Recession, have driven populist movements that seek a return to the seemingly safe sanctuary of the nation-state, much like the economic crises in the Old South led to a desire for independence and a surge in the rhetoric of 'states' rights' in the build-up to the Civil War. However, the United States survived this cataclysmic crisis, which ultimately even led to a new Ackermanian 'constitutional moment.'

From the beginning of this volume I have stressed that critical theory is at its strongest when it rejects the kind of fatalism characteristic of Horkheimer and Adorno's *Dialectic of Enlightenment* (1944). There are certainly many reasons for individuals caught in the 'European vortex' to feel powerless. However, this need not be true of the larger community these individuals compose. As Horkheimer points out in his 1937 statement of the fundamental tenets of critical theory, 'The individual sees himself as passive and dependent, but society, though made up of individuals is an active subject, even if a nonconscious one.'[54] The goal of the critic is to activate European society by making the citizens conscious of their collective ability to struggle against the dominance of international financial capital by coming together and seeking alternatives to neoliberal market fundamentalism.[55]

Through the first decade of the twenty-first century it was still possible to argue in all seriousness that '[s]ome dimensions of European politics suggest that a new epoch may be emerging ... [which] will underpin active citizenship within post-Westphalian arrangements.'[56] This potential has not been lost; it has merely been overpowered by neoliberal interests that have been able use technocratic expertise to do what needs to be done to resolve the crisis brought on by the Great Recession. Instead of leading to passivity, European citizens must actively struggle to find ways to make the new social formations that define the continent's relations at the start of the third millennium work for them by 'guid[ing] some of the advantages of complexity towards the effective renewal and redeployment of economic, political, pedagogical, scientific and cultural resources.'

If the 'transition from overarching forms of legitimacy to a densely articulated network of de-cantered mediations that can coordinate needs, capacities and communication' through active citizenship is going to happen anywhere, postwar Europe is the most likely place.[57] After all, it was the centre of political innovation for the last hundred years. This statement may seem out of place given the fact that the geopolitical rise of the United States has dominated the short twentieth century. Ever since Henry Luce first used the phrase in 1941, the idea of the 1900s as the 'American Century' has stuck.[58] However, while this is undoubtedly true from an economic and military perspective, the United States has not been particularly politically innovative. Its institutions, basic political concepts and forms of governance have remained petrified in eighteenth-century political ideals. This can be seen in the fact that the so-called 'frozen republic' is still using classically modern, statist political concepts in an increasingly interconnected, postmodern world.[59]

In contrast to the classicism of the United States, during its 'century of discontent' Europe has been a hotbed of political innovation.[60] These experiments are not limited to the EU and its creation of shared community institutions. They also include the separate development of the Council of Europe, with the European Court of Human Rights in Strasbourg, as well as many other, smaller initiatives that have sought to increase cross-border cooperation in a number of other policy areas. As a result, there is little doubt that Europe was at the centre of the most important attempts to update systems of political governance to reflect the new conditions of the twentieth century. In Perry Anderson's words, 'Europe has, to a striking extent, become the theoretical proving-ground of contemporary liberalism. Nowhere are the varieties of that liberalism on such vivid display as in the deliberations on the Union.'[61]

If the EU, and its unique political architecture based on supranational 'political practices of mediation and reconciliation,' is to survive into the twenty-first century, it will have to continue the legacy of political innovation it developed in the second half of the twentieth century. Conceptual developments, such as supranationalism, sectoral integration, and spill-over, will have to be supplemented by increased moves towards transnational democracy at the European level based on a shared historical imaginary that can survive the loss of the founding generation and its direct, personal memories of the ruputure of 1945.[62] However, it is important to remember that in addition to acting as threats, crises are also opportunities. With the proper leadership – supported by the activism of the European peoples – the EU has the track record and the potential to develop collective solutions to the collective problems shared by the European community as a whole.

Notes

1 J. Neyer and A. Wiener, *Political Theory of the European Union* (New York: Oxford University Press, 2011).

2 T. Isiksel, *Europe's Functional Constitution: A Theory of Constitutionalism Beyond the State* (Oxford: Oxford University Press, 2016); Habermas, *Zur Verfassung Europas*. Even Eurosceptics like the leading Brexiteer Richard Tuck agree that the EU is best understood as creating constitutional constraints on the member-states at a supranational level. See R. Tuck, 'For the British Left to Succeed, the UK Must Leave the European Union,' *Vox* (12 July 2016), www.vox.com/2016/7/12/12159936/brexit-british-left (accessed 17 July 2016).

3 R. Bellamy and D. Castiglione, 'Building the Union: The Nature of Sovereignty in the Political Architecture of Europe,' *Law and Philosophy*, 16:4 (1997), 444.

4 Kaufman, *Modern Hatreds*; Kalyvas, *The Logic of Violence in Civil War*, 401–411; Mearsheimer, 'Back to the Future'.

5 J. Rifkin, *The European Dream: How Europe's Vision of the Future is Quietly Eclipsing the American Dream* (New York: Penguin, 2004), 385. Bellamy and Castiglione, 'Legitimizing the Euro-"polity" and its "Regime"'; Diez, 'Constructing the Self and Changing Others'; I. Manners, 'The European Union as a Normative Power: A Response to Thomas Diez,' *Millennium – Journal of International Studies*, 1:167 (2006).

6 M. Gauchet, 'Le problème Européen,' *Le Débat*, 129 (2004), 66, translation mine; Judt, *Postwar*, 799.

7 Linklater, *The Transformation of Political Community*, 204.

8 Shapiro, 'The Moralized Economy in Hard Times.'

9 B. S. Frey and F. Oberholzer-Gee, 'The Cost of Price Incentives: An Empirical Analysis of Motivation Crowding-Out,' *The American Economic Review*, 87:4 (1997), 746. Also R. M. Titmuss, *The Gift Relationship: From Human Blood to Social Policy* (London: Allen & Unwin, 1970); B. S. Frey, 'How Intrinsic Motivation is Crowded Out and In,' *Rationality and Society*, 6:3 (1994), 334–352.

10 J. Delors, 'Speech by Jacques Delors (Luxembourg, 9 September 1985),' Bulletin of the European Communities (20 October 2012), www.cvce.eu/obj/speech_by_jacques_delors_luxembourg_9_september_1985-en-423d6913-b4e2–4395-9157-fe70b3ca8521.html (accessed 30 July 2019).

11 J. A. Frank, *Constituent Moments: Enacting the People in Postrevolutionary America* (Durham, NC: Duke University Press, 2010), 8.

12 W. Leiss, 'The Critical Theory of Society: Present Situation and Future Tasks,' in Paul Breines (ed), *Critical Interruptions; New Left Perspectives on Herbert Marcuse* (New York: Herder and Herder, 1970), 93.

13 J. A. Frank, 'Publius and Political Imagination,' *Political Theory*, 37:1 (2009), 76, 78.

14 D. Hume, *A Treatise of Human Nature*, ed. L. A. Selby-Bigge (New York: Oxford University Press, 1978), 566.

15 Frank, 'Publius and Political Imagination,' 70, 90.

16 J. E. Cooke (ed), *The Federalist* (Middletown: Wesleyan University Press, 1961), 298.

17 Ackerman, *We the People*, 193; also B. A. Ackerman, 'Constitutional Politics/Constitutional Law,' *The Yale Law Journal*, 99:3 (1989).

18 Ackerman, *We the People*, 204–205; A. Arato, 'Carl Schmitt and the Revival of the Doctrine of the Constituent Power in the United States,' *Cardozo Law Review*, 5–6:21 (2000), 1739–1747.

19 J. G. A. Pocock, *The Machiavellian Moment* (Princeton: Princeton University Press, 1975), viii. Pocock's 'Machiavellian moment' has been followed by the development of an understanding of the 'Lockean moment,' which stresses the importance of forgetting in the founding of new republics. See T. H. Breen, *The Lockean Moment: The Language of Rights on the Eve of the American Revolution, an Inaugural Lecture Delivered before the University of Oxford on 15 May 2001* (Oxford: Oxford University Press, 2001).

20 M. M. Mathes, *Rape of Lucretia and the Founding of Republics* (University Park: Pennsylvania University Press, 2000), 8. See also B. J. Smith, *Politics and Remembrance: Republican Themes in Machiavelli, Burke, and Tocqueville* (Princeton: Princeton University Press, 1985).

21 Arendt, *Essays in Understanding*, 391; also Benhabib, *The Reluctant Modernism of Hannah Arendt*, 86–95. For more on the connection between Arendt and Habermas, see P. J. Verovšek, 'A Case of Communicative Learning: Rereading Habermas's Philosophical Project through an Arendtian Lens,' *Polity*, 51:3 (2019), 597–627.

22 Frank, *Constituent Moments*, ch. 1.

23 Verovšek, 'Unexpected Support for European Integration,' 389–413.

24 H. Arendt, *On Revolution* (New York: Penguin Classics, 1990), 204.

25 S. Benhabib, 'Democratic Exclusions and Democratic Iterations: Dilemmas of "Just Membership" and Prospects of Cosmopolitan Federalism,' *European Journal of Political Theory*, 6:4 (2007), 445–462.

26 J. Habermas, 'Constitutional Democracy: A Paradoxical Union of Contradictory Principles?' *Political Theory*, 29:6 (2001), 768, 774; F. I. Michelman, 'How Can the People Ever Make the Laws? A Critique of Deliberative Democracy,' in J. Bohman and W. Rehg (eds), *Deliberative Democracy: Essays on Reason and Politics* (Cambridge, MA: MIT Press, 1997), 145–171. For more on this debate, see Frank, *Constituent Moments*, 240–244.

27 Habermas, 'Constitutional Democracy,' 775.

28 B. Honig, *Democracy and the Foreigner* (Princeton: Princeton University Press, 2001), 139; B. Honig, 'Declarations of Independence: Arendt and Derrida on the Problem of Founding a Republic,' *The American Political Science Review*, 85:1 (1991), 97–113.

29 B. A. Ackerman, 'Prologue: Hope and Fear in Constitutional Law,' in E. O. Eriksen, J. E. Fossum, and A. J. Menéndez (eds), *Developing a Constitution for Europe* (London: Routledge, 2004), xiv, xii.

30 Arendt, *On Revolution*, 195.

31 J. G. A. Pocock, 'Deconstructing Europe,' *London Review of Books*, 13:24 (1991), 6–10.

32 Ackerman, 'Prologue,' xii, xiii.

33 Frank, 'Publius and Political Imagination,' 70. Publius argues, '[A]n intimate intercourse under the same government will promote a gradual assimilation, of temper and sentiment.' Cooke, *The Federalist*, 405.

34 Ackerman, 'Prologue,' xiii, xiv.

35 Frank, *Constituent Moments*, 12–13.

36 *Ibid.*, 19–30.

37 A. Lincoln, 'Address before the Young Men's Lyceum of Springfield, Illinois' (27 January 1838).

38 Smith, *Stories of Peoplehood*.

39 P. Rosanvallon, *Democracy Past and Future*, trans. S. Moyn (New York: Columbia University Press, 2006), 92.

40 Fligstein, *Euro-Clash*.

41 Weiler, 'A Quiet Revolution'; Weiler, 'The Reformation of European Constitutionalism'; J. H. H. Weiler, 'Federalism and Constitutionalism: Europe's Sonderweg,' *Jean Monnet Working Paper*, 10 (2000).

42 Cooke, *The Federalist*, 108.

43 See H. S. Stout, *Upon the Altar of the Nation: A Moral History of the American Civil War* (New York: Viking, 2006); D. R. Goldfield, *America Aflame: How the Civil War Created a Nation* (New York: Bloomsbury Press, 2011).

44 Lincoln, 'Address before the Young Men's Lyceum.'

45 Norwegian Nobel Committee, 'The Nobel Peace Prize 2012 – Press Release.'

46 J. Habermas, 'Oslo's Call to Europe,' *La Repubblica* (15 October 2012).

47 The English translation of the Adorno lectures is available as Streeck, *Buying Time: The Delayed Crisis of Democratic Capitalism*. I borrow the image of the EU as a shield and Trojan horse from J. Borrell, 'The Decline of the Left in Europe,' speech at the Center for European Studies, Harvard University, Cambridge, MA, USA, 17 October 2014.

48 W. Streeck, *Gekaufte Zeit: Die vertagte Krise des demokratischen Kapitalismus* (Berlin: Suhrkamp, 2013), 236.

49 J. Habermas, 'Demokratie oder Kapitalismus? Vom Elend der nationalstaatlichen Fragmentierung in einer kapitalistisch integrierten Weltgesellschaft,' *Blätter für Deutsche und internationale Politik* 58:5 (2013), 62; Streeck, 'Small-State Nostalgia?' 218.

50 See W. Streeck, 'Reflections on Political Scale,' *Jurisprudence*, 10:1 (2019), 1–14.

51 W. Streeck, 'How Will Capitalism End?' *New Left Review*, 87 (2014), 35–64.

52 Held, *Introduction to Critical Theory*, 284.

53 U. Beck, 'Cooperate or Fail! The Way Out of the Euro Crisis,' *Dissent* (2011).

54 Horkheimer, 'Traditional and Critical Theory,' 200; also Marcuse, *Reason and Revolution*, 300; Aglietta, 'The European Vortex,' 15–36.

55 Biebricher and Vogelmann, 'Die Zukunft Europas,' 6–8.

56 A. Linklater, *Critical Theory and World Politics: Citizenship, Sovereignty and Humanity* (London: Routledge, 2007), 108; Falk, 'The Making of Global Citizenship,' 136–137.

57 Schecter, *Critical Theory in the Twenty-First Century*, 199.

58 H. R. Luce, 'The American Century,' *Life Magazine* (17 February 1941), 61–65; H. Evans, *The American Century* (New York: Knopf, 1998); W. LaFeber, R. Polenberg, and N. Woloch, *The American Century: A History of the United States since the 1890s* (New York: M. E. Sharpe, 1998); R. L. Moore and M. Vaudagna, *The American Century in Europe* (Ithaca, NY: Cornell University Press, 2003); A. J. Bacevich, *The Short American Century: A Postmortem* (Cambridge, MA: Harvard University Press, 2012).

59 D. Lazare, *The Frozen Republic: How the Constitution is Paralyzing Democracy* (New York: Harcourt Brace, 1996).

60 S. Avineri and Z. Sternhell, *Europe's Century of Discontent: The Legacies of Fascism, Nazism, and Communism* (Jerusalem: Hebrew University Magnes Press, 2003).

61 Anderson, *The New Old World*, 132–133.

62 Bellamy and Castiglione, 'Building the Union,' 444; T. Ball, J. Farr, and R. L. Hanson (eds), *Political Innovation and Conceptual Change* (Cambridge: Cambridge University Press, 1989).

Concluding remarks: a plea for politics at the European level

In regard to the essential kind of change at which critical theory aims, there can be no ... conception of it until it actually comes about. If the proof of the pudding is in the eating, the eating here is still in the future.

Max Horkheimer, 'Traditional and Critical Theory' (1937)

Integration and the European rupture

This book elucidates the origins, development, and future of one of the most interesting and important political innovations of the twentieth century: the European Union. My basic thesis is that the EU's foundation as an autonomous, community-based institution with decision-making powers outside the constitutional infrastructure of its member-states would not have occurred without the transnationally shared, collective memories of Europe's age of total war (1914–45), which forced Europeans across the continent to re-evaluate the previously dominant historical narratives of nationalism after 1945. The critical theory of memory I developed in chapter 1 provided the philosophical basis for my argument by detailing how broad historical ruptures that shatter existing understandings of the past allow individuals and communities to reconstruct these shards into new narratives.

Building on this foundation, Part I applied this theory to the EU by showing how the rupture of 1945 provided the cognitive, motivational, and justificatory resources for European integration 'beyond the nation-state.'[1] Proceeding chronologically, chapters 2 and 3 documented the important role the collective memory of war and atrocity played in the creation and development of the European Communities between 1945 and 2003, despite the opposition of individuals like Charles de Gaulle and member-states like the

Concluding remarks

United Kingdom. I argued that the EU continued to evolve on the community model – not as an intergovernmental organisation or a confederation – primarily because integrationist leaders, whose remembrance of the past led them to believe in the necessity of pooling decision-making powers, pushed the project forward at crucial moments.

In chapter 4, the final section of the explanatory-diagnostic part of the book, I claimed that the EU's problems at the start of the third millennium – while heightened by the financial, monetary, and political crisis brought on by the Great Recession – are tied to the fragmentation and loss of the collective remembrance of the rupture of 1945. For the generations that experienced the continent's age of total war, the movement towards deeper and broader integration was a moral and political imperative that drew its impetus from their memories of war, suffering, and atrocity between 1914 and 1945. As the global economic downturn that started in 2008 put ever greater pressure on the welfare state, a new cohort of leaders born after the end of the war increasingly sought to calculate their European interests in terms of nationalistic, short-range economic cost–benefit analysis.

Having diagnosed the essential problems that underlie the crisis of the EU at the start of the twenty-first century, Part II explored possible treatments for these pathologies. I argued that by acting according to their short-term economic self-interest, the first generation of leaders that has no memory of the rupture of 1945 has undermined the institutional and political resources that represent Europe's best hope to preserve its prosperity and influence in an era of increasing globalisation and multiculturalism. The basic thesis of Part II was that the best hope for the future of Europe is to be found in the cohorts that have come of age during what I refer to as the 'second phase of integration.' By building on their transnationally shared collective memories of growing up in a continent of open borders, these generations – including my own – can construct a new historical imaginary that no longer relies on personal memories of war and atrocity, much like the United States was forced to do when it faced the loss of its generations of experience in the middle of the nineteenth century.

My concluding thoughts are divided into three sections. In the first, I apply my critical theory of memory to the revival of the symbols and policies associated with the fascist movements in the aftermath of the Great Recession. This 'return of the repressed' represents a profound threat to the new European order and its normative foundations. I then consider the possible elements that would make up a realistic European narrative that could carry the project forward despite the loss of the generations that had personal memories of the rupture of 1945. I argue that such a narrative will need a forward-looking component to complement its backward-looking foundations in the continental experience of total war. More specifically, I suggest that the EU show its peoples that it pays to be a European citizen by deploying its powers in order to exert some measure of control over global economic forces at a time when international markets have demonstrated that they can override the political powers of the nation-state.

I conclude by reflecting on the importance of critical theory at the start of the twenty-first century. The unstable geoeconomic and geopolitical situation at the start of the third millennium calls out for a revival of this approach, with its emphasis on the need for 'critical histories of the present' that aim not merely at explanation and understanding, but at the construction of a 'social science with a practical intent.'[2] Although postwar critical theory has increasingly moved towards the analysis of social and cultural issues, the crises of the present have increasingly taken economic form, calling for a renewed attention to the role of economics in political life.[3]

Collective memory and the return of fascism

I have devoted much of this project to demonstrating how the rupture of 1945 provided postwar leaders with the cognitive, motivational, and justificatory resources of transnationally shared collective memory, which allowed them to recombine the pieces of the shattered past to form a new historical narrative of European integration as a moral and political necessity. However, as detailed in Part II, the European project is increasingly imperilled at a time when it not only faces the greatest economic downturn since the Great Depression, but also the loss of its founding generations. As the cohorts with direct memories of the war leave public life, the normative resources of the past that have driven integration have dried up.

As a political project achieved by economic means, integration has always had a Janus-like quality. While Janus is often evoked as a metaphor for being two-faced, it is important to remember that Janus is the Roman deity of beginnings, of gates and doorways. He is the god of transitions, with one face turned to the past, the other to the future. Like Janus, the architects of a community-based Europe always had to strike a balance between past and future, between the political ideals of unity, solidarity, and supranationalism on the one hand and the pragmatic concerns of economics on the other.

Concluding remarks

For previous generations with personal memories of Europe's age of total war, transnationally shared collective remembrance provided a corrective balance to the narrow, nationalistic cost–benefit calculations of short-term economic gain. Today this is no longer the case. In the wake of the Great Recession, Europe has witnessed a 'return of the repressed.' Although it was founded on the opposition to the Nazism of the Third Reich and the elimination of the preconditions that brought it to power, at the start of the twenty-first century it appears that 'fascism has returned to the West.'[4] Summing up this unwelcome phenomenon, Seyla Benhabib notes,

> the rise of far-right extremists not just in Germany, but all over Europe, from the Golden Dawn in Greece to neo-Nazis in Ukraine. Some, like the National Front in France and Britain First in the United Kingdom, have entered the political mainstream. Many sit in the EU Parliament, using the funds of an organisation whose destruction they seek. And all draw from the memories of Europe's fascist past, in the period between the two World Wars, seeking answers to Europe's contemporary problems.[5]

The reinvigoration of these symbols and policies represents a repudiation of the lessons of the postwar era. It also signals a return to the negative mode of collective memory that I introduced in chapter 1 and mentioned again in chapter 5. In contrast to the European project, which was designed to provide a solution to the continent's long-standing conflicts, 'the rise of far-right nationalism is a reaction to the European Union, which sparked a backlash from an older generation of people who fear the loss of their identities as white Christians. As refugees streamed into Europe, those diffuse sentiments for a vanishing past have found easily identifiable targets.'[6] In the face of a supranational integration that certain older segments of the population feel has failed them, Europe is confronted with a desire shared by many across the continent to return to the old 'container [*Behälter*] of the nation-state.'[7]

The exact characterisation of the reinvigoration of the far right in Europe is controversial. Some commentators argue that these movements are populist, others that they are fascist, while a third group has coined neologisms like 'populist authoritarianism' to describe the French National Rally, the United Kingdom Independence Party, the Golden Dawn, True Finn, Italy's League, Spain's Vox, and the other parties that fit into this broader right-wing turn in Europe.[8] Regardless of the label, what these movements and parties all share is 'a type of politics that wants to suppress and even kill its opponents rather than arguing with them, that prefers an authoritarian state over democracy, and that pits an aggressively exclusionary idea of the nation against a pluralism that prioritises difference.'[9] Although they are not fascist in the classical sense, they are the result of the same social pathologies that the Frankfurt School thinker Erich Fromm diagnosed in the 1930s: tiredness and loneliness, as well as the exhaustion and failure of the left.[10]

Much like the Great Depression of the early 1930s, the proximate cause of the current rise of fascism is the economic crisis brought on by the Great Recession. However, the true causes lie deeper. According to Sheri Berman, the problem is 'not the economic suffering it caused – although that was bad enough – but the failure of democratic institutions to respond to it.' Echoing these thoughts, Geoff Eley concludes that this threat derives from a dual, interlocking crisis of representation and consent 'in which two separate things happen together. First, the given political arrangements no longer work in a way that enables stable governing to occur. Second, those governing arrangements malfunction so badly that they forfeit the consent of the people.'[11]

This focus on the return of fascism to Europe also helps to explain the demographic underpinnings of support for the far right. Through an examination of recent polling data, Robert Inglehart and Pippa Norris show that '[o]lder voters are much likelier than younger voters to support these parties, although unemployment rates are higher among the young.'[12] In line with my own arguments, Inglehart and Norris are referring to individuals of the 'baby boom' generation, who were born shortly after the war and grew up at a time when the EU and its effects were not particularly visible in the everyday lives of Europeans. In contrast to millennials (born 1981–96) and younger cohorts, who see themselves as European as a result of their experiences growing up on a continent of open borders, this older 'baby boom' generation associates the EU with the end of the economic boom known as the *Wirtschaftswunder* or the *trente glorieuses* (1945–75).

This understanding of the generational dynamics of memory helps to explain the vulnerability of the first postwar cohort of Europeans to backward-looking electoral slogans that look to 'take back control,' as the catchphrase of the 2016 'Vote Leave' campaign for Britain to leave the EU so successfully put it.[13] This desire to go back to the past drives not only a broader yearning to return to the comfortable confines of the nation-state, but also an increasing scepticism towards democratic self-government. As Roberto Foa and Yascha Mounk point out, 'Over the last three decades, trust in political institutions such as parliaments or the courts has precipitously declined across the established democracies of North America and Western Europe.' Combined with decreasing voter turnout and an increasing loss of faith in the ability of democracy to protect the interests of its citizens, these dynamics leads to what they call a broader 'democratic deconsolidation.' This 'legitimation crisis' – to use Habermas's vocabulary – threatens many of the gains of the postwar period, as '[c]itizens who once accepted democracy as the only legitimate form of government could become more open to authoritarian alternatives.'[14]

Despite these problems, not all hope is lost. Although the Great Recession and the crisis of the Eurozone have been traumatic, they have not yet fulfilled the criteria of repeated, violent delegitimation of the existing system that I laid out as the preconditions for rupture in chapter 1. In fact, the dangers Europe faces at the start of the third millennium pale in comparison to those of the interwar years; in spite of everything, a third world war does not appear to be on the horizon.[15] Given that many of the cultural threats driving the rise of the far right in Europe are enabled by the perception of economic instability rooted in rising global inequality, the EU needs to address these problems through the 'existing European framework for collective deliberation,' as well as by developing new mechanisms that can cope with these issues.[16]

Doing so will require the EU to take its social policies more seriously by developing a more robust model of economic government, a form of rule that not only seeks to enable ever-purer market competition, but that also takes social policies and workers' rights into account. Some steps in this direction have already been taken. Although the French government has been arguing for the need for *gouvernement économique* – an 'economic government' as opposed to mere 'economic governance' – for some time, recently even the traditionally reluctant Germans have started to speak of *Wirtschaftsregierung*. Although these moves are still in the early stages, Luuk van Middelaar argues that this development is important because 'battles over words very often help us to grasp underlying political forces.' Overall, he contends that this testifies to a 'return to politics' driven by the realisation that 'rules alone cannot constitute an economic policy.' The abandonment of rules in favour of an approach that recognises the need for 'crisis mechanisms, permanent political guidance and a common understanding of its needs' is signified precisely in the semantic shift from governance to government.[17]

Despite their necessity, this transformation will not come easily. In fact, it will require a number of changes to current practices. For example, Sigmar Gabriel, a leading figure in the German Social Democratic Party, points out that developing economic government in Europe will require combating the image of Germany as the 'packhorse of Europe.' He notes, 'The root of the problem is purely national narratives in the member states of the European Union, particularly in our country. Whereas the truth is that Germany is the chief profiteer, indeed the net *beneficiary*, of the European Union.' This is visible not only in the fact that European unification was a prerequisite for German reunification after 1989, but also in the fact that Germany's status as an export champion depends on production lines and markets that extend throughout the EU.[18]

In addition to combating these nationalistic narratives, the move towards greater economic government will also require a revitalised, transnational political understanding of solidarity. As Habermas points out, 'Solidarity is not charity. Solidarity – united action supportive of one's allies – means accepting certain disadvantages for the sake of one's long-term self-interest, trusting that one's partners will act similarly in comparable situations.' Although it is difficult, Habermas argues that Europe has much to gain by opposing nationalistic economic narratives, particularly if Europeans want to fight back against the interests of global capital and maintain a voice on the global geopolitical stage: 'there is no natural or inevitable reason why issues of redistributive fairness should stop at national borders and should not also be discussed within the European community of nations.'[19]

How exactly this can be achieved is an open question. Thomas Piketty has advocated the creation of 'an original form of a European bicameral system based on one hand on the EP (elected directly by the citizens) and on the other on a Parliamentary Chamber comprising representatives from the national parliaments in proportion to the population of each country and the political groups present in each Parliament.' Much like Habermas, Piketty argues that this form of bicameralism will give the EP the necessary democratic backing and legitimacy to engage in transnational welfare and social policy to a much greater degree than it has to date.[20]

Along similar lines, Ulrike Guérot seeks to build on the federalist ideals of the EU's founding fathers, arguing that such changes cannot be brought about by national leaders. Instead, she argues that what Europe needs is a European republic created by and for a truly European citizenry. By contrast, Yannis Varoufakis, the former Greek Finance Minister, has proposed to democratise European economic governance through the creation of a European Investment Bank that would encourage spending and investment rather than austerity.[21] Whatever concrete solutions the peoples of Europe decide to adopt, it is clear that politics must move up to the European level if it is to develop the ability to face the complex, global problems of the twenty-first century.

Concluding remarks

A European story of peoplehood

In the aftermath of the fall of the Iron Curtain and the 'return to Europe' of the postcommunist states of East-Central Europe, it was possible to argue that a European identity existed based on the fact that Europeans were increasingly engaging in common debates mediated through their national public spheres.[22] Two decades later, these optimistic conclusions appear unreasonably Panglossian at best. Although it is true that both the clashes of memory brought about by the accession of the postcommunist member-states and the crisis of the Eurozone have encouraged debate about common issues and problems, these discussions have not resulted in greater solidarity and understanding. Instead, they have merely served to reinforce national divisions and stereotypes between different parts of Europe.

This demonstrable lack of a common identity has reinvigorated the 'no demos thesis,' which holds that the EU and its institutions cannot effectively or legitimately undertake political functions 'because there is as yet no European people.'[23] The issues facing Europe in the aftermath of the Great Recession and the populist, neo-fascist revival it has spawned, have also exacerbated the questions of the 'democratic deficit' that have haunted the European Communities from the start. Much of the EU's basic structure, such as its unelected executive commission, which is only partially responsible to an assembly of representatives from the nation-states, has persisted since the 1950s. From this perspective it is understandable why many see the EU's enduring democratic deficit as the '*faut de M. Monnet.*'[24]

However, the EU has taken certain steps towards greater democratic legitimacy. To start, although the structures of the EU clearly do not meet the criteria for national democracies, it has been able to draw some legitimacy from its constituent parts. Most of its leading functions – such as central banking, constitutional adjudication, civil prosecution, economic diplomacy, and technical administration – have traditionally been of little electoral salience and are usually delegated to expert committees in most states on the national level.[25] Additionally, it is undeniable that the EU has become more democratic over the course of its development, even in terms of popular sovereignty. The institutional deepening since 1985 has gradually accorded more power to the directly elected EP. Since the inauguration of the European Council in 1974 the EU has also been able to draw more democratic legitimacy from leaders elected on the national level, since most important decisions have to be approved by heads of government with a domestic electoral mandate.[26]

Concluding remarks

There are limits, however, to how far integration can go without developing its own democratic legitimacy through common, supranational practices of opinion- and will-formation. Although many of the EU's activities are technocratic, this argument has lost its force as the Eurozone crisis has pushed Europe to expand its competencies into more democratically salient policy areas, such as banking regulation and fiscal policy. The EU's increasing tendency to act as a political union must also be complemented by democratic decision-making procedures that resemble a political community as well.

In order to take this step, the EU will also need to build a common identity based on the idea of an ethically constitutive identity that allows its citizens to act together as a single, coherent, and powerful agent in the world. Ever since the Schuman Declaration of 1950, the narrative of a community-based, supranational Europe as a product of the experience of war and suffering in the first half of the twentieth century has dominated the continent's political discourse.[27] However, this backward-looking answer to the basic legitimation demand seems to have lost its force, particularly since the fall of communism in 1989. Unfortunately, once it has been achieved, peace is 'quiet'; it is easily forgotten and taken for granted.[28] New, forward-looking resources that go beyond the mere achievement of order are necessary precisely because the old ones no longer seem capable of legitimising the steps the EU needs to take at the start of the twentieth century.

What the EU needs is a new narrative that links the 'space of experience' incorporated into the present through collective memory and the 'horizons of expectations' for the future in effective and attractive ways that can ground what Rogers Smith refers to as 'a story of peoplehood.' As I have already pointed out, in the past the EU has traditionally relied on narratives of security and prosperity to legitimise its existence. The first justification seems to have been exhausted. Similarly, the second seems laughable in the aftermath of the greatest economic crisis since the Great Depression. As Smith points out, it is 'risky to attempt to "sell" a vision of political community strictly in terms of its economic benefits. Inevitably, economic bad times will come, to some or many of their core constituents.'[29] However, this does not mean that welfare can no longer play a role in justifying the EU, just as its success in achieving peace does not mean that security is no longer salient either. On the contrary, both of these factors remain important; they just need to be reconceptualised in ways that account for these difficulties.

Unfortunately, in light of the crisis of the Eurozone and the transnational return of fascism, retreat is not an option. The globalisation of economic interests, which have successfully moved beyond the nation-state and generated protectionist responses across Europe, have not been matched by an expansion of politics to a similar level. On the contrary, developments since the end of the Cold War show that the power of the state to control events within its borders, which is crucial to the traditional doctrine of sovereignty, is in decline. According to Matti Koskenneimi, 'The pattern of influence and decision-making that rules the world has an increasingly marginal connection with sovereignty.'[30]

In the face of these developments, I argue that the existing European legal and political order can legitimise itself by showing that it can protect its citizens against the encroachment of external economic forces. This narrative combines the security and welfare justifications for integration by reconceptualising these ideas. Instead of focusing on warfare as the primary threat to internal economic prosperity within the state, it justifies postnational governance as a necessary response to threats to the welfare of citizens posed by transnational economic interests that can no longer be harnessed by the state. In this sense, a realistic European story of peoplehood would be based on what Habermas describes as the need for politics 'to catch up with globalized markets … in institutional forms that do not regress below the legitimacy conditions for democratic self-determination.'[31]

There is already some evidence that the EU has started to develop in the direction suggested by Habermas's critical theory of what he refers to as the 'postnational constellation.' These moves towards greater European political control over international market forces are already visible in the emergence of two differing models of globalisation in the post-Cold War world. The first, American path is driven by bilateral agreements, limited planning, and the idea that the power of multinational corporations and other economic interests should predominate 'without organizing or even supervising, markets.'[32] This approach builds on the United States' hegemonic position in global politics to support its vision of globalisation based on market liberalisation.

In contrast, Europe has developed a second, alternative approach. The European form of 'managed globalization' seeks to embed economic policy within multilateral agreements that allow for intervention by supranational politicians and bureaucrats based on codified rules and an awareness of the economic consequences of market liberalisation. Simon Reich and Richard Ned Lebow observe, 'In contrast to the American neoliberal theories that profits are ultimately good for everyone because prosperity will trickle down, the European approach is rooted in a more egalitarian theory of justice … [that] make it compatible with a more just social democratic model of society.'[33] In addition to its anti-trust cases against Google, another example of this is the development and passage into law of the General Data Protection Regulation (GDPR), which seeks to give individuals control over the use of their private online data. Because it applies to any enterprise that deals with subjects located within the EU regardless of citizenship, it has had a profound effect on global data-sharing practices.

Despite its successes, the basic problem is that European institutions have not succeeded in translating these developments into a clear narrative that can legitimise their actions. My argument implies not only that supranational political cooperation to influence global markets is needed to answer the European demand for legitimation; it is also necessary for the survival of the EU. During the crisis of the Eurozone international financial markets and large financial institutions were able to dictate policy to the EU and its member-states, which found themselves dependent on these actors for capital in the middle of an economic downturn. In order to reassert political control over these impersonal financial forces, the EU will have to develop its own mechanisms of economic governance, including mutual borrowing, fiscal transfers from richer to poorer regions, and the presence of a lender of last resort.

Although the EMU was 'initially conceived as a technocratic exercise,' in response to the crisis it 'is now rapidly transforming the EU into a federal entity.'[34] While these changes are undesirable on a certain level, the necessity to integration in order to reassert control over economic and financial forces that operate beyond the nation-state could potentially help to ground a new European historical imaginary. Although such a narrative of identity would clearly be a construction, all such narratives are constructed as part of an active 'politics of people-building.' As Habermas points out, such constructions lose the 'stigma of randomness' if they are accompanied by an act of 'self-conscious appropriation.'[35] Achieving the goal of self-conscious appropriation of a politics that will allow for Europeans to regain control over the market forces that are increasingly exercising control over their lives is the key task of European politics today.

A critical theory of the contemporary moment

In discussing collective memory and its role in the origins and development of European integration, I have repeatedly returned to the methodological issues raised by the Frankfurt School of social and political theory. In addition to contributing to the burgeoning literature on memory and normative EU studies, my goal was to demonstrate the enduring potential of critical theory as an engaged form of social analysis that not only seeks to identify but also to suggest possible solutions to the social pathologies of the present. Insofar as my substantive arguments have been convincing, I hope that this will also serve as an endorsement of the critical theory developed by the Frankfurt School.

The situation at the start of the third millennium calls for a revival of critical theory. Horkheimer, Adorno, and the other thinkers associated with the first generation of the Frankfurt School initially formulated their understanding of critical theory in order to understand the problems facing interwar Europe, including the economic suffering brought on by the Great Depression, the rise of fascism, the endurance of prejudice (particularly in the form of anti-Semitism), the mechanisation of the economy, the failure of the workers' movement, and the threat of total war. Although it is certainly possible to normatively reconstruct the history of the past hundred years as part of a progressive learning process, many of the same problems that plagued the 1920s and 1930s still persist, albeit in different guises.

Perhaps the most striking parallel between the interwar years and the world at the start of the twenty-first century is to be found in the economic realm. While critical theory moved away from its focus on capitalism towards an analysis of injustice after the passing of the first generation, today it is once again clear that an economic focus on '[e]mancipation, not justice, is the urgent job of critique.'[36] Although they are separated by almost a hundred years, both of these periods have been defined by a global collapse of financial capitalism. The very names for these two crises – the Great Depression and the Great Recession – put this comparison front and centre.

In both of these situations, economics has taken precedence over politics, making individuals and communities feel powerless in the face of the systemic forces of capitalism. For much of the population the excesses of global finance stand as the paradigmatic example of this disturbing trend: 'Today every endangered large bank has to be upheld by means of state aid … while in former times measures of this kind were an exception.' These words from Friedrich Pollock – written in 1932! – could just as easily describe the situation in 2008. He continues,

> Today, many enterprises in industry and banking have grown so gigantically, that no state power, no matter how liberally it behaves, can stand by and witness their

downfall. Above a certain size of capital, the enterprise may continue to claim the profit for itself, but the risk is unrolled to the mass of tax-payers, since its collapse would bring about the most severe consequences – both for the body economic and political situation.[37]

It is precisely the impotence that citizens feel when faced with this kind of technocratic logic that critical theory sought to combat at the time of its creation at the Institute for Social Research during the interwar years. In 1937 Herbert Marcuse argued, 'The philosophical element within [critical] theory is a form of protest against the new "economism": against an isolation of the economic struggle, against the division maintained between the economic and the political.'[38] This economic rationality, which subordinates collective political decisions to the impartial needs of the capitalist system, has continued to develop since Marcuse first identified it in the time leading up to the start of the Second World War. It received its definitive statement in the oft-repeated refrain used to justify austerity and bailing out overleveraged banks at the taxpayers' expense in the aftermath of the Great Recession: 'there is no alternative' (TINA).

The reduction of reason to an instrumental form of thinking that only considers how to preserve the existing system signals the end of politics as a collective form of decision-making. Once reason lost its ability to consider ends, Marcuse notes, 'Rationality is transformed from a critical force into one of adjustment and compliance. Autonomy of reason loses its meaning in the same measure as the thoughts, feelings and actions of men are shaped by the technical requirements of the apparatus which they themselves have created.'[39]

As Horkheimer points out in the epigraph I quoted at the beginning of this chapter, critical theory will never be able to predict the concrete form that future social emancipation will take, since this requires the concrete action of individuals in the world. However, engaged thinkers following in the tradition of the Frankfurt School must continue to make use of it to identify the social pathologies of the present and to encourage individuals to take concrete action to bring about better, more autonomous forms of life. Spurring an awareness of the pathologies of present in order to stimulate social change is the mission of the critical theorist as 'non-conformist intellectual.'[40]

European integration was originally designed to emancipate the citizens of the continent from the forces that had led them into two world wars and a decade-long depression between 1914 and 1945. Given these lofty goals, it is particularly

Concluding remarks

disappointing to see the EU fall victim to TINA narratives. However, the message of a critical theory of the contemporary moment is that it is still possible for the EU to fulfil its promise in the future if the people take the concrete action necessary to forge alternatives that currently appear not to exist. Perhaps the fallout of the memory clashes between eastern and western member-states, and the suffering brought about by the Great Recession and the Eurozone crisis can act as a non-military rupture to spur the cognitive, motivational, and justificatory resources that are necessary to bring about new forms of political innovation vis-à-vis international market forces in the twenty-first century.

Notes

1 Haas, *Beyond the Nation-State*.
2 Hoy and McCarthy, *Critical Theory*, 229–230; Benhabib, *Critique, Norm, and Utopia*, 253; J. Habermas, *Knowledge and Human Interests*, trans. J. J. Shapiro (Boston: Beacon Press, 1971).
3 P. Anderson, *Considerations on Western Marxism* (London: New Left Books, 1976).
4 W. Streeck, 'The Return of the Repressed,' *New Left Review*, 104 (2017); S. Amin, 'The Return of Fascism in Contemporary Capitalism,' *Monthly Review*, 4:1 (2014), 12.
5 S. Benhabib, 'The Return of Fascism,' *The New Republic* (29 September 2017).
6 *Ibid.*
7 U. Beck and E. Grande, *Das kosmopolitische Europa: Gesellschaft und Politik in der zweiten Moderne* (Frankfurt am Main: Suhrkamp, 2004).
8 See S. Berman, 'Populism is Not Fascism: But it could be a Harbinger,' *Foreign Affairs* (2016); Amin, 'The Return of Fascism in Contemporary Capitalism'; Inglehart and Norris, 'Trump and the Populist Authoritarian Parties.' See R. Eatwell, 'Populism and Fascism,' in C. R. Kaltwasser, P. A. Taggart, P. Ochoa Espejo, and P. Ostiguy (eds), *The Oxford Handbook of Populism* (Oxford: Oxford University Press, 2017); Koronaiou *et al.*, 'Golden Dawn, Austerity and Young People'.
9 G. Eley, 'Is Trump a Fascist?' *Hate 2.0*, November 2016, https://hate2point0.com/2016/11/21/is-trump-a-fascist/amp/ (accessed 3 December 2016); also Eley, 'Fascism and Antifascism, 1920–2020: Slogan, Impulse, Theory, Strategy,' talk delivered at Leuphana University Lüneburg, 1 November 2017.
10 E. Fromm, *Escape from Freedom* (New York: Holt, Rinehart and Winston, 1941).
11 Berman, 'Populism is Not Fascism,' 41; Eley, 'Is Trump a Fascist?'.
12 Inglehart and Norris, 'Trump and the Populist Authoritarian Parties,' 446.
13 M. Goodwin and O. Heath, 'The 2016 Referendum, Brexit and the Left Behind: An Aggregate-Level Analysis of the Result,' *The Political Quarterly*, 87:3 (2016).
14 Foa and Mounk, 'The Dangers of Deconsolidation,' 6, 15; Habermas, *Legitimation Crisis*.
15 Berman, 'Populism is Not Fascism,' 43.
16 T. Piketty, 'Reconstructing Europe After Brexit,' *Le Blog de Thomas Piketty*, 30 June 2016, http://piketty.blog.lemonde.fr/2016/06/30/reconstructing-europe-after-brexit/ (accessed 4 July 2016).
17 Van Middelaar, 'The Return of Politics,' 501, 500.

Concluding remarks

18 S. Gabriel, J. Habermas, and E. Macron, 'Rethinking Europe: A Discussion between Jürgen Habermas, Sigmar Gabriel and Emmanuel Macron,' *Eurozine* (4 April 2017), www.eurozine.com/jurgen-habermas-sigmar-gabriel-e-emmanuel-macron-sulleuropa-da-ripensare/ (accessed 6 April 2017).

19 *Ibid.*

20 Piketty, 'Reconstructing Europe after Brexit.'

21 U. Guérot, *Warum Europa eine Republik werden muss! Eine politische Utopie* (Bonn: J.H.W. Dietz, 2016); Y. Varoufakis, 'Our Plan to Revive Europe Can Succeed Where Macron and Picketty Failed,' *The Guardian* (13 December 2018).

22 F. Andriessen, *Prosperity and Stability in a Wider Europe*, speech at the Atlantic CEO Institute (Dobris, Czechoslovakia: Europa Press Release, 10 June 1991), http://europa.eu/rapid/pressReleasesAction.do?reference=SPEECH/91/71&format=HTML&aged=1&language=EN&guiLanguage=en (accessed 27 February 2012); T. Risse, '"Let's Argue!": Communicative Action in World Politics,' *International Organization*, 54:1 (2000).

23 D. Grimm, 'Does Europe Need a Constitution?,' *European Law Journal*, 1:3 (1995), 295.

24 J.-P. Chevènement, *La faute de M. Monnet: La république et l'Europe* (Paris: Fayard, 2006). Also A. S. Milward, *The European Rescue of the Nation-State* (London: Routledge, 1992), 336; K. Featherstone, 'Jean Monnet and the "Democratic Deficit" in the European Union,' *Journal of Common Market Studies*, 32:2 (1994), 149–170.

25 A. Moravcsik, 'In Defense of the "Democratic Deficit": Reassessing Legitimacy in the European Union,' *Journal of Common Market Studies*, 40:4 (2002), 603–624; P. Rosanvallon, *Democratic Legitimacy: Impartiality, Reflexivity, Proximity* (Princeton: Princeton University Press, 2011).

26 M. Pensky, *The Ends of Solidarity: Discourse Theory in Ethics and Politics* (Albany: State University of New York Press, 2008); R. Bellamy and S. Kröger, 'Domesticating the Democratic Deficit? The Role of National Parliaments and Parties in the EU's System of Governance,' *Parliamentary Affairs*, 67:2 (2014), 437–457.

27 D. Dinan, 'The Historiography of European Integration,' in D. Dinan (ed), *Origins and Evolution of the European Union* (Oxford: Oxford University Press, 2006), 297.

28 L. G. Feldman, 'Reconciliation and Legitimacy: Foreign Relations and Enlargement of the European Union,' in T. Banchoff and M. Smith (eds), *Legitimacy and the European Union: The Contested Polity* (London: Routledge, 1999), 66.

29 Smith, *Stories of Peoplehood*, 82.

30 M. Koskenniemi, 'What use for Sovereignty Today?' *Asian Journal of International Law*, 1 (2011), 63; J. Habermas, 'The Postnational Constellation and the Future of Democracy,' in *The Postnational Constellation: Political Essays*, trans. Max Pensky (Cambridge, MA: MIT Press, 2001).

31 Habermas, 'The Postnational Constellation and the Future of Democracy,' 84.

32 R. Abdelal and S. Meunier, 'Managed Globalization: Doctrine, Practice and Promise,' *Journal of European Public Policy*, 17:3 (2010), 351.

33 S. Reich and R. N. Lebow, *Good-Bye Hegemony: Power and Influence in the Global System* (Princeton: Princeton University Press, 2014), 61, 64.

34 W. Streeck, 'Markets and Peoples: Democratic Capitalism and European Integration,' *New Left Review*, 73 (2012), 67.

35 Habermas, 'The Postnational Constellation and the Future of Democracy,' 64; Smith, *Stories of Peoplehood*, 36–37; Habermas, 'February 15,' 12, 10.

36 Azmanova, 'Crisis?' 358.

Concluding remarks

37   F. Pollock, 'Die gegenwärtige Lage des Kapitalismus und die Aussichten einer planwirtschaftlichen Neuordnung,' *Zeitschrift für Sozialforschung*, 1 (1932), 12.

38   Herbert Marcuse, 'Philosophie und kritische Theorie,' *Zeitschrift für Sozialforschung*, 6 (1937), 646, quoted in Dubiel, *Theory and Politics: Studies in the Development of Critical Theory*, 65.

39   Marcuse, 'Some Social Implications of Modern Technology,' *Zeitschrift für Sozialforschung*, 9 (1941), 422.

40   A. Demirović, *Der nonkonformistische Intellektuelle: Die Entwicklung der kritischen Theorie zur Frankfurter Schule* (Frankfurt am Main: Suhrkamp, 1999).

Select bibliography

Abdelal, Rawi, and Sophie Meunier. 'Managed Globalization: Doctrine, Practice and Promise.' *Journal of European Public Policy* 17, no. 3 (2010): 350–367.

Ackerman, Bruce A. 'Prologue: Hope and Fear in Constitutional Law.' In *Developing a Constitution for Europe*. Edited by Erik Oddvar Eriksen, John Erik Fossum, and Agustín José Menéndez. London: Routledge, 2004.

———. *We the People*. Cambridge, MA: Belknap Press of Harvard University Press, 1991.

———. 'Constitutional Politics/Constitutional Law.' *The Yale Law Journal* 99, no. 3 (December, 1989): 453–547.

Adenauer, Konrad. *Briefe, 1953–1955*, edited by Rudolf Morsey and Hans-Peter Schwarz. Berlin: Siedler Verlag, 1995.

———. *Briefe, 1949–1951*, edited by Rudolf Morsey and Hans-Peter Schwarz. Berlin: Siedler Verlag, 1985.

———. *Briefe 1945–1947*, edited by Rudolf Morsey and Hans Peter Mensing. Berlin: Siedler Verlag, 1983.

———. *Briefe über Deutschland, 1945–1951*, edited by Hans Peter Mensing. Berlin: Corso, 1983.

———. *Memoirs 1945–53*, translated by Beate Ruhm von Oppen. Chicago: Henry Regnery Company, 1966.

Adenauer, Konrad, and Theodor Heuss. *Unter vier Augen: Gespräche aus den Gründerjahren 1949–1959*, edited by Hans Peter Mensing. Berlin: Siedler Verlag, 1997.

Adorno, Theodor W. *Kulturkritik und Gesellschaft. Prismen. Ohne Leitbild*. Gesammelte Schriften Bd. 10. Darmstadt: Wissenschaftliche Buchgesellschaft, 1998.

———. 'What does Coming to Terms with the Past Mean?' In *Bitburg in Moral and Political Perspective*. Edited by Geoffrey H. Hartman. Bloomington: Indiana University Press, 1986.

———. *Gesammelte Schriften, Band 8: Soziologische Schriften 1*. Frankfurt am Main: Suhrkamp Verlag, 1972.

———. 'Scientific Experiences of a European Scholar in America.' In *The Intellectual Migration: Europe and America, 1930–1960*. Edited by Donald Fleming and Bernard Bailyn. Cambridge, MA: Harvard University Press, 1969.

———. *Stichworte: Kritische Modelle 2*. Frankfurt am Main: Suhrkamp, 1969.

———. 'Negative Dialektik.' In *Gesammelte Schriften, Band 6*. Frankfurt am Main: Suhrkamp Verlag, 1966.

Select bibliography

Adorno, Theodor W., Else Frenkel-Brunswik, Daniel Levinson, and Nevitt Sanford. *The Authoritarian Personality*. London: Verso, 2019.

Agüero, Felipe. *Soldiers, Civilians, and Democracy: Post-Franco Spain in Comparative Perspective*. Baltimore: Johns Hopkins University Press, 1995.

Ahonen, Pertti. *After the Expulsion: West Germany and Eastern Europe, 1945–1990*. Oxford: Oxford University Press, 2003.

——. 'Domestic Constraints on West German Ostpolitik: The Role of the Expellee Organizations in the Adenauer Era.' *Central European History* 31, no. 1/2 (1998): 31–63.

Amin, Samir. 'The Return of Fascism in Contemporary Capitalism.' *Monthly Review* 66, no. 4 (2014): 1–12.

Ammert, Niklas. 'To Bridge Time: Historical Consciousness in Swedish History Textbooks.' *Journal of Educational Media, Memory, and Society* 2, no. 1 (Spring, 2010): 17–30.

Anastasakis, Othon, Kalypso Nicolaïdis, and Kerem Öktem. *In the Long Shadow of Europe: Greeks and Turks in the Era of Postnationalism*. Boston: Martinus Nijhoff, 2009.

Anderson, Perry. *The New Old World*. London: Verso, 2009.

——. 'Under the Sign of the Interim.' *London Review of Books* 18, no. 1 (1996): 13–17.

——. *Considerations on Western Marxism*. London: New Left Books, 1976.

Annan, Noel Gilroy. *Changing Enemies: The Defeat and Regeneration of Germany*. New York: W. W. Norton & Co., 1996.

Appiah, Anthony. *Cosmopolitanism: Ethics in a World of Strangers*. New York: W. W. Norton & Company, 2007.

Arendt, Hannah. *The Human Condition*. Chicago: University of Chicago Press, 1998.

——. 'Approaching the German Question.' In *Essays in Understanding, 1930–1954*. Edited by Jerome Kohn. New York: Harcourt, Brace & Co., 1994.

——. 'Dream and Nightmare.' In *Essays in Understanding, 1930–1954*. New York: Harcourt, Brace & Co., 1994.

——. *Essays in Understanding, 1930–1954*. New York: Harcourt, Brace & Co., 1994.

——. *On Revolution*. New York: Penguin Classics, 1990.

——. 'Walter Benjamin: 1892–1940.' In *Illuminations: Essays and Reflections*. Edited by Walter Benjamin. New York: Schocken Books, 1977.

——. 'Reflections on Violence.' *Journal of International Affairs* 23, no. 1 (1969): 1–35.

——. *The Origins of Totalitarianism*. New York: Brace Harcourt, 1951.

Armstrong, Karen. 'Ambiguity and Remembrance: Individual and Collective Memory in Finland.' *American Ethnologist* 27, no. 3 (2000): 591–608.

Aronsson, Peter. 'Uses of the Past – Nordic Historical Cultures in a Comparative Perspective.' *Culture Unbound* 2 (2010): 553–563.

Assmann, Aleida. 'Europe: A Community of Memory?' *GHI Bulletin* 40 (Spring, 2007): 11–25.

Avineri, Shlomo, and Zeev Sternhell. *Europe's Century of Discontent: The Legacies of Fascism, Nazism, and Communism*. Jerusalem: Hebrew University Magnes Press, 2003.

Azmanova, Albena. 'Crisis? Capitalism is Doing Very Well, How is Critical Theory?' *Constellations* 21, no. 3 (2014): 351–365.

Bacevich, Andrew J., ed. *The Short American Century: A Postmortem*. Cambridge, MA: Harvard University Press, 2012.

Badiou, Alain. *The Communist Hypothesis*. New York: Verso, 2010.

Bakiner, Onur. *Truth Commissions: Memory, Power, and Legitimacy*. Philadelphia: University of Pennsylvania Press, 2016.

Select bibliography

Ball, Terence, James Farr, and Russell L. Hanson, eds. *Political Innovation and Conceptual Change*. Cambridge: Cambridge University Press, 1989.

Ballinger, Pamela. *History in Exile: Memory and Identity at the Borders of the Balkans*. Princeton: Princeton University Press, 2003.

Barkan, Elazar, and Alexander Karn. 'Group Apology as Ethical Imperative.' In *Taking Wrongs Seriously: Apologies and Reconciliation*. Edited by Elazar Barkan and Alexander Karn. Stanford: Stanford University Press, 2006.

Bauman, Zygmunt, and Carlo Bordoni. *State of Crisis*. Cambridge: Polity, 2014.

Baylis, John. 'Britain, the Brussels Pact and the Continental Commitment.' *International Affairs* 60, no. 4 (Autumn, 1984): 615–629.

Beasley, Alessandra. 'Public Discourse and Cosmopolitan Political Identity: Imagining the European Union Citizen.' *Futures* 38 (2006): 133–145.

Beck, Ulrich. *German Europe*. New York: Polity, 2013.

——. 'Cooperate Or Fail! The Way Out of the Euro Crisis.' *Dissent*, 7 February 2011.

——. 'The Cosmopolitan Condition: Why Methodological Nationalism Fails.' *Theory, Culture & Society* 24, no. 7–8 (2007): 286–290.

Becker, Avi. 'Building Up a Memory: Austria, Switzerland, and Europe Face the Holocaust.' In *Power and the Past: Collective Memory and International Relations*. Edited by Eric Langenbacher and Yossi Shain. Washington, DC: Georgetown University Press, 2010.

Bell, Duncan. *Memory, Trauma and World Politics: Reflections on the Relationship between Past and Present*. New York: Palgrave Macmillan, 2006.

Bellamy, Richard, and Dario Castiglione. 'Legitimizing the Euro-"polity" and its "Regime": The Normative Turn in EU Studies.' *European Journal of Political Theory* 2, no. 1 (2003): 7–34.

——. 'Building the Union: The Nature of Sovereignty in the Political Architecture of Europe.' *Law and Philosophy* 16, no. 4 (July, 1997): 421–445.

Bellamy, Richard, and Sandra Kröger. 'Domesticating the Democratic Deficit? The Role of National Parliaments and Parties in the EU's System of Governance.' *Parliamentary Affairs* 67, no. 2 (April, 2014): 437–457.

Bellamy, Richard, and Alex Warleigh. 'From an Ethics of Integration to an Ethics of Participation: Citizenship and the Future of the European Union.' *Millennium* 27, no. 3 (September, 1998): 447–468.

Beloff, Nora. *The General Says No: Britain's Exclusion from Europe*. Baltimore: Penguin Books, 1963.

Benhabib, Seyla. 'The Return of Fascism.' *The New Republic*, 29 September 2017.

——. 'The New Sovereigntism and Transnational Law: Legal Utopianism, Democratic Scepticism and Statist Realism.' *Global Constitutionalism* 5, no. 1 (2016): 109–144.

——. 'Arendt and Adorno: The Elusiveness of the Particular and the Benjaminian Moment.' In *Understanding Political Modernity: Comparative Perspectives on Adorno and Arendt*. Edited by Lars Rensmann and Samir Gandesha. Stanford: Stanford University Press, 2012.

——. 'Democratic Exclusions and Democratic Iterations: Dilemmas of "Just Membership" and Prospects of Cosmopolitan Federalism.' *European Journal of Political Theory* 6, no. 4 (2007): 445–462.

——. *The Reluctant Modernism of Hannah Arendt*. Lanham: Rowman & Littlefield, 2003.

——. *The Claims of Culture: Equality and Diversity in the Global Era*. Princeton: Princeton University Press, 2002.

——. *Critique, Norm, and Utopia: A Study of the Foundations of Critical Theory*. New York: Columbia University Press, 1986.

Benhabib, Seyla, and Türküler Isiksel. 'Ancient Battles, New Prejudices, and Future Perspectives: Turkey and the EU.' *Constellations* 13, no. 2 (2006): 218–233.

Benjamin, Walter. *The Arcades Project.* Cambridge, MA: Belknap Press, 1999.

——. *Illuminations: Essays and Reflections*, edited by Hannah Arendt. New York: Schocken Books, 1977.

——. 'Theses on the Philosophy of History.' In *Illuminations: Essays and Reflections.* Translated by Harry Zohn, edited by Hannah Arendt. New York: Schocken Books, 1977.

Berger, Thomas U. *War, Guilt, and World Politics After World War II.* Cambridge: Cambridge University Press, 2012.

Berman, Sheri. 'Populism is Not Fascism: But it could be a Harbinger.' *Foreign Affairs* 95, no. 6 (November/December, 2016): 39–44.

Betz, Hans G., and Stefan Immerfall. *The New Politics of the Right: Neo-Populist Parties and Movements in Established Democracies.* London: Macmillan, 1998.

Bischof, Günter. 'Victims? Perpetrators? "Punching Bags" of European Historical Memory? the Austrians and their World War II Legacies.' *German Studies Review* 27, no. 1 (February, 2004): 17–32.

Bitsch, Marie-Thérèse. *Robert Schuman, apôtre de l'Europe, 1953–1963.* Brussels: P.I.E. Peter Lang, 2010.

Black, Jeremy. *The Age of Total War, 1860–1945.* Westport: Praeger Security International, 2006.

Blankenhorn, Herbert. *Verständnis und Verständigung: Blätter eines politischen Tagebuchs, 1949 bis 1979.* Frankfurt am Main: Propyläen Verlag, 1980.

Blight, David W. 'The Memory Boom: Why and Why Now?' In *Memory in Mind and Culture.* Edited by Pascal Boyer and James V. Wertsch. Cambridge: Cambridge University Press, 2009.

Blustein, Jeffrey. *The Moral Demands of Memory.* Cambridge: Cambridge University Press, 2008.

Blyth, Mark. *Austerity: The History of a Dangerous Idea.* Oxford: Oxford University Press, 2013.

Bohman, Jonathan. 'The European Union Democratic Deficit: Federalists, Skeptics, and Revisionists.' *European Journal of Political Theory* 5, no. 2 (2006): 191–212.

Bottici, Chiara. 'Europe, War and Remembrance.' In *The Search for a European Identity: Values, Policies and Legitimacy of the European Union.* Edited by Furio Cerutti and Sonia Lucarelli. London: Routledge, 2008.

Bottici, Chiara, and Benoît Challand. *Imagining Europe: Myth, Memory, and Identity.* New York: Cambridge University Press, 2013.

Bratsis, Peter. 'Legitimation Crisis and the Greek Explosion.' *International Journal of Urban and Regional Research* 34, no. 1 (2010): 190–196.

Bromberger, Merry, and Serge Bromberger. *Jean Monnet and the United States of Europe.* New York: Coward-McCann, 1969.

Browning, Christopher R. *Ordinary Men: Reserve Police Battalion 11 and the Final Solution in Poland.* New York: Penguin, 2001.

Brubaker, Rogers. *Ethnicity without Groups.* Cambridge, MA: Harvard University Press, 2006.

Brugmans, Henri. *Le message européen de Robert Schuman.* Lausanne: Fondation Jean Monnet pour l'Europe, 1965.

Bull, Hedley. 'Civilian Power Europe: A Contradiction in Terms?' *Journal of Common Market Studies* 21, no. 2 (1982): 149–164.

Calligaro, Oriane. *Negotiating Europe: EU Promotion of Europeanness since the 1950s.* New York: Palgrave Macmillan, 2013.

Select bibliography

Challand, Benoit. 'European Identity and its External Others in History Textbooks (1950–2005).' *The Journal of Educational Media, Memory and Society* 1, no. 2 (2009): 60–96.

Chalmers, Adam. 'Refiguring the European Union's Historical Dimension.' *European Journal of Political Theory* 5, no. 4 (2006): 437–454.

Charmley, John. *Splendid Isolation? Britain, the Balance of Power and the Origins of the First World War*. London: Hodder & Stoughton, 1999.

Chevènement, Jean-Pierre. *La faute de M. Monnet: La république et l'Europe*. Paris: Fayard, 2006.

Christnacker, Daniel. *Les interventions de Robert Schuman au Conseil de l'Europe (1949–1951)*. Strasbourg: Mémoire IEP, 1975.

Connerton, Paul. *How Societies Remember*. New York: Cambridge University Press, 1989.

Conquest, Robert. *Reflections on a Ravaged Century*. New York: W. W. Norton, 2000.

Cooke, Maeve. *Re-Presenting the Good Society*. Cambridge, MA: MIT Press, 2006.

Curtice, John. 'Brexit: Behind the Referendum.' *Political Insight* 7, no. 2 (2016): 4–7.

De Gaulle, Charles. *Complete War Memoirs of Charles de Gaulle*. New York: Simon & Schuster, 1967.

———. *Major Addresses, Statements and Press Conferences of Charles de Gaulle: May 19, 1958–January 31, 1964*. New York: French Embassy, 1964.

———. *The Call to Honor: Documents 1940–1942*. New York: Simon & Schuster, 1955.

———. *France and Her Army*. London: Hutchinson, 1945.

———. *The Army of the Future*. Philadelphia: Lippincott, 1941.

Deighton, Anne. *Building Postwar Europe: National Decision-Makers and European Institutions, 1948–63*. New York: St. Martin's Press, 1995.

Delanty, Gerard, and Chris Rumford. *Rethinking Europe: Social Theory and the Implications of Europeanization*. London: Routledge, 2005.

Delors, Jacques. *L'unité d'un homme*. Paris: Odile Jacob, 1994.

Delors, Jacques, and Jean-Louis Arnaud. *Mémoires*. Paris: Plon, 2004.

Derrida, Jacques. *On Cosmopolitanism and Forgiveness*, translated by Mark Dooley and Michael Hughes. New York: Routledge, 2001.

———. 'Force of Law: The Mystical Foundation of Authority.' In *Deconstruction and the Possibility of Justice*. Edited by Drucilla Cornell and Michael Rosenfeld. New York: Routledge, 1992.

Deutsch, Karl Wolfgang. *Nationalism and Social Communication: An Inquiry into the Foundations of Nationality*. Cambridge: Cambridge University Press, 1953.

Diekmann, Kai, and Ralf Georg Reuth. *Kohl: Ich wollte Deutschlands Einheit*. Berlin: Propyläen, 1996.

Diez, Thomas. 'Constructing the Self and Changing Others: Reconsidering "Normative Power Europe".' *Millennium – Journal of International Studies* 33, no. 3 (2005): 613–636.

Diez, Thomas, Mathias Albert, and Stephan Stetter, eds. *The European Union and Border Conflicts: The Power of Integration and Association*. Cambridge: Cambridge University Press, 2008.

Díez Medrano, Juan. *Framing Europe: Attitudes to European Integration in Germany, Spain, and the United Kingdom*. Princeton: Princeton University Press, 2003.

Dinan, Desmond. 'The Historiography of European Integration.' In *Origins and Evolution of the European Union*. Edited by Desmond Dinan. Oxford: Oxford University Press, 2006.

———. *Europe Recast: A History of European Union*. Boulder: Lynne Rienner, 2004.

Diner, Dan. *Zivilisationsbruch: Denken nach Auschwitz*. Berlin: Fischer Taschenbuch, 1988.

Dubiel, Helmut. *Theory and Politics: Studies in the Development of Critical Theory*. Cambridge, MA: MIT Press, 1985.

Duchêne, François. *Jean Monnet: The First Statesman of Interdependence*. New York: Norton, 1994.

Select bibliography

Dullien, Sebastian, and Ulrike Guérot. 'The Long Shadow of Ordoliberalism: Germany's Approach to the Euro Crisis.' *ECFR Policy Brief* 49 (2012): 1–15.

Dyson, Kenneth H. F. *Elusive Union: The Process of Economic and Monetary Union in Europe.* New York: Longman, 1994.

Eco, Umberto. 'An Uncertain Europe between Rebirth and Decline.' In *Old Europe, New Europe, Core Europe: Transatlantic Relations After the Iraq War.* Edited by Daniel Levy, Max Pensky, and John C. Torpey. London: Verso, 2005.

Elias, Norbert. *The Germans: Power Struggles and the Development of Habitus in the Nineteenth and Twentieth Centuries,* translated by Eric Dunning and Stephen Mennell. New York: Polity Press, 1996.

Erdmann, Karl Dietrich. *Adenauer in der Rheinlandpolitik nach dem Ersten Weltkrieg.* Stuttgart: E. Klett Verlag, 1966.

Eriksen, Anne, and Jón Viðar Sigurðsson. *Negotiating Pasts in the Nordic Countries: Interdisciplinary Studies in History and Memory.* Sweden: Nordic Academic Press, 2009.

Eriksen, Erik O. *The Unfinished Democratization of Europe.* Oxford: Oxford University Press, 2009.

Eriksen, Erik Oddvar, John Erik Fossum, and Agustín José Menéndez. *Developing a Constitution for Europe.* London: Routledge, 2004.

Evans, Harold. *The American Century.* New York: Knopf, 1998.

Falk, Richard. 'The Making of Global Citizenship.' In *The Condition of Citizenship.* Edited by Bart van Steenbergen. London: Sage Publications, 1994.

Featherstone, Kevin. 'Jean Monnet and the "Democratic Deficit" in the European Union.' *Journal of Common Market Studies* 32, no. 2 (1994): 149–170.

——. *Socialist Parties and European Integration: A Comparative History.* New York: St. Martin's Press, 1988.

Ferrara, Alessandro. 'Europe as a "Special Area for Human Hope".' *Constellations* 14, no. 3 (2007): 315–331.

Fierke, K. M., and A. Wiener. 'Constructing Institutional Interests: EU and NATO Enlargement.' *Journal of European Public Policy* 6, no. 5 (December, 1999): 721–742.

Fimister, Alan Paul. *Robert Schuman: Neo-Scholastic Humanism and the Reunification of Europe.* Brussels: Peter Lang, 2008.

Finkelstein, Norman G. *The Holocaust Industry: Reflection on the Exploitation of Jewish Suffering.* New York: Verso, 2000.

Finney, Patrick. 'The Ubiquitous Presence of the Past? Collective Memory and International History.' *The International History Review* 36, no. 3 (2014): 443–472.

Fligstein, Neil. *Euro-Clash: The EU, European Identity, and the Future of Europe.* Oxford: Oxford University Press, 2008.

Foa, Roberto Stefan, and Yascha Mounk. 'The Dangers of Deconsolidation: The Democratic Disconnect.' *Journal of Democracy* 27, no. 3 (2016): 5–17.

Fondation Jean Monnet pour l'Europe. *L'Europe: Une longue marche.* Lausanne: Fondation Jean Monnet pour l'Europe, 1985.

Forst, Rainer. *The Right to Justification: Elements of a Constructivist Theory of Justice,* translated by Jeffrey Flynn. New York: Columbia University Press, 2012.

Foucault, Michel. *Language, Counter-Memory, Practice.* Ithaca, NY: Cornell University Press, 1977.

Frank, Jason A. *Constituent Moments: Enacting the People in Postrevolutionary America.* Durham, NC: Duke University Press, 2010.

——. 'Publius and Political Imagination.' *Political Theory* 37, no. 1 (February, 2009): 69–98.

Select bibliography

Frankel, Joseph. *British Foreign Policy 1945–1973*. London: Oxford University Press, 1975.

Fransen, Frederic J. *The Supranational Politics of Jean Monnet: Ideas and Origins of the European Community*. Westport: Greenwood Press, 2001.

Frei, Norbert. 'Deutschlands Vergangenheit und Europas Gedächnis.' In *Europas Gedächnis: Das neue Europa zwischen nationalen Errinnerungen und gemeinsamer Identität*. Edited by Helmut König, Julia Schmidt, and Manfred Sickling. Bielefeld: transcript Verlag, 2008.

———. *Vergangenheitspolitik: Die Anfänge der Bundesrepublik und die NS-Vergangenheit*. Munich: Beck, 1996.

Friis, Lykke, and Anna Murphy. 'The European Union and Central and Eastern Europe: Governance and Boundaries.' *Journal of Common Market Studies* 37, no. 2 (1999): 211–232.

Fromm, Erich. *Escape from Freedom*. New York: Holt, Rinehart and Winston, 1941.

Furet, François. *Interpreting the French Revolution*. Cambridge: Cambridge University Press, 1981.

Fussell, Paul. *The Great War and Modern Memory*. Oxford: Oxford University Press, 1975.

Gadamer, Hans-Georg. *Truth and Method*, translated by Joel Weinsheimer and Donald G. Marshall. London: Continuum, 2004.

———. 'Concerning Empty and Ful-Filled Time.' *Southern Journal of Philosophy* 8, no. 4 (1970): 341–353.

Gaffney, John. *Political Leadership in France: From Charles de Gaulle to Nicholas Sarkozy*. New York: Palgrave Macmillan, 2010.

Gardner Feldman, Lily. 'Reconciliation and Legitimacy: Foreign Relations and Enlargement of the European Union.' In *Legitimacy and the European Union: The Contested Polity*. Edited by Thomas Banchoff and Mitchell Smith. London: Routledge, 1999.

Gebert, Konstanty. 'Projecting Poland and its Past.' *Eurozone*, 27 April 2018.

Gerbet, Pierre. *La genèse du Plan Schuman*. Lausanne: Fondation Jean Monnet pour l'Europe, 1962.

Geuss, Raymond. *Philosophy and Real Politics*. Princeton: Princeton University Press, 2008.

———. *The Idea of a Critical Theory: Habermas and the Frankfurt School*. Cambridge: Cambridge University Press, 1981.

Giddens, Anthony. *Turbulent and Mighty Continent: What Future for Europe?* Cambridge: Polity, 2013.

Gillingham, John. *European Integration, 1950–2003: Superstate or New Market Economy?* Cambridge: Cambridge University Press, 2003.

———. 'Jean Monnet and the Origins of European Monetary Union.' In *The European Union: From Jean Monnet to the Euro*. Edited by Dean J. Kotlowski. Athens, OH: Ohio University Press, 2000.

———. 'Jean Monnet and the European Coal and Steel Community: A Preliminary Appraisal.' In *Jean Monnet: The Path to European Unity*. Edited by Douglas Brinkley and Clifford P. Hackett. Houndmills: Macmillan, 1991.

Glaurdić, Josip. *The Hour of Europe: Western Powers and the Breakup of Yugoslavia*. New Haven: Yale University Press, 2011.

Goldfield, David R. *America Aflame: How the Civil War Created a Nation*. New York: Bloomsbury Press, 2011.

Goodwin, Matthew, and Oliver Heath. 'The 2016 Referendum, Brexit and the Left Behind: An Aggregate-Level Analysis of the Result.' *The Political Quarterly* 87, no. 3 (2016): 323–332.

Granieri, Ronald J. *The Ambivalent Alliance: Konrad Adenauer, the CDU/CSU, and the West, 1949–1966*. New York: Berghahn Books, 2003.

Grant, Charles. *Delors: Inside the House that Jacques Built.* London: Nicholas Brealey, 1994.

Grimm, Dieter. 'Does Europe Need a Constitution?' *European Law Journal* 1, no. 3 (29 November 1995): 282–302.

Gross, Jan T. *Neighbors: The Destruction of the Jewish Community in Jedwabne, Poland.* Princeton: Princeton University Press, 2001.

Grosser, Alfred. 'General de Gaulle and the Foreign Policy of the Fifth Republic.' *International Affairs* 39, no. 2 (1963): 198–213.

Guérot, Ulrike. *Warum Europa eine Republik werden muss! Eine politische Utopie.* Bonn: J. H. W. Dietz, 2016.

———. 'The Euro Debate in Germany: Towards Political Union?' *European Council on Foreign Relations: Reinvention of Europe Project* (September, 2012): 1–9.

Guisan, Catherine. 'EMU Political Leadership Vs. Greek Civil Society: How Shall we Live Together?' *Mediterranean Politics* 21, no. 3 (2016): 387–406.

———. *A Political Theory of Identity in European Integration: Memory and Policies.* New York: Routledge, 2012.

———. 'From the European Coal and Steel Community to Kosovo: Reconciliation and its Discontents.' *Journal of Common Market Studies* 49, no. 3 (2011): 541–562.

Haakonssen, Knud. 'The Structure of Hume's Political Theory.' In *The Cambridge Companion to Hume.* Edited by David Fate Norton. New York: Cambridge University Press, 1993.

Haas, Ernst B. *The Uniting of Europe: Political, Social, and Economic Forces, 1950–1957.* Notre Dame: University of Notre Dame Press, 2004.

———. *Beyond the Nation-State: Functionalism and International Organization.* Stanford: Stanford University Press, 1964.

———. 'International Integration: The European and the Universal Process.' *International Organization* 15, no. 3 (1961): 366–392.

Habermas, Jürgen. 'Zur Prinzipienkonkurrenz von Bürgergleichheit und Staatengleichheit im supranationalen Gemeinwesen. Eine Notiz aus Anlass der Frage nach der Legitimität der ungleichen Repräsentation der Bürger im europäischen Parlament.' *Der Staat* 53, no. 2 (2014): 167–192.

———. 'Demokratie oder Kapitalismus? Vom Elend der nationalstaatlichen Fragmentierung in einer kapitalistisch integrierten Weltgesellschaft.' *Blätter für Deutsche und internationale Politik* 58, no. 5 (2013): 59–70.

———. *The Crisis of the European Union: A Response*, translated by Ciaran Cronin. Cambridge: Polity Press, 2012.

———. *Zur Verfassung Europas: Ein Essay.* Berlin: Suhrkamp Verlag, 2011.

———. *Europe: The Faltering Project*, translated by Ciaran Cronin. Cambridge: Polity Press, 2009.

———. 'Public Space and Political Public Sphere: The Biographical Roots of Two Motifs in My Thought.' In *Between Naturalism and Religion.* London: Polity, 2008.

———. 'Does Europe Need a Constitution?' In *Time of Transitions.* Translated by Cronin Ciaran and Max Pensky. Cambridge: Polity, 2006.

———. 'Why Europe Needs a Constitution.' In *Developing a Constitution for Europe.* Edited by Erik Oddvar Eriksen, John Erik Fossum, and Agustín José Menéndez. London: Routledge, 2004.

———. 'Constitutional Democracy: A Paradoxical Union of Contradictory Principles?' *Political Theory* 29, no. 6 (December, 2001): 766–781.

———. 'The Postnational Constellation and the Future of Democracy.' In *The Postnational Constellation: Political Essays.* Translated by Max Pensky. Cambridge, MA: MIT Press, 2001.

Select bibliography

——. *The Theory of Communicative Action*, translated by Thomas A. McCarthy. Boston: Beacon Press, 1984/1987.

——. 'What does Crisis Mean Today? Legitimation Problems in Late Capitalism.' *Social Research* 51, no. 1/2 (1984): 39–64.

——. *Legitimation Crisis*. Boston: Beacon Press, 1975.

——. *Knowledge and Human Interests*, translated by Jeremy J. Shapiro. Boston: Beacon Press, 1971.

Habermas, Jürgen, and Jacques Derrida. 'February 15, or what Binds Europeans Together: A Plea for a Common Foreign Policy, Beginning in the Core of Europe.' *Constellations* 10, no. 3 (2003): 291–297.

Halbwachs, Maurice. *On Collective Memory*, translated by Lewis A. Coser. Chicago: University of Chicago Press, 1992.

Hallstein, Walter. *Europäische Reden*, edited by Thomas Oppermann and Joachim Kohler. Stuttgart: Deutsche Verlags-Anstalt, 1979.

Haynes-Renshaw, Fiona, and Helen Wallace. 'Changing the Course of European Integration – Or Not?' In *Visions, Votes and Vetoes: The Empty Chair Crisis and the Luxembourg Compromise Forty Years On*. Edited by Jean-Marie Palayret, Helen Wallace, and Pascaline Winand. Brussels: Peter Lang, 2006.

Hazareesingh, Sudhir, and Karma Nabulsi. 'Using Archival Sources to Theorize about Politics.' In *Political Theory: Methods and Approaches*. Edited by David Leopold and Marc Stears. Oxford: Oxford University Press, 2008.

Hegel, Georg Wilhelm Friedrich. *Phenomenology of Spirit*, translated by Arnold V. Miller, edited by J. N. Findlay. Oxford: Clarendon Press, 1977.

Held, David. *Introduction to Critical Theory: Horkheimer to Habermas*. Berkeley: University of California Press, 1980.

Henderson, Karen. *Back to Europe: Central and Eastern Europe and the European Union*. London: UCL Press, 1999.

Herf, Jeffrey. *Divided Memory: The Nazi Past in the Two Germanys*. Cambridge, MA: Harvard University Press, 1997.

Hirsch, Étienne. *Ainsi va la vie*. Lausanne: Fondation Jean Monnet pour l'Europe, 1988.

Hobolt, Sara B. 'The Brexit Vote: A Divided Nation, a Divided Continent.' *Journal of European Public Policy* 23, no. 9 (2016): 1259–1277.

Hobsbawm, E. J., and T. O. Ranger. *The Invention of Tradition*. Cambridge: Cambridge University Press, 1992.

Hoffmann, Stanley. *The European Sisyphus: Essays on Europe, 1964–1994*. Boulder: Westview Press, 1995.

——. 'The Effects of World War II on French Society and Politics.' *French Historical Studies* 2, no. 1 (1961): 28–63.

Hoffmann, Stanley, and Inge Hoffmann. 'The Will to Grandeur: De Gaulle as Political Artist.' *Daedalus* 97, no. 3 (1968): 829–887.

Holton, R. J. 'The Idea of Crisis in Modern Society.' *The British Journal of Sociology* 38, no. 4 (1987): 502–520.

Honig, Bonnie. *Democracy and the Foreigner*. Princeton: Princeton University Press, 2001.

——. 'Declarations of Independence: Arendt and Derrida on the Problem of Founding a Republic.' *The American Political Science Review* 85, no. 1 (1991): 97–113.

Hooghe, Lisbet, and Gary Marks. 'A Postfunctionalist Theory of European Integration: From Permissive Consensus to Constraining Dissensus.' *British Journal of Political Science* 39, no. 1 (2008): 1–23.

Select bibliography

Horkheimer, Max. 'Notes on Science and the Crisis.' In *Critical Theory: Selected Essays*. Translated by Matthew J. O'Connell. New York: Continuum Publishing Company, 1972.

——. *Sozialphilosophische Studien. Aufsätze, Reden und Vorträge 1930–1972*. Frankfurt am Main: Athenäum Fischer Taschenbuch Verlag, 1972.

——. 'Traditional and Critical Theory.' In *Critical Theory: Selected Essays*. Translated by Matthew J. O'Connell. New York: Continuum Publishing Company, 1972.

——. *Eclipse of Reason*. New York: Oxford University Press, 1947.

Horkheimer, Max, and Theodor W. Adorno. *Dialectic of Enlightenment: Philosophical Fragments*, translated by Gunzelin Schmid Noerr. Stanford: Stanford University Press, 2002.

Horne, Alistair. *Harold MacMillan: Volume II, 1957–1986*. London: Penguin, 1989.

Hoy, David Couzens, and Thomas A. McCarthy. *Critical Theory*. Oxford: Blackwell, 1994.

Hume, David. *Essays, Moral, Political, and Literary*, edited by Eugene F. Miller. Indianapolis: Liberty Fund, 1985.

——. *A Treatise of Human Nature*, edited by Lewis Amherst Selby-Bigge. New York: Oxford University Press, 1978.

Inglehart, Ronald. *The Silent Revolution: Changing Values and Political Styles among Western Publics*. Princeton: Princeton University Press, 1977.

Inglehart, Ronald, and Pippa Norris. 'Trump and the Populist Authoritarian Parties: The Silent Revolution in Reverse.' *Perspectives on Politics* 15, no. 2 (2017): 443–454.

Insdorf, Annette. *Indelible Shadows: Film and the Holocaust*. Cambridge: Cambridge University Press, 1983.

Iser, Mattias. *Empörung und Fortschritt: Grundlagen einer kritischen Theorie der Gesellschaft*. Frankfurt: Campus Verlag, 2008.

Isiksel, Turkuler. *Europe's Functional Constitution: A Theory of Constitutionalism Beyond the State*. Oxford: Oxford University Press, 2016.

Jabko, Nicolas. *Playing the Market: A Political Strategy for Uniting Europe, 1985–2005*. Ithaca, NY: Cornell University Press, 2006.

Jaeger, Hans. 'Generationen in der Geschichte. Überlegungen zu einer umstrittenen Konzeption.' *Geschichte und Gesellschaft* 3, no. 4 (1977): 429–452.

Janitschek, Hans. *Mário Soares: Portrait of a Hero*. London: Weidenfeld & Nicolson, 1985.

Jarausch, Konrad H. 'Zeitgeschichte zwischen Nation und Europa. Eine transnationale Herausforderung.' *Aus Politik und Zeitgeschichte* 54, no. B39 (2004): 3–10.

Jaspers, Karl. *The Question of German Guilt*, translated by E. B. Ashton, edited by Joseph W. Koterski SJ. New York: Fordham University Press, 2001.

Jay, Martin. *Songs of Experience: Modern American and European Variations on a Universal Theme*. Berkeley: University of California Press, 2005.

——. *The Dialectical Imagination: A History of the Frankfurt School and the Institute of Social Research, 1923–1950*. Boston: Little, Brown and Company, 1973.

Joerges, Christian. 'Law and Politics in Europe's Crisis: On the History of the Impact of an Unfortunate Configuration.' *Constellations* 21, no. 2 (2014): 249–261.

Joly, Marc. *Le mythe Jean Monnet: Contribution à une sociologie historique de la construction européenne*. Paris: CNRS Éditions, 2007.

Jouve, Edmond. *Le général de Gaulle et la construction de l'Europe (1940–1966)*. Paris: Librairie generale de droit et de jurisprudence, R. Pichon et R. Durand-Auzias, 1967.

Judt, Tony. *Postwar: A History of Europe since 1945*. New York: Penguin Press, 2005.

——. 'The Past is another Country: Myth and Memory in Postwar Europe.' *Daedalus* 121, no. 4 (1992): 83–118.

Select bibliography

Kagan, Robert. *Of Paradise and Power: America and Europe in the New World Order.* New York: Vintage Books, 2004.

Kaiser, Wolfram. 'From Great Men to Ordinary Citizens? The Biographical Approach to Narrating European Integration in Museums.' *Culture Unbound: Journal of Current Cultural Research* 3 (2011): 385–400.

———. 'Transnational Christian Democracy: From the *Nouvelles equipes internationales* to the European People's Party.' In *Christian Democracy in Europe since 1945.* Edited by Michael Gehler and Wolfram Kaiser. London: Routledge, 2004.

Kalyvas, Stathis N. 'The Intellectual Impact of the Euro Crisis.' *European Politics and Society Newsletter* Summer (2012): 11–12.

———. *The Logic of Violence in Civil War.* New York: Cambridge University Press, 2006.

Kansteiner, Wulf. 'Losing the War, Winning the Memory Battle: The Legacy of Nazism, World War II, and the Holocaust in the Federal Republic of Germany.' In *The Politics of Memory in Postwar Europe.* Edited by Richard Ned Lebow, Wulf Kansteiner, and Claudio Fogu. Durham, NC: Duke University Press, 2006.

———. 'Between Politics and Memory: The *Historikerstreit* and the West German Historical Culture of the 1980s.' In *Fascism's Return: Scandal, Revision, Ideology.* Edited by Richard J. Golsan. Lincoln: University of Nebraska Press, 1998.

Kattago, Siobhan. 'Agreeing to Disagree on the Legacies of Recent History.' *European Journal of Social Theory* 12, no. 3 (2009): 375–395.

Kaufman, Stuart J. *Modern Hatreds: The Symbolic Politics of Ethnic War.* New York: Cornell University Press, 2001.

Kauppinen, Antti. 'Reason, Recognition, and Internal Critique.' *Inquiry* 45, no. 4 (2002): 479–498.

Khong, Yuen Foong. *Analogies at War: Korea, Munich, Dien Bien Phu, and the Vietnam Decisions of 1965.* Princeton: Princeton University Press, 1992.

Klein, Kerwin Lee. 'On the Emergence of Memory in Historical Discourse.' *Representations* 69 (2000): 127–155.

Kohl, Helmut. *Aus Sorge um Europa: Ein Appell.* Munich: Verlag Droemer Knaur, 2014.

Köhler, Henning. *Adenauer: Eine politische Biographie.* Frankfurt am Main: Propyläen, 1994.

König, Helmut. *Politik und Gedächtnis.* Weilerswist: Velbrück Wissenschaft, 2008.

Koronaiou, Alexandra, Evangelos Lagos, Alexandros Sakellariou, Stelios Kymionis, and Irini Chiotaki-Poulou. 'Golden Dawn, Austerity and Young People: The Rise of Fascist Extremism among Young People in Contemporary Greek Society.' *The Sociological Review* 63, no. 2 (2015): 231–249.

Koselleck, Reinhart. *The Practice of Conceptual History: Timing History, Spacing Concepts,* translated by Todd Samuel Presner. Stanford: Stanford University Press, 2002.

———. *Futures Past: On the Semantics of Historical Time,* translated by Keith Tribe. Cambridge, MA: MIT Press, 1985.

Koskenniemi, Martti. 'What use for Sovereignty Today?' *Asian Journal of International Law* 1 (2011): 61–70.

Kundera, Milan. 'The Tragedy of Central Europe.' *The New York Review of Books* 31, no. 7 (26 April 1984): 33–38.

Küsters, Hanns Jürgen. 'Jean Monnet and the European Union: Idea and Reality of the Integration Process.' In *Jean Monnet et l'Europe d'aujourd'hui.* Edited by Giandomenico Majone, Emile Noël, and Peter van den Bossche. Baden-Baden: Nomos, 1989.

Lacouture, Jean. *De Gaulle: The Ruler 1945–1970,* translated by Patrick O'Brian. New York: W. W. Norton, 1991.

——. *De Gaulle: The Rebel 1890–1944*, translated by Patrick O'Brian. New York: W. W. Norton, 1990.

LaFeber, Walter, Richard Polenberg, and Nancy Woloch. *The American Century: A History of the United States since the 1890s*. New York: M. E. Sharpe, 1998.

Langenbacher, Eric. 'Changing Memory Regimes in Contemporary Germany?' *German Politics & Society* 21, no. 2 (2003): 46–68.

Langenbacher, Eric, and Yossi Shain, eds. *Power and the Past: Collective Memory and International Relations*. Washington, DC: Georgetown University Press, 2010.

Lapavitsas, Costas et al. *Crisis in the Eurozone*. London: Verso, 2012.

Lašas, Ainius. *European Union and NATO Expansion*. New York: Palgrave Macmillan, 2010.

——. 'Restituting Victims: EU and NATO Enlargements through the Lenses of Collective Guilt.' *Journal of European Public Policy* 15, no. 1 (2008): 98–116.

Lazare, Daniel. *The Frozen Republic: How the Constitution is Paralyzing Democracy*. New York: Harcourt Brace, 1996.

Lebow, Richard Ned, Wulf Kansteiner, and Claudio Fogu. *The Politics of Memory in Postwar Europe*. Durham, NC: Duke University Press, 2006.

Lejeune, René. *Robert Schuman (1886–1963), Père de l'Europe: La politique, chemin de sainteté*. Paris: Fayard, 2000.

——. *Robert Schuman: Une âme pour l'Europe*. Paris: Editions Saint-Paul, 1986.

Lenz, Otto. *Im Zentrum der Macht: Das Tagebuch von Staatssekretär Lenz, 1951–1953*, edited by Klaus Gotto, Hans-Otto Kleinmann, and Reinhard Schreiner. Düsseldorf: Droste, 1989.

Leopold, David, and Marc Stears, eds. *Political Theory: Methods and Approaches*. Oxford: Oxford University Press, 2008.

Levy, Daniel, and Natan Sznaider. 'Memory Unbound: The Holocaust and the Formation of Cosmopolitan Memory.' *European Journal of Social Theory* 5, no. 1 (2002): 87–106.

Linklater, Andrew. *Critical Theory and World Politics: Citizenship, Sovereignty and Humanity*. London: Routledge, 2007.

——. *The Transformation of Political Community: Ethical Foundations of the Post-Westphalian Era*. Columbia: University of South Carolina Press, 1998.

Lipset, Seymour Martin. *Political Man: The Social Bases of Politics*. Garden City: Doubleday, 1960.

Lipstadt, Deborah E. *Denying the Holocaust: The Growing Assault on Truth and Memory*. New York: The Free Press, 2012.

Littoz-Monnet, Annabelle. 'The EU Politics of Remembrance: Can Europeans Remember Together?' *West European Politics* 35, no. 5 (2012): 1182–1202.

London, Frederic. 'The Logic and Limits of *Désinflation Competitive*: French Economic Policy from 1983.' *Oxford Review of Economic Policy* 14, no. 1 (1998): 96–114.

Lord, Christopher. '"With but Not of": Britain and the Schuman Plan, a Reinterpretation.' *Journal of European Integration History* 4, no. 2 (1998): 23–46.

Loriaux, Michael. *European Union and the Deconstruction of the Rhineland Frontier*. Cambridge: Cambridge University Press, 2008.

Loth, Wilfried. *Crises and Compromises: The European Project 1963–1969*. Brussels: Bruylant, 2001.

Lowe, Keith. *Savage Continent: Europe in the Aftermath of World War II*. New York: St. Martin's Press, 2012.

Löwenthal, Leo. *An Unmastered Past*. Berkeley: University of California Press, 1987.

Luce, Henry R. The American Century. *Life Magazine*, 17 February 1941.

Lücker, Hans August, and Jean Seitlinger. *Robert Schuman und die Einigung Europas*. Luxemburg: Editions Saint-Paul, 2000.

Select bibliography

Macmillan, Harold. *Tides of Fortune, 1945–1955*. New York: Harper & Row, 1969.

Mahoney, Daniel J. *De Gaulle: Statesmanship, Grandeur, and Modern Democracy*. Westport: Praeger, 1996.

Maier, Charles S. 'Hot Memory … Cold Memory: On the Political Half-Life of Fascist and Communist Memory.' *Transit – Europäisches Revue* 22 (2002): 153–165.

——. 'A Surfeit of Memory? Reflections on History, Melancholy and Denial.' *History and Memory* 5, no. 2 (1993): 136–152.

Majone, Giandomenico. 'Europe's "Democratic Deficit": The Question of Standards.' *European Journal of Law* 4, no. 1 (1998): 5–28.

Malraux, André. *Felled Oaks: Conversation with De Gaulle*. New York: Holt, Rinehart and Winston, 1971.

Manent, Pierre. 'De Gaulle as Hero.' *Perspectives on Political Science* 21, no. 4 (1992): 201–206.

Manners, Ian. 'The European Union as a Normative Power: A Response to Thomas Diez.' *Millennium – Journal of International Studies* 1, no. 167 (2006): 167–180.

——. 'Normative Power Europe: A Contradiction in Terms?' *Journal of Common Market Studies* 40, no. 2 (2002): 235–258.

Mannheim, Karl. *Essays on the Sociology of Knowledge*. London: Routledge & Kegan Paul, 1952.

Marcuse, Herbert. 'Some Social Implications of Modern Technology.' In *The Essential Frankfurt School Reader*. Edited by Andrew Arato and Eike Gerhardt. New York: Urizen Books, 1977.

——. *Eros and Civilization: A Philosophical Inquiry into Freud*. Boston: Beacon Press, 1966.

——. *One-Dimensional Man: Studies in the Ideology of Advanced Industrial Society*. New York: Routledge Classics, 1964.

——. *Soviet Marxism: A Critical Analysis*. Boston: Beacon Press, 1964.

——. *Reason and Revolution*. Boston: Beacon Press, 1960.

Mark, James. *The Unfinished Revolution: Making Sense of the Communist Past in Central-Eastern Europe*. New Haven: Yale University Press, 2010.

Marsh, David. *Europe's Deadlock: How the Euro Crisis could be Solved, and Why it Won't Happen*. New Haven: Yale University Press, 2013.

——. *The Euro: The Battle for the New Global Currency*. New Haven: Yale University Press, 2011.

Mathes, Melissa M. *Rape of Lucretia and the Founding of Republics*. University Park: Pennsylvania University Press, 2000.

McCarthy, Thomas A. *Race, Empire, and the Idea of Human Development*. New York: Cambridge University Press, 2009.

McGrattan, Cillian, and Stephen Hopkins. 'Memory in Post-Conflict Societies: From Contention to Integration?' *Ethnopolitics* 16, no. 5 (2017): 488–499.

McNamara, Kathleen R. *The Politics of Everyday Europe: Constructing Authority in the European Union*. Oxford: Oxford University Press, 2015.

Mearsheimer, John J. 'Back to the Future: Instability in Europe After the Cold War.' *International Security* 15, no. 1 (1990): 5–56.

Merleau-Ponty, Maurice. *Les adventures de la dialectique*. Paris: Gallimard, 1955.

Meunier, Sophie, and Milada Anna Vachudova. 'Liberal Intergovernmentalism, Illiberalism and the Potential Superpower of the European Union.' *JCMS: Journal of Common Market Studies* 56, no. 7 (2018): 1631–1647.

Michelman, Frank I. 'How can the People Ever make the Laws? A Critique of Deliberative Democracy.' In *Deliberative Democracy: Essays on Reason and Politics*. Edited by James Bohman and William Rehg. Cambridge, MA: MIT Press, 1997.

Milward, Alan S. *The European Rescue of the Nation-State*. London: Routledge, 1992.

Select bibliography

——. *The Reconstruction of Western Europe, 1945–51*. Berkeley: University of California Press, 1984.

Minow, Martha, ed. *Breaking the Cycles of Hatred: Memory, Law, and Repair*. Princeton: Princeton University Press, 2002.

Mioche, Philippe. 'L'Invention du Plan Monnet.' In *Modernisation ou décadence*. Edited by Bernard Cayes and Philippe Mioche. Aix-en-Provence: Publications de l'Université de Provence, 1990.

Misztal, Barbara A. *Theories of Social Remembering*. Philadelphia, PA: Open University Press, 2003.

Monnet, Jean. *Memoirs*. London: Collins, 1978.

——. *Speeches Delivered by Jean Monnet, President of the High Authority at the Inauguration of the High Authority on August 10th, 1952 [and] at the Opening Session of the Assembly on Sept 11th, 1952*. Strasbourg: European Coal and Steel Community, 1952.

Monnet, Jean, and Robert Schuman. *Jean Monnet, Robert Schuman: Correspondance, 1947–1953*. Lausanne: Fondation Jean Monnet pour l'Europe, 1986.

Moore, R. Laurence, and Maurizio Vaudagna. *The American Century in Europe*. Ithaca, NY: Cornell University Press, 2003.

Moravcsik, Andrew. 'In Defense of the "Democratic Deficit": Reassessing Legitimacy in the European Union.' *Journal of Common Market Studies* 40, no. 4 (2002): 603–624.

——. *The Choice for Europe: Social Purpose and State Power from Messina to Maastricht*. Ithaca, NY: Cornell University Press, 1998.

Morgan, Glyn. 'European Political Integration and the Need for Justification.' *Constellations* 14, no. 3 (2007): 332–346.

——. *The Idea of a European Superstate: Public Justification and European Integration*. Princeton: Princeton University Press, 2005.

Müller, Guido, and Vanessa Plichta. 'Zwischen Rhein und Donau. Abendländisches denken zwischen deutsch-französischen Verständigungsinitiativen und konservativ-katholischen Integrationsmodellen 1923–1957.' *Journal of European Integration History* 5, no. 2 (1999): 17–47.

Müller, Jan-Werner. *What is Populism?* Philadelphia: Pennsylvania University Press, 2016.

——. *Memory and Power in Post-War Europe: Studies in the Presence of the Past*. New York: Cambridge University Press, 2002.

Nelsen, Brent F., and James L. Guth. *Religion and the Struggle for European Union: Confessional Culture and the Limits of Integration*. Washington, DC: Georgetown University Press, 2015.

Neyer, Jürgen. *The Justification of Europe: A Political Theory of Supranational Integration*. Oxford: Oxford University Press, 2012.

Neyer, Jürgen, and Antje Wiener. *Political Theory of the European Union*. Oxford and New York: Oxford University Press, 2011.

Nicholson, Frances, and Roger East. *From the Six to the Twelve: The Enlargement of the European Communities*. Essex: Longman Group UK Limited, 1987.

Nietzsche, Friedrich. *On the Geneology of Morals; Ecce Homo*, edited by Walter Kaufmann. New York: Vintage Books, 1989.

Nora, Pierre. *Les lieux de mémoire*. Paris: Gallimard, 1984.

Northedge, F. S. *Descent from Power: British Foreign Policy, 1945–1973*. London: G. Allen & Unwin, 1974.

Nuti, Alasia. *Injustice and the Reproduction of History: Structural Inequalities, Gender and Redress*. Cambridge: Cambridge University Press, 2019.

O'Brennan, John. *The Eastern Enlargement of the European Union*. New York: Routledge, 2006.

Select bibliography

——. 'The Democratic Welfare State in an Integrating Europe.' In *Democracy Beyond the State? The European Dilemma and the Emerging Global Order*. Edited by Michael Th. Greven and Louis W. Pauly. Lanham: Rowman & Littlefield, 2000.

——. *Contradictions of the Welfare State*. Cambridge, MA: MIT Press, 1984.

Olick, Jeffrey K. *The Politics of Regret: On Collective Memory and Historical Responsibility*. New York: Routledge, 2007.

——. 'Memory and the Nation: Continuities, Conflicts, and Transformations.' *Social Science History* 22, no. 4 (1998): 377–387.

——. 'What does it Mean to Normalize the Past? Official Memory in German Politics since 1989.' *Social Science History* 22, no. 4 (1998): 547–571.

Olick, Jeffrey K., and Daniel Levy. 'Collective Memory and Cultural Constraint: Holocaust Myth and Rationality in German Politics.' *American Sociological Review* 62, no. 6 (1997): 921–936.

Olick, Jeffrey K., Vered Vinitzky-Seroussi, and Daniel Levy, eds. *The Collective Memory Reader*. Oxford: Oxford University Press, 2011.

Paasi, Anssi. 'Geographical Perspectives on Finnish National Identity.' *GeoJournal* 43, no. 1 (1997): 41–50.

——. *Territories, Boundaries, and Consciousness: The Changing Geographies of the Finnish-Russian Boundary*. Chichester and New York: J. Wiley & Sons, 1996.

Pagden, Anthony. 'Europe: Conceptualizing a Continent.' In *The Idea of Europe: From Antiquity to the European Union*. Edited by Anthony Pagden. New York: Cambridge University Press, 2002.

Parsons, Craig. 'The Triumph of Community Europe.' In *Origins and Evolution of the European Union*. Edited by Desmond Dinan. Oxford: Oxford University Press, 2006.

——. *A Certain Idea of Europe*. Ithaca: Cornell University Press, 2003.

Pennera, Christian. *Robert Schuman: La jeunesse et les débuts politiques d'un grand européen de 1886 à 1924*. Paris: Editions Pierron, 1985.

Pensky, Max. 'Solidarity with the Past and the Work of Translation: Reflections on Memory Politics and the Postsecular.' In *Habermas and Religion*. Edited by Craig J. Calhoun, Eduardo Mendieta, and Jonathan VanAntwerpen. Cambridge: Polity, 2013.

——. 'Contributions Toward a Theory of Storms: Historical Knowing and Historical Progress in Kant and Benjamin.' *The Philosophical Forum* 41, no. 1–2 (2010): 149–174.

——. *The Ends of Solidarity: Discourse Theory in Ethics and Politics*. Albany: State University of New York Press, 2008.

Piketty, Thomas. *Capital in the Twenty-First Century*, translated by Arthur Goldhammer. Cambridge, MA: The Belknap Press of Harvard University Press, 2014.

Piris, Jean-Claude. *The Future of Europe: Towards a Two-Speed EU?* Cambridge: Cambridge University Press, 2012.

Pocock, J. G. A. 'Deconstructing Europe.' *London Review of Books* 13, no. 24 (1991): 6–10.

——. *The Machiavellian Moment*. Princeton: Princeton University Press, 1975.

Poidevin, Raymond. *Robert Schuman: Homme d'état, 1886–1963*. Paris: Impr. nationale, 1986.

Pond, Elizabeth. *The Rebirth of Europe*. Washington, DC: Brookings Institution Press, 2002.

Postone, Moishe. 'Political Theory and Historical Analysis.' In *Habermas and the Public Sphere*. Edited by Craig J. Calhoun. Cambridge, MA: MIT Press, 1992.

Preston, Paul. *The Triumph of Democracy in Spain*. London: Methuen, 1986.

Prutsch, Marcus J. *European Historical Memory: Policy Challenges and Perspectives*. Brussels: Directorate-General for Internal Policies: Culture and Education, 2013.

Select bibliography

Reich, Simon, and Richard Ned Lebow. *Good-Bye Hegemony: Power and Influence in the Global System*. Princeton: Princeton University Press, 2014.

Resina, Joan Ramon. *Disremembering the Dictatorship: The Politics of Memory in the Spanish Transition to Democracy*. Atlanta: Rodopi, 2000.

Resnik, Julia. '"Sites of Memory" of the Holocaust: Shaping National Memory in the Education System in Israel.' *Nations and Nationalism* 9, no. 2 (2003): 297–317.

Ricœur, Paul. 'The Human Experience of Time and Narrative.' In *A Ricoeur Reader: Reflection and Imagination*. Edited by Mario J. Valdés. Toronto: Toronto University Press, 1991.

Rieben, Henri. *Des guerres européennes à l'Union de l'Europe*. Lausanne: Fondation Jean Monnet pour l'Europe, 1987.

Rifkin, Jeremy. *The European Dream: How Europe's Vision of the Future is Quietly Eclipsing the American Dream*. New York: Penguin, 2004.

Risse, Thomas. *A Community of Europeans? Transnational Identities and Public Spheres*. Ithaca, NY: Cornell University Press, 2010.

———. '"Let's Argue!": Communicative Action in World Politics.' *International Organization* 54, no. 1 (2000): 1–39.

Rochefort, Robert. *Robert Schuman*. Paris: Les Éditions du Cerf, 1968.

Rodrik, Dani. *The Globalization Paradox: Democracy and the Future of the World Economy*. New York: W. W. Norton & Company, 2011.

Rosanvallon, Pierre. *Democratic Legitimacy: Impartiality, Reflexivity, Proximity*. Princeton: Princeton University Press, 2011.

———. *Counter-Democracy: Politics in an Age of Distrust*, translated by Arthur Goldhammer. Cambridge: Cambridge University Press, 2008.

———. *Democracy Past and Future*, translated by Samuel Moyn. New York: Columbia University Press, 2006.

Ross, George. *Jacques Delors and European Integration*. New York: Oxford University Press, 1995.

Roth, François. *Robert Schuman, 1886–1963: Du Lorrain des frontières au père de l'Europe*. Paris: Fayard, 2008.

Rousso, Henry. *The Vichy Syndrome: History and Memory in France since 1944*. Cambridge, MA: Harvard University Press, 1991.

Sakellaropoulos, Spyros, and Panagiotis Sotiris. 'Postcards from the Future: The Greek Debt Crisis, the Struggle Against the EU-IMF Austerity Package and the Open Questions for Left Strategy.' *Constellations* 21, no. 2 (2014): 262–273.

Schacter, Daniel L. *The Seven Sins of Memory: How the Mind Forgets and Remembers*. Boston: Houghton Mifflin, 2001.

Schecter, Darrow. *Critical Theory in the Twenty-First Century*. New York: Bloomsbury Academic, 2013.

Schimmelfennig, Frank. *The EU, NATO and the Integration of Europe: Rules and Rhetoric*. Cambridge: Cambridge University Press, 2003.

Schissler, Hanna, and Yasemin Nuhoğlu Soysal. *The Nation, Europe, and the World: Textbooks and Curricula in Transition*. New York: Berghahn Books, 2005.

Schneider, Christina J. *Conflict, Negotiation and European Union Enlargement*. New York: Cambridge University Press, 2009.

Schönwald, Matthias. 'Walter Hallstein and the "Empty Chair" Crisis 1965/66.' In *Crises and Compromises: The European Project 1963–1969*. Edited by Wilfried Loth. Vol. Bd. 8. Brussels: Bruylant, 2001.

Schudson, Michael. 'The Present in the Past Versus the Past in the Present.' *Communication* 11 (1989): 105–113.

Select bibliography

Schuman, Robert. *For Europe*. Paris: Nagel Editions SA, 2010.

Schwartz, Thomas Alan. *America's Germany: John J. McCloy and the Federal Republic of Germany*. Cambridge, MA: Harvard University Press, 1991.

Schwarz, Hans-Peter. *Konrad Adenauer: A German Politician and Statesman in a Period of War, Revolution, and Reconstruction*. Vol. 1: *From the German Empire to the Federal Republic, 1876–1952*. Providence: Berghahn Books, 1995.

Sedelmeier, Ulrich. 'Sectoral Dynamics of EU Enlargement: Advocacy, Access and Alliances in a Composite Policy.' *Journal of European Public Policy* 9, no. 4 (2002): 627–649.

Shennan, Andrew. *De Gaulle*. New York: Longman, 1993.

Sierp, Aline. *History, Memory, and Trans-European Identity: Unifying Divisions*. London: Routledge, 2017.

——. 'Drawing Lessons from the Past: Mapping Change in Central and South-Eastern Europe.' *East European Politics and Societies* 30, no. 1 (2016): 3–9.

Sierp, Aline, and Jenny Wüstenberg. 'Linking the Local and the Transnational: Rethinking Memory Politics in Europe.' *Journal of Contemporary European Studies* 23, no. 3 (2015): 321–329.

Simonian, Haig. *The Privileged Partnership: Franco-German Relations in the European Community, 1969–1984*. Oxford: Clarendon Press, 1985.

Sjursen, Helene. *Questioning EU Enlargement: Europe in Search of Identity*. London: Routledge, 2007.

——. 'Why Expand? The Question of Legitimacy and Justification in the EU's Enlargement Policy.' *Journal of Common Market Studies* 40, no. 3 (2002): 491–513.

Smith, Bruce James. *Politics and Remembrance: Republican Themes in Machiavelli, Burke, and Tocqueville*. Princeton: Princeton University Press, 1985.

Smith, Rogers M. *Stories of Peoplehood: The Politics and Morals of Political Membership*. New York: Cambridge University Press, 2003.

Snyder, Timothy. *The Road to Unfreedom: Russia, Europe, America*. London: Bodley Head, 2018.

——. *Bloodlands*. New York: Basic Books, 2010.

——. 'Balancing the Books.' *Index on Censorship* 34, no. 2 (2005): 72–75.

Soros, George. *Financial Turmoil in Europe and the United States*. New York: PublicAffairs, 2012.

Soros, George, and Gregor Peter Schmitz. *The Tragedy of the European Union: Disintegration or Revival?* New York: Public Affairs, 2014.

Spiegel, Gabrielle M. 'Memory and History: Liturgical Time and Historical Time.' *History and Theory* 41, no. 2 (2002): 149–162.

Sternberger, Dolf. 'Die deutsche Frage.' *Der Monat* 8/9 (1949): 16–21.

——. 'Versuch zu einem Fazit.' *Die Wandlung* 4 (1949): 700–710.

Stirk, Peter M. R. *Critical Theory, Politics and Society: An Introduction*. New York: Continuum, 2000.

Stout, Harry S. *Upon the Altar of the Nation: A Moral History of the American Civil War*. New York: Viking, 2006.

Streeck, Wolfgang. 'The Return of the Repressed.' *New Left Review* 104 (2017): 5–18.

——. *Buying Time: The Delayed Crisis of Democratic Capitalism*, translated by Patrick Camiller. London: Verso, 2014.

——. 'How Will Capitalism End?' *New Left Review* 87 (2014): 35–64.

——. 'Small-State Nostalgia? The Currency Union, Germany, and Europe: A Reply to Jürgen Habermas.' *Constellations* 21, no. 2 (2014): 213–221.

——. 'Markets and Peoples: Democratic Capitalism and European Integration.' *New Left Review* 73 (2012): 63–71.

——. 'The Crises of Democratic Capitalism.' *New Left Review* 71 (2011): 5–29.

Select bibliography

Strydom, Piet. *Contemporary Critical Theory and Methodology*. London: Routledge, 2013.

Suny, Ronald Grigor. *The Revenge of the Past: Nationalism, Revolution, and the Collapse of the Soviet Union*. Stanford: Stanford University Press, 1993.

Swoboda, Hans, and Jan Marinus Wiersma, eds. *Politics of the Past: The Use and Abuse of History*. Brussels: The Socialist Group in the European Parliament and the Renner Institute, 2009.

Ther, Philipp. 'Die Last der Geschichte und die Falle der Erinnerung.' *Transit – Europäisches Revue* 30 (2006): 70–87.

Tocci, Nathalie. *The EU and Conflict Resolution: Promoting Peace in the Backyard*. London: Routledge, 2007.

Torreblanca, José I. *The Reuniting of Europe: Promises, Negotiations and Compromises*. Aldershot: Ashgate, 2001.

Trenz, Hans-Jörg, and Klaus Eder. 'The Democratizing Dynamics of a European Public Sphere: Towards a Theory of Democratic Functionalism.' *European Journal of Social Theory* 7, no. 1 (2004): 5–25.

Troebst, Stefan. 'Halecki Revisited: Europe's Conflicting Cultures of Remembrance.' In *A European Memory? Contested Histories and Politics of Remembrance*. Edited by Małgorzata Pakier and Bo Stråth. New York: Berghahn Books, 2010.

Ugland, Trygve. *Jean Monnet and Canada: Early Travels and the Idea of European Unity*. Toronto: University of Toronto Press, 2011.

Uhl, Heidemarie. 'From Victim Myth to Co-Responsibility Thesis: Nazi Rule, World War II, and the Holocaust in Austrian Memory.' In *The Politics of Memory in Postwar Europe*. Translated by Tom Appleton and Eli Lebow, edited by Richard Ned Lebow, Wulf Kansteiner, and Claudio Fogu. Durham, NC: Duke University Press, 2006.

van Middelaar, Luuk. 'The Return of Politics: The European Union After the Crises in the Eurozone and Ukraine.' *Journal of Common Market Studies* 54, no. 3 (2016): 495–507.

——. *The Passage to Europe*. New Haven: Yale University Press, 2013.

Verdun, Amy. 'The Role of the Delors Committee in the Creation of EMU: An Epistemic Community?' *Journal of European Public Policy* 6, no. 2 (1999): 308–328.

Verovšek, Peter J. 'Memory, Narrative, and Rupture: The Power of the Past as a Resource for Political Change.' *Memory Studies* 13, no. 2 (2020).

——. 'Integration After Totalitarianism: Arendt and Habermas on the Postwar Imperatives of Memory.' *Journal of International Political Theory* 16, no. 1 (2020): 2–24.

——. 'A Case of Communicative Learning: Rereading Habermas's Philosophical Project through an Arendtian Lens.' *Polity* 51, no. 3 (2019): 597–627.

——. 'Critical Theory as Medicine? On the Diagnosis and Treatment of Social Pathology.' *Thesis Eleven* 155, no. 1 (2019): 109–126.

——. 'Impure Theorizing in an Imperfect World: Politics, Utopophobia and Critical Theory in Geuss's Realism.' *Philosophy & Social Criticism* 45, no. 3 (2019): 265–283.

——. 'La memoria è essenziale per la democrazia.' *VoxEurop*, 8 March 2019, https://voxeurop.eu/it/2019/gli-europei-e-la-storia-5122733 (accessed 9 March 2019).

——. 'The Loss of European Memory.' *Social Europe Journal*, 12 February 2019, www.socialeurope.eu/the-loss-of-european-memory (accessed 12 February 2019).

——. 'Historical Criticism without Progress: Memory as an Emancipatory Resource for Critical Theory.' *Constellations* 26, no. 1 (2019): 132–147.

——. 'Lexit undermines the Left: It will be no Prize for Labour.' *LSE Brexit Blog*, 16 October 2018, https://blogs.lse.ac.uk/brexit/2018/10/16/lexit-undermines-the-left-it-will-be-no-prize-for-labour/ (accessed 17 October 2018).

Select bibliography

——. 'Memory and Forgetting in Central Europe.' *Social Europe Journal*, 20 December 2018, www.socialeurope.eu/migration-and-forgetting-in-central-europe (accessed 3 February 2019).

——. 'Screening Migrants in the Early Cold War: The Geopolitics of U.S. Immigration Policy,' *Journal of Cold War Studies* 20, no. 4 (2018): 154–179.

——. 'Habermas's Theological Turn and European Integration,' *The European Legacy* 22, no. 5 (2017): 528–548.

——. 'The Immanent Potential of Economic Integration: A Critical Reading of the Eurozone Crisis.' *Perspectives on Politics* 15, no. 2 (2017): 396–410.

——. 'Collective Memory, Politics, and the Influence of the Past: The Politics of Memory as a Research Paradigm.' *Politics, Groups, and Identities* 4, no. 3 (2016): 529–543.

——. 'Expanding Europe through Memory: The Shifting Content of the Ever-Salient Past.' *Millennium – Journal of International Studies* 43, no. 2 (2015): 531–550.

——. 'Memory and the Euro-Crisis of Leadership: The Effects of Generational Change in Germany and the EU.' *Constellations* 21, no. 2 (2014): 239–248.

——. 'Unexpected Support for European Integration: Memory, Rupture and Totalitarianism in Arendt's Political Theory.' *The Review of Politics* 76, no. 3 (2014): 389–413.

——. 'Meeting Principles and Lifeworlds Halfway: Jürgen Habermas on the Future of Europe.' *Political Studies* 60, no. 2 (2012): 363–380.

Waldron, Jeremy. 'Superseding Historic Injustice.' *Ethics* 103, no. 1 (1992): 4–28.

Wallace, Helen, and Pascaline Winand. 'The Empty Chair Crisis and the Luxembourg Compromise Revisited.' In *Visions, Votes and Vetoes: The Empty Chair Crisis and the Luxembourg Compromise Forty Years On*. Edited by Jean-Marie Palayret, Helen Wallace, and Pascaline Winand. Brussels: Peter Lang, 2006.

Weber, Eugen Joseph. *The Nationalist Revival in France, 1905–1914*. Vol. 60. Berkeley: University of California Press, 1959.

Weiler, J. H. H. 'Federalism and Constitutionalism: Europe's Sonderweg.' *Jean Monnet Working Paper* 10 (2000).

——. 'The Reformation of European Constitutionalism.' *Journal of Common Market Studies* 35, no. 1 (1997): 97–131.

——. 'A Quiet Revolution: The European Court of Justice and its Interlocutors.' *Comparative Political Studies* 26, no. 4 (1994): 510–534.

Wells, Sherrill Brown. *Jean Monnet: Unconventional Statesman*. Boulder: Lynne Rienner Publishers, 2011.

Wertsch, James V., and Henry L. Roediger. 'Collective Memory: Conceptual Foundations and Theoretical Approaches.' *Memory* 16, no. 3 (2008): 318–326.

Wesseling, H. L. *Certain Ideas of France: Essays on French History and Civilization*. Westport: Greenwood Press, 2002.

Weymar, Paul. *Konrad Adenauer. Die autorisierte Biographie*. Munich: Kindler, 1955.

Whitman, Richard G., and Stefan Wolff. *The European Union as a Global Conflict Manager*. London: Routledge, 2012.

Winter, Jay. *Dreams of Peace and Freedom: Utopian Moments in the Twentieth Century*. New Haven: Yale University Press, 2006.

——. 'The Generation of Memory: Reflections on the Memory Boom in Contemporary Historical Studies.' *Bulletin of the German Historical Institute* (2000): 69–92.

——. *Sites of Memory, Sites of Mourning: The Great War in European Cultural History*. New York: Cambridge University Press, 1995.

Select bibliography

Wolf, Joan B. *Harnessing the Holocaust: The Politics of Memory in France*. Stanford: Stanford University Press, 2004.

Wolfrum, Edgar. *Geschichtspolitik in der Bundesrepublik Deutschland: Der weg zur Bundesrepublikanischen Erinnerung 1948–1990*. Darmstadt: Wissenschaftliche Buchgesellschaft, 1999.

Young, Iris Marion. *Justice and the Politics of Difference*. Princeton: Princeton University Press, 1990.

Zurcher, Arnold John. *The Struggle to Unite Europe, 1940–1958: An Historical Account of the Development of the Contemporary European Movement from its Origin in the Pan-European Union to the Drafting of the Treaties for Euratom and the European Common Market*. New York: New York University Press, 1958.

Index

Index

Index

Index

EU authorised representative for GPSR:
Easy Access System Europe, Mustamäe tee 50,
10621 Tallinn, Estonia
gpsr.requests@easproject.com

9 781526 163769